PUBLICATIONS

OF THE

NAVY RECORDS SOCIETY

Vol. LIV

THE LIFE AND WORKS

OF

SIR HENRY MAINWARING

Vol. I

THE LIFE AND WORKS OF
SIR HENRY MAINWARING

EDITED BY

G. E. MANWARING

Vol. I

PUBLISHED BY ROUTLEDGE FOR THE NAVY RECORDS SOCIETY
1920

First published 1920 for the Navy Records Society

Published 2019 by Routledge
2 Park Square, Milton Park, Abingdon, Oxon OX14 4RN
52 Vanderbilt Avenue, New York, NY 10017

Routledge is an imprint of the Taylor & Francis Group, an informa business

ISBN 13: 978-1-9112-4878-1 (pbk)
ISBN 13: 978-1-296-54638-0 (hbk)

THE COUNCIL

OF THE

NAVY RECORDS SOCIETY

1920-1921

———◆———

PATRON
THE KING

PRESIDENT
THE LORD GEORGE HAMILTON, P.C., G.C.S.I.

VICE-PRESIDENTS

CUSTANCE, ADMIRAL SIR REGINALD N., G.C.B., K.C.M.G., C.V.O., D.C.L.

MARSDEN, R. G.

NEWBOLT, SIR HENRY, D.Litt.

RICHMOND, REAR - ADMIRAL HERBERT W.

COUNCILLORS

ATKINSON, C. T.

BADDELEY, V. W., C.B.

BRINDLEY, HAROLD H., F.S.A.

BROCK, VICE - ADMIRAL SIR OSMOND DE B., K.C.B., K.C.M.G., K.C.V.O.

BROWNING, ADMIRAL SIR MONTAGUE E., G.C.M.G., K.C.B., M.V.O.

CALLENDER, GEOFFREY A. R.

CORBETT, SIR JULIAN S., F.S.A.

DARTMOUTH, THE EARL OF, P.C., K.C.B.

DESART, THE EARL OF, P.C., K.P., K.C.B.

DEWAR, CAPTAIN ALFRED C., O.B.E., R.N.

FIRTH, PROFESSOR C. H., LL.D., F.B.A.

GOUGH - CALTHORPE, ADMIRAL THE HON. SIR SOMERSET A., G.C.M.G., K.C.B., C.V.O.

GRAY, SIR ALBERT, K.C.B., K.C.

HALDANE, THE VISCOUNT, P.C., K.T., O.M., K.C.

KENYON, LIEUT. - COL. SIR FREDERICK G., K.C.B., P.B.A., D.Litt., LL.D.

KILBRACKEN, THE LORD, G.C.B.

LEYLAND, JOHN

MURRAY, SIR OSWYN A. R., K.C.B.

OTTLEY, REAR-ADMIRAL SIR CHARLES L., K.C.M.G., C.B., M.V.O.

ROSE, PROFESSOR J. HOLLAND, D.Litt.

SLADE, ADMIRAL SIR EDMOND J. W., K.C.I.E., K.C.V.O.

TARLETON, CAPTAIN ALFRED H., M.V.O., R.N.

WESTER WEMYSS, ADMIRAL OF THE FLEET LORD, G.C.B., C.M.G., M.V.O., D.C.L.

WHITE, CAPTAIN JOHN BELL, C.B.E., R.N.R.

SECRETARY
W. G. PERRIN, Admiralty, S.W.

HON. TREASURER
SIR W. GRAHAM GREENE, K.C.B., Ministry of Munitions, S.W.

INTRODUCTION

THE historian who sets himself the task of writing about the Elizabethan navy must inevitably centre his labours round the foremost of its seamen, Sir Francis Drake, and in like manner the naval history of the first two Stuarts can be written round the life of Sir Henry Mainwaring.[1]

In some respects Mainwaring was no unworthy successor of the Elizabethan hero, though owing to the fact that he did not take to the sea until after the peace with Spain, the same opportunities of glory and distinction did not present themselves. To this may be attributed the circumstance of his name having barely escaped oblivion, for no account of him is to be found in the Dictionary of National Biography. Had he been born a generation earlier he would have probably filled such another page in history as his brilliant compatriot. As it is, his career is typical of the sea-life of the first half of the 17th century, and its significance as throwing light on a dark period of our naval history between

---

[1] With two exceptions, Mansell's Expedition to Algiers in 1620, and Cecil's Voyage to Cadiz five years later, this volume is entirely representative of the naval history of the time.

viii INTRODUCTION

the Spanish and Dutch wars cannot be over-
estimated.

The period in question was devoid of any
really great naval operations, and it is chiefly
due to this that it has not been a favourite
one with writers of naval history.[1] Nevertheless,
it was an epoch of considerable importance. It
was, in fact, a period when many fertile seeds
were sown—a period of preparation when the
bold bids of both the Dutch and the French
for naval supremacy, awakened us from the
comfortable feeling of security following on the
naval reputation acquired in Elizabeth's reign.

It is to this period that we owe the doctrine
of the Sovereignty of the Narrow Seas, and the
first attempt to create a standing navy to enforce
that doctrine. For such is the significance of
the ship-money fleets and of the reorganisation
of naval administration, both by reforms in the
Admiralty itself and by a process of unification
under which the Cinque Ports lost their independ-
ence. It was a great advance; not only did
it set in motion the final departure from the
mediaeval ideas of a navy—the final supersession
of the naval militia by a regular fleet—but for
the first time it proclaimed the doctrine of unity
of command as the fundamental postulate of
sound naval defence.

Side by side with the birth of these essentially
modern ideas there was a decided advance in the

---

[1] The most detailed accounts of the navy during this
period are to be found in Sir Julian Corbett's *England in the
Mediterranean* ; Mr. Oppenheim's *History of the Administration
of the Navy* ; Mr. T. W. Fulton's *Sovereignty of the Sea* ; and
Clowes' *History of the Royal Navy*, vol. ii. Since the completion
of my own work there has appeared *The Navy under the Early
Stuarts*, by Mr. C. D. Penn, a veritable mine of information.

material and practical aspects of the naval art, which was nourished by the growing scientific spirit of the age. In naval architecture there was a definite breaking away from the traditional forms that, so far as is known, had lasted with little modification since early Tudor times. A similar movement in tactics can be clearly seen in the instructions issued to the ship-money fleets, in which appears the first groping after a tactical system—the first attempts to handle a fleet as a whole in the manner in which the scientific soldiers of the time were developing the handling of armies.

Finally, it was to the period of Mainwaring's activity that belongs our first attempts to exert diplomatic influence on the continent by operations in the Mediterranean. With all these advances he was intimately brought into contact, but it was in the process of widening out the horizon of a national policy in the Mediterranean that he was probably most conspicuous. He was certainly one of the pioneers of political adventure ' within the Straits.'

When James the First brought to an end the operations that had been carried on against the Spaniards since the days of the Armada, the livelihood of those who followed the call of the sea as privateers was seriously threatened. In the summer of 1603 a proclamation was issued recalling all letters of marque, which was followed two years later by another forbidding English seamen to seek service in foreign ships.[1] Up till then English vessels had found a plausible excuse for sailing armed to the Mediterranean and other parts, though their operations in most cases were not

[1] Corbett, *Successors of Drake*, 401-2.

above suspicion. The pursuit was found to be both exciting and lucrative, and therefore they were naturally unwilling to abandon it for something more peaceful and less profitable. The result was that in spite of proclamations many of them continued to scour the seas. The situation produced is thus ably summed up by a contemporary[1] :

> After the death of our most gracious Queen Elizabeth . . . King James, who from his infancy had reigned in peace with all nations, had no employment for those men of war, so that those that were rich rested with what they had ; those that were poor and had nothing but from hand to mouth turned pirates ; some, because they became slighted of those for whom they had got much wealth ; some, for that they could not get their due ; some, that had lived bravely, would not abase themselves to poverty ; some vainly, only to get a name ; others for revenge, covetousness, or as ill.

Piracy was then a school for seamanship, and it is as a pirate that the first chapter of Mainwaring's sea-career opens. The circumstance does not appear to have been due to choice, and it was more by accident than design that he took to the ' trade.' So diligently did he apply himself to it that he soon rose to a position as distinctive as it was unique, and, like Drake and Raleigh, he made himself the enemy of the Spaniards, to whom he proved a scourge and a terror. His reputation as a pirate was such, that ' for nautical skill, for fighting his ship, for his mode of boarding, and for resisting the enemy ' he was said to be without equal in England. Seeing then that as a result of the Spanish war the English Navy was the most renowned in Europe, it is no small wonder that Mainwaring's services were eagerly sought

[1] Captain John Smith, *Works*, 1884 ed., p. 914.

after on the continent. Spain in particular was anxious to come to an agreement with him, and through her ambassador in England she offered Mainwaring a pardon and a high command if he would enlist his services under the Spanish flag ; but tempting as the bait was it failed to attract him, for the advisers of James were equally alive to securing the services of such men and also had offers to make. Mainwaring and his like were primarily patriotic and had little love for Spain. Without much difficulty, therefore, he was brought to see the error of his ways, and received a pardon and knighthood.

Henceforth he devoted himself to his country's service and to an active ambition to rise in it. As a thank-offering he presented the King with his first literary effort, a 'Discourse' on the suppression of piracy. James, who was highly impressed by Mainwaring's ability, having no appointment worthy of his acceptance at home, strongly recommended him for service under the Venetian Republic. The opportunity occurred during the year 1618, at a time when the Venetians were greatly alarmed by the warlike preparations Spain was making against them. In consequence they sought the assistance of James, asking him for a loan of some of his merchant shipping for the purposes of defence. Mainwaring being 'the first and foremost seaman that England possessed,' it is only natural that they should have solicited his aid regarding the hiring of suitable vessels. The command of this little squadron, the sailing of which ushered in the birth of England as a naval power in the Mediterranean, would have undoubtedly been given to Mainwaring but for the violent opposition of the Spanish ambassador, who saw in Mainwaring a formidable opponent.

Accordingly he appeared at the Council table and strongly objected to Mainwaring serving a state that was hostile to the King of Spain. Not content with this, he actually sued him for 80,000 ducats, that being the sum he estimated Mainwaring had taken from the Spaniards. By these and other sinister methods Mainwaring was prevented from receiving the command of the ships, though he was able to render considerable assistance to the Venetian Government by journeying overland to them, and placing his maritime knowledge at their disposal.

As an exponent of the art of naval warfare he was far ahead of his time, and the paper which he drew up for the benefit of the Republic on the relative fighting value of large and small ships is printed with other documents relating to the event in this volume.

On Mainwaring's return he was given the important post of Lieutenant of Dover Castle and Deputy Warden of the Cinque Ports, a position which was then of considerable importance in naval affairs. This he held from 1620 to 1623, and whatever leisure the post afforded him was occupied in rescuing from oblivion the language of the sea, and preserving it for the benefit of future generations.

His next employment was in 1623, when a squadron of ten warships was sent to bring the Prince of Wales home from Spain. In accordance with the custom of the time of appointing noblemen as admirals of a fleet, the command was given to the Earl of Rutland, though frequently, as in the case of Rutland, they were ignorant of naval affairs. The real seaman commander was found in Mainwaring, who, in the words of the King, was ' the first Sea-Captain of our Admiral's choice.' The good service Mainwaring rendered in this capacity certainly justified his appointment, and the account contained in this book of the journey of the fleet to and from Spain is believed to be the fullest that has yet appeared. At the time of the expedition to Cadiz in 1625 Mainwaring presented a paper to Buckingham, then the Lord High Admiral, on the adaptability of Portsmouth as a naval base. In view of the important position that Portsmouth holds in the naval world to-day, this paper cannot fail to be of interest to the student of naval history.

From 1626 to 1627 Mainwaring was actively engaged on the Naval Commission of Enquiry, and the documents concerning it that have been brought together in this volume help to throw an interesting light on the condition of the Navy at the time, and incidentally reveal some of the main causes of the failure of the expeditions of 1625-6. In 1627 a fleet was despatched to the Isle of Rhé, and Mainwaring was fully occupied in surveying and hastening the various ships that were employed. A similar office was entrusted to him in the following year, when the two unsuccessful expeditions were fitted out for Rochelle. By Mainwaring's letters we are able to see the delays that were encountered in setting out a fleet during the Stuart *régime*. The lack of efficient seamen, the unwholesome condition of the food that was placed aboard ship, and the unseaworthy state of the ships themselves, were some of the difficulties that had to be surmounted.

In 1629 Charles made peace with France, and the welcome truce was devoted to reorganising the naval arm and carrying into effect the reforms that had been suggested by the Commission two years previously. Mainwaring was not idle at the time, and he is found at the meetings of the Brethren of the Trinity House, participating in the various duties that came under the jurisdiction of the Corporation.

The next stage of Mainwaring's career brings us into touch with an important development in our naval policy, the inauguration of the famous ship-money fleets. With the exception of the first, which was sent out in 1635, Mainwaring saw service in all of them, and in those of 1639 and 1640 he was appointed Vice-Admiral. The significance of these yearly naval demonstrations by Charles I has been treated at some length in this volume, and Mainwaring's evidence regarding the inefficiency of the fleet of 1636, and his account of the action between the Spanish and Dutch in the Downs in 1639, add to our knowledge of the naval history of the time. Complete lists of the ship-money fleets from 1635 to 1641 are given in this volume. Considerable time has been given to their compilation and, with the exception of those for 1635 and 1636, they have never been printed before. From these lists much interesting light is thrown on the early careers of seamen such as Batten and Popham, who afterwards achieved fame in the Parliament's service ; or who, like Mennes, Slingsby, and Carteret, lived to reap the reward of their loyalty to the King by being appointed at the Restoration to high administrative posts in the Navy.

The condition of the seamen during the 17th century was pitiable in the extreme, and the inhuman treatment to which they were subjected under the first two Stuarts had much to do in influencing the Navy to the side of the Parliament on the eve of the Civil War. A typical instance is given by Mainwaring when in command of the Unicorn in 1636. His ship, he tells us, was manned by ' men of poor and wretched person, without clothes or ability of body.' Of the victuals supplied the dry salted beef ' was blue and white mouldy.' ' One hogshead of pork stank.' . . . Both the ling and haberdine were very bad, so much so that ' when it was boiled the men would not eat it, but threw it overboard.' The musty bread sent aboard, he informs us, ' caused a soreness of the mouths and throats of the crew.' When sick, the seamen had to be kept aboard, or if turned ashore they were in danger of starvation. To quote his own words, ' some have been seen to die upon the strand for lack of relief.' Wages were not forthcoming, and many of the seamen for want of clothes were unable ' to stand to their labours upon the deck, or to keep their watches in winter.'

On the outbreak of the Civil War, Mainwaring took the side of the King, and his ship assisted in the defence of the last royalist stronghold in the west of England. After this he was attached to the suite of Prince Charles, and it was probably to Mainwaring that the Prince owed the foundation of that nautical knowledge which so distinguished him as Charles II.

Now that the history of the 17th century is being re-written in the light of modern research, the personality of Mainwaring is slowly but surely emerging from the obscurity into which it has fallen. Sir Julian Corbett in his ' England in the Mediterranean ' has written of Mainwaring's connection with the Barbary corsairs [1] ; while Mr. Pearsall Smith [2] and Mr. Allen Hinds [3] have

[1] Vol. i. pp. 56–9.
[2] *Life and Letters of Sir H. Wotton*, vol. ii. pp. 471–2.
[3] *Cal. of State Papers*, Venice, 1617–9.

thrown much light on Mainwaring's negotiations
with the Venetian Republic. Mr. David Hannay,
in his interesting volume entitled 'Ships and
Men,' has taken Mainwaring as a typical pirate,
and has also used and quoted Mainwaring's
'Discourse of Pirates' in a later book.[1] The
'Discourse of Pirates' was printed for the first
time in the United Service Magazine of 1913,[2]
with an introduction by Mr. L. G. Carr Laughton.

Sir Henry Mainwaring has frequently been
confused with others of the same name, an
error which is perhaps pardonable, when we
consider the frequency with which the surname
is met with in documents of the 16th and 17th
centuries.[3] Besides being credited with commanding a ship against the Spanish Armada,[4]
Mainwaring is stated to have served under
Monson and Leveson on the coast of Portugal
in 1602, as captain of the Dreadnought.[5] The
late Samuel Smiles, however, is responsible for
an error that is quite unpardonable, in describing
Mainwaring as half-brother to the ill-fated
Raleigh.[6] An incident of Mainwaring's career
in 1623 has been immortalised by Ainsworth,
and occupies some thirteen pages in that author's
stirring romance, 'The Spanish Match.'

Before completing this volume I had hoped
to discover a portrait of Sir Henry Mainwaring,
but after a fruitless search in many quarters I
am convinced that none exist.

---

[1] *The Sea-trader*, pp. 235–42.
[2] November and December, 1913.
[3] Mainwaring always used the form 'Maynwaringe.'
[4] Chatterton, *Sailing Ships*, p. 198.
[5] *Navy Rec. Soc.*, vol. ii. 335. The ship in question was
commanded by Captain Edmond Mainwaring.
[6] *Men of Invention*, p. 43.

In conclusion, there only remains for me the congenial duty of recording my gratitude to all who have assisted me in the preparation of my book, first and foremost among whom I must name Sir Julian Corbett. Not only has he read through the whole of the manuscript, but he has freely given me the benefit of his advice and criticism, a debt which I cannot too fully acknowledge. Mr. David Hannay and other gentlemen have also perused my book in manuscript, and whatever perfection it may have achieved it is due in no small degree to their kindly aid and suggestions.

Finally, I have to express my sincere thanks to Lieut.-Col. W. G. Perrin, O.B.E., for the interest he has taken in the preparation of this volume, and for his kindness in reading the proofs. His intimate knowledge of the period has enabled me to escape many pitfalls, and I cannot sufficiently thank him for the valuable assistance he has rendered.

G. E. MANWARING.

May, 1920.

CONTENTS

OF

THE FIRST VOLUME

xix

CHRONOLOGICAL TABLE OF EVENTS, ETC., IN THE LIFE OF SIR HENRY MAINWARING

1587. Birth.
1599. Matriculates at Brasenose College, Oxford.
1602. Receives his degree of B.A.
1604. November. Admitted a student of the Inner Temple.
1611. John Davies, of Hereford, writes sonnet to Mainwaring.
1611. Grant (promissory) of the Captaincy of St. Andrew's Castle, Hants.
1611. Commission from the Lord Admiral against the pirates.
1612. Intends accompanying Sir Robert Shirley on his return embassy to Persia.
(1612 ?). Puts to sea in the Resistance, under the pretext of plundering the Spaniards beyond ' the line.'
(Between 1612–15). Plunders a French ship.
1614. Seizes two ships belonging to Calais and Lubeck.
1614. On the Newfoundland coast with five ships.
1614. Mainwaring's name used as a decoy by Sir William Monson to capture a pirate's stronghold on the Irish coast.
1615. Defeats five of the Spanish royal fleet.
1615. On the coast of Ireland with two ships.
1616. Takes a ship belonging to Lubeck.
1616. Receives the royal pardon.
1616. Captures a ' Turkish pirate ' in the Thames
1618. ' Discourse of Pirates ' presented to the King.
1618. March 20th. Knighted by James I at Woking, Surrey.
1618. Gentleman of the Bedchamber to James I.
1618. Sir Henry Peyton and Mainwaring try for the command of the fleet enlisted in the service of the Venetian Republic.
1619. January. Offers his services to Venice.

1619. February. Suggests to the King the loan of warships to the Venetians.

1619. Returns from Venice.

1620-3. Lieutenant of Dover Castle.

1620. Letter on Sir Henry Wotton's poem to the Queen of Bohemia.

1620. Member of the Committee of the Virginia Company.

1620-3. Composes his 'Nomenclator Navalis,' or 'Seaman's Dictionary.'

1621-2. Member of Parliament for Dover.

1623. Discharged from Lieutenancy of Dover Castle.

1623. Appointed Captain of the Prince Royal, to fetch Prince Charles home from Spain.

1624. Opposes Sir Edward Cecil as M.P. for Dover.

1625. Suggests Portsmouth as a harbour for the fleet, and presents a paper on the subject to Buckingham.

1626-7. Member of the Special Commission on naval abuses.

1627. Brother of the Trinity House.

1627-8. Helps to prepare the fleet for the expeditions to Rhé and La Rochelle.

1629. Romantic wooing of a wealthy widow.

1630. Presents discourse to Sir John Coke on the evils of allowing the French to fish at the Sowe.

1630. Marriage to a daughter of Sir Thomas Gardiner at the 'Topp of Paules.'

1630. Master of the Corporation of Trinity House.

1630. Petitions the King for a grant of the Island of Fernando do Noronha.

1633. Death of Lady Mainwaring.

1636. Report on the condition of the Navy.

1637. Rear-Admiral.

1638. Unsuccessful candidate for the Surveyorship of the Navy.

1639. Vice-Admiral under Sir John Penington in the expedition to Scotland.

1639. Meets the Spanish and Dutch fleets in the Downs.

1642. Master of the Corporation of Trinity House.

1643. Created a Doctor of Physic by Oxford University.

1643. Helps in the defence of Pendennis Castle against Fairfax.

1644. His 'Seaman's Dictionary' published.

1647-8. At Jersey with Prince Charles, afterwards Charles II.

1649. At the Hague with Charles II.

1651. Returns to England and makes a composition with the Committee for compounding the estates of the Royalists.

1653. May. Death, and burial at St. Giles', Camberwell.

THE LIFE AND WORKS

OF

SIR HENRY MAINWARING

CHAPTER I

1587–1616

ANCESTRY—BIRTH—PIRACY

To 1587, the year that witnessed Drake's daring exploits on the Spanish coast, the birth of the subject of this memoir may be assigned. The family—a branch of the Mainwarings of Peover in Cheshire [1]—migrated during the 15th century into the neighbouring county of Shropshire, and settled at Ightfield, some four miles south-east of Whitchurch. Among the brasses in the church of St. John the Baptist at Ightfield are two which record the names of members of the family who flourished at this period. The first, *circa* 1495, is to Dame Margery Calveley, daughter of William Maynwaryng of Ightfield, and widow of Philip Egerton, with four sons and four daughters beside her effigy. The second, *circa*

---

[1] The reputed founder of the family in England was one Ranulphus de Mesnilwarin, who came over in the train of William the Conqueror, and for his services received fifteen lordships in Cheshire, with that of Waburne in Norfolk (Ormerod, *Cheshire*, iii. 226).

1497, is to ' The Good ' William Maynwaryng, second son of Hawkyn Maynwaryng and Margaret his wife, daughter and heir of Grffyn Warren of Ightfield.[1]

In a description of the banners of those who entered France, 16th of June, 1513, the following entry occurs :

> Sir John Maynwaryng of Ightfield bareth gold an Ass head haltered sable and a crescent upon the same ; and Rondell Maynwaryng his Petty Captain.[2]

In the early part of the 16th century Ightfield boasted an extensive park, and Leland in his ' Itinerary,' undertaken in or about the years 1535–43, mentions the following under Shropshire :

> Sir Richard Mainwaring, chief of that name, dwelleth a iii miles by east from Price (*i.e.* Press) village at a village called Ightfield, having a park and a great plenty of wood about him.[3]

A moated 15th or 16th century manor house at Ightfield is now a farm, and bloodstains are shown on the floor of a bedroom of one of its former owners—a Mainwaring.[4]

During the 16th century various members of the family filled important posts in the county, and between 1504 and 1576 they supplied no fewer than seven sheriffs for Shropshire.[5] The last member to hold that office was Sir Arthur Mainwaring,[6] and by the marriage of this Sir Arthur to Margaret, daughter and co-heiress of

---

[1] Haines, *Monumental Brasses*, ii. 178.
[2] *Shropshire Visitation*, ii. (Harleian Soc.). Sir John was Knighted by the King at Lille.
[3] Leland, 1910 ed., pt. ix. p. 17.
[4] Hare, *Shropshire*, p. 253.
[5] Public Record Office Lists, ix. 119.
[6] Sheriff also in 1562.

Sir Randle Mainwaring of Peover, the two branches of the family once more became united. They had issue, three daughters and a son George, who eventually inherited the Ightfield estates. This son married Anne, second daughter of Sir William More of Loseley, Surrey, and was knighted in 1595. The More family were originally settled in Derbyshire, but in 1532 they purchased the Loseley estate, with its park of 200 acres. William More mentioned above was born on the 30th of January, 1520, and knighted on the 14th of May, 1576, in the presence of Queen Elizabeth. He sat in Parliament several times as member for Guildford, and was knight of the shire for Surrey, as well as sheriff of the counties of Surrey and Sussex.[1] That he was held in high esteem is proved by the fact that Elizabeth honoured him with her presence at Loseley on several occasions, and Sir John Oglander, who married a grand-daughter of Sir William, records that ' the Queen was wont to come to Loseley to Sir William More's very often, whom she called her black husband.' [2]

To Sir George Mainwaring and his wife were born four sons and two daughters.[3] The birth of the second son Henry took place, as we have seen, in stirring times, when the one topic of the day was the threatened invasion of England by the Spaniards. It was a period in which the feeling of the country was violently anti-Spanish, and its influence on his subsequent career cannot be over-estimated. As a boy he probably paid frequent visits to his maternal grandfather

[1] Britton and Brayley, *Surrey*, i. 410–12.
[2] *Oglander Memoirs*, ed. W. H. Long, p. 138. Sir William died 20th July, 1600, being then in his 81st year.
[3] See Note on the family in Vol. II.

at Loseley, and as Sir William More held the important post of Vice-Admiral of Sussex, it is only natural to presume that he would have entertained his grandson with stories of the sea. We can picture young Mainwaring on these occasions, seated at the feet of his grandsire in the library at Loseley, eagerly listening to the heroic and daring exploits of the Elizabethan sea-dogs, expounded possibly from the pages of Master Hakluyt, whose ' Principal Navigations of the English Nation ' had just been given to the world. From that great ' prose epic,' and the personal reminiscences of his grandfather, the boy probably owed his infatuation for the sea and ships — an infatuation which so distinguished him in the years to come, and stamped him as no unworthy successor of his Elizabethan heroes.

The rudiments of his education were probably received at the hands of a tutor, and, like the rest of his brothers, he was afterwards sent to Brasenose College, Oxford. The usual age for young men to enter either of the Universities was from fourteen to sixteen, but ' many parents,' to quote a contemporary,

take them from school, as birds out of the nest, ere they be fledged and send them so young to the University, that scarce one among twenty proveth aught . . . so these young things, of twelve, thirteen, or fourteen, that have no more care than to expect the next carrier, and where to sup on Fridays and Fasting nights : no further thought of study, than to trim up their studies with pictures, and place the fairest books in openest view, which, poor lads, they scarce ever opened, or understand not.[1]

[1] Peacham, *Compleat Gentleman*, 1634 (reprinted 1906), p. 33.

Mainwaring was certainly one of those to whom the first part of this criticism was applicable, for, at the time of his matriculation, he was only twelve years of age.[1]

During the latter part of the 16th century, when Dean Nowell and Thomas Singleton were successively Principals of Brasenose, little is known of the social life of the college. The furnishing of the undergraduate's room was of the simplest character, and of comfort he knew little.[2]   The top floors of the college were probably split up into dormitories, in which a student was often forced to share his bed with another ; while the lower chambers, about the year 1596, were reported ' dampish and unwholesome, being unboarded.'[3]   Even if the student had a desire for knowledge, the books in the library at this period were few. Mainwaring, however, was assiduous in his studies, and books were more to him than objects to be placed in ' openest view ' and seldom read. On the 15th of July, 1602, after a residence of a little over three years, he received his degree of Bachelor of Arts.[4]

After leaving the University it was customary for young men to receive a short course of legal training, and in November 1604 Mainwaring was admitted as a student of the Inner Temple.[5] About this time, or very shortly afterwards, he became a pupil of John Davies of Hereford, the most famous writing-master of his day, whose pupils were drawn from the noblest families in

[1] *Brasenose Register*, ' Matr. *eq.* 27 April, 1599, aged 12.'
[2] Buchan, *Brasenose College*, p. 45.
[3] Churton, *Life of Nowell*, p. 427.
[4] *Brasenose Register*.
[5] List of students admitted to Inner Temple, 1571–1625, p. 97.

the land, and whose skill in penmanship was
said to have been unequalled. That Mainwaring
was an apt pupil is proved by the fact that
Davies, when he published his ' Scourge of Folly '
in 1611, inscribed the following epigram ' To
my most dear pupil, Mr. Henry Mainwaring.' [1]

Your soul (dear Sir, for I can judge of sprights
Though not judge souls) is like (besides her sire)
Those ever-beaming eye delighting lights
Which do heav'ns body inwardly attire ;
For her superior part (your spotless mind)
Hath nought therein that's not angelical ;
As high, as lowly, in a diverse kind,
And kind in either ; so belov'd of all.
    Then (noble Henry) love me as thine own,
    That lives but (with thy worths) to make thee known.

While the more wealthy finished their education
by making the grand tour, the adventurous
spirits during the reign of James sought the
profession of arms, and enlisted their services
in the wars in the Low Countries. Probably
Mainwaring was among the latter, and it is
even possible that he was one of the 4000 Englishmen serving under Sir Edward Cecil at the siege
of Juliers in 1610. At all events, Mainwaring
must have qualified himself in some such capacity,
for in June 1611 he was deemed sufficiently worthy
for the post of Captain of St. Andrew's Castle,
a fortress which then existed at Hamble Point,
near Southampton.[2] Though promised the position, there is no evidence that he ever filled it,
for in the same year he received a commission
from the Lord Admiral to proceed against the

[1] *Works*, ed. Grosart, 1878. Davies had a house in
Fleet Street about this time.
[2] *S.P. Dom.*, James I, lxiv. 25.

pirates who were infesting the Bristol Channel. In the February of 1610 it was reported that Peter Easton, a notorious pirate, was hovering on the coast, and fears were entertained that all the shipping in the King Road, a roadstead at the mouth of the Avon, might be captured by him.[1] This incessant plundering had driven the Bristol merchants to seek the aid of the Lord Admiral, the Earl of Nottingham, and from the State Papers of the period it appears that the Earl had promised them his personal assistance, but a few days afterwards granted the commission to Captain Mainwaring.[2] Nottingham was then in his 75th year, and was evidently of the opinion that the task required a younger man. What result attended the commission is unknown, but by this time it is clear that Mainwaring had developed an insatiable love for adventure on the high seas.

There arrived in England during the following year a picturesque personality whose adventures at the Persian Court figured largely in the gossip of the day, and whose subsequent dealings altered the whole course of Mainwaring's career. This was Sir Robert Shirley, the youngest of the three famous brothers, who after spending several years in Persia had been sent by the Shah on a mission to Europe, to solicit the aid of the Christian Princes against the Turks, and to foster commercial relations. Shirley was handsomely entertained by James I at Hampton Court, but was unsuccessful in his mission, and towards the end of 1612 preparations were made for his return. Such a swashbuckling adventurer could not fail to attract the youth of the time, and Mainwaring was one of those who were

[1] *S.P. Dom.*, James I, lii. 50.
[2] *Ibid.*, Addenda, Oct. 1611 (lxvi. 107).

chosen or volunteered to accompany him on his
return embassy to Persia. This occasioned his
old tutor, John Davies, to write a farewell ode
in his honour, which is inscribed thus:

To my most dear, and no less worthily-beloved
Friend and Pupil, Henry Mainwaring, Esquire, with the
truly-noble and venturous Knight Sir Henry Thynne,
accompanying, into Persia, the meritoriously-far-
renowned Knight; Sir Robert Shirley, Englishman;
yet Lord Ambassador sent from the great Persian
Potentate to all Christian Princes for the good of Christen-
dom.[1]

Heroic Pupil, and most honor'd Friend,
    to thee, as to my Moiety, I bequeath
Half the other half; beginning at mine end,
    to make (I hope) me triumph over death.

My Son (sole Son; and, all I ever had)
    unto thy Care and Service I commend;
So, make me sonless, till you make me glad
    with your Return from this World's further end.

The Absence of so dear a Son as thou,
    must needs affect thine honor'd Sire with Grief;
But for thy good, he doth his grief subdue:
    so, doe I mine, by his, sith his is chief:
Then, with my Son, take thou my Heart and these
Celestial Charms, in Storms, to calm the Seas.

There is evidence of Sir Henry Thynne returning in the ambassador's train, but not of Mainwaring. It was originally intended that three
or four ships loaned by merchant adventurers
should accompany Shirley, but owing to a belief
that the vessels would eventually be used for

[1] *Muse's Sacrifice*, Works, ed. Grosart, ii. It would
appear from the above that Davies's son also accompanied
Shirley.

piracy, the offer was withdrawn. The Spanish envoy in England sent word to his government that four ships had been fitted out to sail to Persia nominally, but their real intention, he wrote, was to go buccaneering to the Indies. Finally, an agreement was drawn up with Sir Henry Thynne, who undertook to provide a ship, the Expedition, of 200 tons, commanded by Captain Newport,[1] for the conveyance of the Ambassador and his suite, who embarked from Dover in January 1613. Thynne was evidently in the ship, as before the Expedition sailed, power was granted to him ' to use martial law in his voyage to Persia.'[2] Had the merchant ships been hired, there is evidence to prove that they would have sailed under the command of Mainwaring. As it was, through the embargo placed on them by the Spanish Ambassador, Mainwaring eventually took to piracy,[3] and it is to this year that the birth of his career as a corsair may be assigned. He himself assured the King that ' he fell not purposely but by mischance into those courses,' but being in them, he strove to do all the service he could to the State.

At this period the English pirates had established themselves at Mamora, at the mouth of the Sebu River on the Barbary coast, and their adventures in the Mediterranean will, as Mr. Bruce states, ' bear a good deal more investi-

---

[1] Captain Christopher Newport, born about 1565. In 1592 he was captain of the *Golden Dragon*. Between 1606 and 1611 he made five voyages to Virginia. He entered the service of the East India Co. in 1612, and died in 1617.

[2] *S.P. Dom.*, James I, lxviii. 104; *S.P. Venice*, 1610–13, 666, 767; *Shirley Bros.* (Roxburghe Club), p. 81.

[3] See Wotton's account of Mainwaring on p. 50.

gation.'[1] Many Englishmen furnished themselves with good ships, and took to the high seas and piracy, and among their ranks was found a sprinkling of the aristocracy. Sir Francis Verney, of the ancient Buckinghamshire family of that name, sold his estates in 1608, and went to Algiers to follow the ' trade.'[2] The calling, though fraught with considerable danger and daring, was found to be remunerative, and it became popular, if not strictly fashionable, to turn ' Turk ' and lead the life of a corsair. The ports of England were shut to them, but that did not prevent the English merchants from going to the Barbary coast to trade in secret. Many of the pirates, doubting their offences to be pardonable by law, renounced the Christian faith and embraced Mohammedanism, but Mainwaring to the last refused to take such a step. Chief among the corsairs Stow records the names of Captains Ward, Bishop, Verney, and Glanville. Ward, it is interesting to note, applied himself so diligently to the life, that he was enabled to erect himself a palace at Tunis, ' beautiful with rich marble and alabaster, more fit for a prince than a pirate,' and it was only eclipsed in magnificence by that of the Dey.

In spite of numerous proclamations, piracy increased considerably during the reign of James I, so much so that ' nulli melius piraticam exercent quam Angli' passed into a proverb.[3] Some of the pirates came home in 1611, upon the promise of pardon for life and goods, but the greater

---

[1] *Verney Papers*, ed. J. Bruce, viii.; also Corbett, *England in the Mediterranean*, vol. i. pp. 10–20.

[2] He met a miserable end seven years later, dying in hospital at Messina.

[3] Scaliger. ' None make better pirates than the English.

part took to the Irish coast, because they were only offered pardon for life.[1] Before the arrival of the Englishmen on the Barbary coast, the knowledge possessed by the Moors of naval matters was very trifling, and, according to one eminent authority, they ' knew scarce how to sail a ship,'[2] but by the summer of 1611 Sir Ferdinand Gorges reported that they were possessed of some forty sail, manned by 2000 men.[3]

Details of Mainwaring's early operations at sea are wanting, but, from the evidence that is available, they were evidently fought under the guise of a privateer. To obtain the necessary licence did not present difficulties, for his ability as a seaman had already been favourably noticed by Nottingham, the Lord High Admiral, and, under the thinly veiled pretext of pillaging the Spaniards beyond ' the line,' he was allowed to sail. His ship, the Resistance,[4] though of small dimensions, was chosen on account of her speed and sailing qualities, and whatever she lacked in size was amply compensated for by the fact that she was well armed, and manned by a crew whose knowledge of the sea was second to none. From the first, Mainwaring's real intention was to carry on an indiscriminate warfare against the Spaniards, and ignore ' the line ' altogether. On nearing the Straits of Gibraltar he called his men together, and announced his intention

[1] *Verney Papers*, pp. 95–101. For an interesting study of the pirate, see Mr. D. Hannay's *Ships and Men*, pp. 39–55.

[2] Captain John Smith, *Works*, 1884 ed., p. 914.

[3] *Cal. S.P. Dom.*, July 5, 1611.

[4] Of about 160 tons. Built by Phineas Pett, the well-known shipwright, in 1604, and purchased by Mainwaring in July 1612 for ' 700 and odd pounds ' (*Phineas Pett*, ed. W. G. Perrin, p. 96).

from that day onwards of giving fight to any
Spanish vessel that chanced to cross his path.
As a base he decided to use Mamora, the pirate's
Mecca, for from this port he knew he could safely
reckon on getting supplies and shelter when
necessary. Lying in the track of the great
Spanish carracks off Cape Spartel, he soon proved
himself a scourge and a terror, for hardly a ship
passed his lair without either suffering damage
or capture. By this means he soon found himself
at the head of a powerful fleet, crews to man which
could always be found at Mamora.

Before long Mainwaring's success in this
new mode of life became so pronounced, that
ere many months had passed he reigned supreme
on the Barbary coast. The Spaniards had long
consoled themselves that the spirit and daring
of the old Elizabethan sea-dogs had passed away
with the death of the Queen, yet here was a
man whose every action was the embodiment
of what they firmly believed had long since
ceased to exist—the very reincarnation of ' el
Draque ' himself. Though a pirate, it was part
of Mainwaring's plan of campaign to do all in
his power for the welfare of his own country, and
his reverence for the English flag is shown in all
his actions. While at Mamora, he informs us,
there were some thirty sail of pirate vessels
using the port, but before he allowed any of them
to sail, they had first to pledge their word not
to molest English shipping.[1] One incident connected with his career at this period helps
to illustrate the kind of warfare he carried on.
He had overhauled and stopped two merchantmen bound from Lubeck and Calais respectively,

---

[1] *Discourse of Pirates.*

with cargoes for a Spanish port. After taking what he required of their lading, he dismissed the ships, and left the crews to continue their voyage. As soon as the vessels entered port they reported their loss, and a complaint was afterwards lodged by a Galway merchant, Valentine Blake, that the goods taken out of these foreign vessels were his, and that they were consigned to his factor in Spain, Anthony Lynch, for sale. This was brought to Mainwaring's knowledge, and he forthwith anchored off the port, and sent for the factor to come aboard his ship, in order to test the truth of Blake's statement. Having received satisfactory evidence that such was the case, Mainwaring immediately restored the whole of his plunder, which amounted to about 3000*l.* in value, in fulfilment of his promise not to molest English shipping, or cargoes belonging to English merchants.[1] Though our merchantmen were immune from attack as far as Mainwaring was concerned— which was testified to by the merchants themselves—it was not so with those of Spain, and the ceaseless snapping up of their shipping soon struck terror into the hearts of the Spanish traders. In consequence numerous complaints were lodged at court concerning the depredations committed by Mainwaring, but the Spanish Government were at a loss to know what measures to take in order to satisfy their subjects. Finding that they were unable to capture Mainwaring and his comrades by fair means, they hit on what they thought would be an ingenious plan to bring about his downfall. It was this. Once in possession of his base they

[1] *Cal. S.P. Ireland*, 1614, No. 814.

firmly believed his activities would soon cease. Accordingly they dispatched the Duke of Medina to Mainwaring, with a dish which was as tempting as it was diplomatic. 'If,' the Duke informed Mainwaring, 'you will deliver up Mamora to the King of Spain, his Majesty in return for this gracious favour will be pleased to bestow on you a free pardon and a considerable sum of money.' Then Medina went on to show how generous his catholic Majesty was. 'As for the pardon,' he pointed out, 'it has been drawn up on such benevolent lines, that it will enable you and your fellow corsairs to retain what ships and goods happen to be in your possession.' It was indeed a tempting bait, which might have drawn many smaller fish into the diplomatic net spread by King Philip, but not Mainwaring. As a final effort, Medina played his last card. 'If you agree to my offer,' he informed Mainwaring, 'his Majesty will esteem it an honour to offer you a high command in the Spanish royal fleet.' But still neither monetary considerations nor the various other alluring gifts that the Spanish Government were capable of offering an individual when it suited them, had any effect on Mainwaring, and the Duke of Medina returned to his King with his highly flavoured dishes untasted.[1] Nor was Spain the only continental state that was anxious to secure Mainwaring's services. The Duke of Florence also saw that such a man would be of inestimable value to him, especially as he (the Duke) was about to fit out a fleet of galleys to go privateering, for which purpose he had already enlisted the services of a French corsair.[2]   There-

---

[1] *Discourse of Pirates.*
[2] Cosimo II, de Medici (*Cal. S.P. Venice*, 1613–15).

fore he extended to Mainwaring the hospitality of his palace, and deputed a ship to wait on him, until such time as he thought fit to come in.[1]

These two incidents help to show the feeling with which he was regarded at the various European courts. The boast of one of Mainwaring's compatriots,[2] that 'he would not bow to one king, when he in a way, was a king himself,' equally applies to Mainwaring and pirate captains generally. Even on some parts of the Irish coast his name was almost a household word—the fame of 'valiant Captain Mainwaring' holding an honoured place among the seafaring folk of that country. Certainly they were not over scrupulous in their dealings with pirates, and either by occasional visits himself, or incidents related by seamen who had met him, Mainwaring's notoriety became firmly established there ; so much so, that Sir William Monson was able to exploit his personality as a means of capturing others who adhered to the 'trade.'

Though on the Irish coast a pirate was not openly dealt with, it was the custom of the 'country people' to treat privately with the captain for such victuals and munitions as he might require. The method adopted was this. Having ascertained the needs of a pirate ship that would be lying off the coast, a rendezvous would be arranged, and the required articles deposited there. The captain would then appoint several of his crew to go and bring them aboard, and for this purpose a small boat would leave the ship in the dead of night. Before returning with their cargo, they were expected to leave

---

[1] *Discourse of Pirates.*   [2] Peter Easton.

on shore either goods or money equivalent to
two or three times the value of their purchases.[1]

In 1614 Monson was sent on an expedition
against the pirates, and after a fruitless quest
in the Hebrides, proceeded to Broadhaven in
Ireland, having received information that a
sympathiser and protector of pirates, Cormat
by name, resided there. With four ships in
his company, Monson sailed, but meeting with
heavy seas, his small squadron were soon scattered, and one of his ships eventually foundered.
On the 28th of May he arrived at Broadhaven,
the 'well-head of all pirates,' as he calls it, and
coming to an anchor, he made choice of such of
his company as had formerly been pirates, to
give the least suspicion of his purpose. This
precaution having been satisfactorily completed,
Monson despatched them in a boat to Cormat,
and 'took upon himself to be a pirate, and the
name of Captain Manwaring.' One of the
'pirates,' who no doubt had been specially coached
for the occasion by Monson, extolled the wealth
that 'Manwaring' had on board, and by way
of proving his assertion, gave out how liberal
he always was to those who courteously received
him. The commendations and names of various
other pirates were used to give colour to his
oration, and the women folk, wide eyed and
open mouthed, were deluded with stories to
the effect that 'Captain Manwaring' was on
the best of terms with the various pirate lovers,
and they had entrusted him with a veritable
emporium of presents for distribution among
them. At the moment, of course, they were
on board 'Captain Manwaring's' ship. The

[1] *Discourse of Pirates.*

'gentleman of the place' at first seems to have been suspicious of his visitors, and with a plausible excuse he absented himself, leaving his wife and daughters to entertain his unbidden guests. But this was not for long. The hilarity and good news attracted him, and his tongue became very fluent and voluble. Monson's plan bid fair to be a success. Cormat, after detailing the various favours that he had bestowed on sundry other members of the community of which he was an honoured member, expressed an ardent wish to be of service to 'Captain Manwaring,' having a devotion for his person! The next morning, as a fuller assurance of his fidelity, Cormat sent two men on board 'Manwaring's' ship, to extend to him the hospitality of his humble abode. These ambassadors of peace, after delivering their master's greeting, were promptly put into irons by Monson, much to their chagrin and dismay.

The time had now arrived for Monson to play his trump card, and after announcing that he was coming on shore that very day, three or four hundred men were ordered down to the water's edge to attend him. Three of their number waded through the sea up to their armpits, 'striving who should have the credit to carry him ashore.' Forthwith Monson was conducted to Cormat's abode, and one of the three, falling into discourse, 'told him they knew his friends, and though his name had not discovered it, yet his face did show him to be a Manwaring!' In short, they stated that he might command them and their country, and that no man was ever so welcome as Captain Manwaring! Entering the house, Cormat's three daughters were the first to greet 'Manwaring.' The hall was newly

strewed with rushes, and a harper played merrily
in a corner of the room. Compliments were
passed, and enquiries were made by the ladies,
respecting their pirate sweethearts, while the
two messengers who had been detained by
Monson were suspected of 'drinking and frolick-
ing in the ship,' as was the custom upon the
arrival of pirates. A dance was afterwards
given in 'Manwaring's' honour, and Cormat,
who was in high spirits, offered him the service
of ten mariners of his acquaintance, 'that lay
lurking thereabouts, expecting the coming in of
men-of-war,[1] which he (Cormat) had power to
command.' The offer was accepted, and with
a promise of a reward for their services, Cormat
wrote to his acquaintances in the following
strain :—'Honest brother Dick, and the rest,
we are all made men ; for valiant Captain Manwaring and all his gallant crew are arrived at
this place. Make haste ; for he flourisheth in
wealth, and is most kind to all men. Farewell,
and once again make haste !' Monson himself
took the letter, announcing his intention of dis-
patching a messenger with it at once. Having,
as he informs us, 'now drawn out of the country
all the secret he desired,' he caused the music
to cease, and began to address his pirate audience.
He revealed his identity and mission, informing
them that nothing now remained but for them
to proceed to execution, for which purpose he had
brought a gallows ready framed. Realising that
their position was hopeless, he informs us that
'their mirth was turned into mourning, and
their dancing into lamentation.' However,
Monson tempered mercy with justice, and after

[1] *I.e.* pirates. A man-of-war proper was always designated
as a 'King's ship' or 'Queen's ship' (Monson, *Naval
Tracts*, ed. Oppenheim, vol. iii. p. 63 n).

keeping them four and twenty hours in irons, he released them, on receiving their promise never to ' connive again at pirates.' [1]

In the meantime the real Harry Mainwaring was continuing his unchequered career on the Barbary coast, and was instrumental in making some sort of treaty with the Sallee Moriscoes whereby all Christian prisoners were to be released. Not only Morocco, but Tunis received him with open arms. The Dey, with whom he had ' eat bread and salt,' was particularly anxious to secure his services, and ' swore by his head ' that if Mainwaring would take up his residence with him, he should receive half shares in all prizes. Mainwaring, however, had no intention of becoming a renegado, and this and similar offers of entertainment were all refused. ' I preferred,' as he afterwards informed King James, ' the service of my own country, and my particular obedience to your royal person,' than that of any other ruler. [2]

A favourite recruiting ground for the pirates was Newfoundland, for among the fishing fleet there they knew that both supplies and men were obtainable. Every spring fishermen from the west of England, the Low Countries, and the harbours of Northern Spain, Portugal and France, faced the dangers of the western seas, with its fogs and ice, to gather a harvest on the great fishing banks. The chief commodity of the island is its cod fishery, and to our ancestors, ' the discovery of the fishing grounds of Newfoundland was a veritable God-send, a piscatorial El-Dorado.' [3]

Hardly a season passed without some depre-

[1] Monson, *Naval Tracts*, III., N.R.S., vol. xliii. pp. 59–65; where the story is told at some length

[2] *Discourse of Pirates.*

[3] Prowse, *Newfoundland*, pp. 18–19.

dations being committed on the fishermen, and
Mainwaring himself resolved to try his luck at
the 'Banks.' With eight good ships in his
company (two of which were captured *en route*),
he arrived among the fishing fleet on the 4th
of June, 1614, and Sir Richard Whitbourne, who
knew the island as familiarly as England, records
meeting Mainwaring there in that year, while on
a trading voyage from Newfoundland to Marseilles. Speaking of Mainwaring, Whitbourne
writes : ' He caused me to spend much time
in his company, and from him I returned into
England ; although I was bound from thence
to Marseilles, to make sale of such goods as I
then had.' [1]   What the reason was that occasioned
Whitbourne to return direct to England, instead
of carrying his merchandise to Marseilles, is far
from clear.   It is possible, however, that during
the time he was detained in the ' company '
of Mainwaring, the latter had persuaded him to
return to England, and negotiate a pardon for
him, as Easton had done two years previous.

Though Mainwaring arrived at the island at
the beginning of the summer, he did not take
his departure till the following September, and
during that time he appears to have been particularly active.   His exploits for the period are
fully chronicled in the ' Colonial Records,' which
give a detailed account of the damage, &c., committed by pirates from 1612 to 1621.   The year
1614 is recorded thus :

Captain Mainwaring with divers other captains arrived
in Newfoundland on the 4th of June, having 8 sail of
warlike ships, one whereof they took at the bank, another

. [1] *Purchas Pilgrimes*, 1626, iv. p. 1882, and Whitbourne,
Westward Hoe (reprinted 1870).

upon the main of Newfoundland, from all the harbours whereof they commanded carpenters, mariners, victuals, munitions, and all necessaries from the fishing fleet after this rate—of every six mariners they take one, and the one first part of all their victuals ; from the Portugal ships they took all their wine and other provisions, save their bread ; from a French ship in Harbour de Grace they took 10,000 fish ; some of the company of many ships did run away unto them. They took a French ship fishing in Carboneir, &c., and so after they had continued three months and a half in the country, taking their pleasure of the fishing fleet, the 14th of September, 1614, they departed, having with them from the fishing fleet about 400 mariners and fishermen ; many volunteers, many compelled.[1]

Although Mainwaring and Easton were unquestionably the leading corsairs of their day, no record is extant (as far as I have been able to ascertain) of any action in which they both took part, but their careers at this period appear so identical, that it may not be considered inappropriate to dwell for a moment on that of the 'Arch-Pirate,' as Whitbourne styles Easton. The history of Easton is one of the most remarkable in the annals of piracy. As previously stated, in 1611 he was reported to have command of forty ships ; and in that somewhat free and easy time, with such a squadron fully manned and armed, a pirate was a personage whom no sovereign or state could afford to ignore. The following year saw Easton on the Newfoundland coast with ten ships well furnished and very rich.[2]

[1] *S.P. Colonial* (America and W. Indies), i. 16 Mar. 1621 (cited in Prowse, p. 103). This same record also gives an account of the plunder committed by Sir W. Raleigh's captains in Newfoundland, on their return from his last expedition.

[2] *Purchas*, iv. p. 1882, where the year is given as 1611, evidently in error, as Guy's statement points to the year 1612.

John Guy, who was governor of the island
at the time, helps us with details regarding his
sojourn there. Until the 17th of July, Easton
remained in Harbour de Grace, trimming and
repairing his ships, commanding the carpenters
of every vessel in the harbour to come to his aid.
He also appropriated victuals and munitions,
together with one hundred men to man his
squadron.[1]

Whitbourne at this period chanced to be at
the island, and Easton, as he tells us, kept him
‘ eleven weeks under his command,’ during which
time he severely admonished Easton on the
wickedness of piracy. Strange as it may seem,
this lecture seems to have borne fruit, and the
pirate finally entreated Whitbourne to return
to England, ‘ to some friends of his, and solicit
them to become humble petitioners to the King
for his pardon.’[2] This Whitbourne undertook
to do, though, as in the case of Mainwaring, he
was bound on another trading voyage. With
the offer of ‘ much wealth,’ which was discreetly
refused, Whitbourne started, claiming as a small
recompense for his trouble the release of a ship
belonging to Fowey, Cornwall. In order to learn
the terms on which a pardon would be granted,
Easton despatched one of his captains, Harvey
by name, to Ireland, while he himself mustered
his squadron at Ferryland, some forty miles
south of St. John’s. This having been successfully accomplished, he resolved to play his last
card before capitulating, and accordingly he
shaped his course for the Azores, with the idea
of intercepting the Spanish Plate fleet. In the
meantime Captain Harvey was nearing the

---

[1] *Purchas*, xix. (Hakluyt Soc.) ; Guy's Rept., 29 July. 1612.
[2] Whitbourne, pp. 41–2.

Irish coast, and apparently no sooner had he entered home waters than he divulged his master's intention, much to the annoyance of Whitbourne, who found on reaching England that a pardon had already been despatched.[1] Nevertheless, the anxiety of the Government to secure Easton's surrender was not destined to meet with success, for the bearer of the pardon, to use Whitbourne's own words, ' by a too much delaying of time,' caused Easton to lose hope ; and, after waiting patiently off the Barbary coast, with his ships full of treasure, he sailed for the Straits of Gibraltar, finally entering the service of the Duke of Savoy, under whom he lived in palatial luxury.[2] The total amount of damage done to the shipping of various nations, both at and around Newfoundland, by Easton and his fellow corsairs, was stated to exceed 20,000*l*.[3]

During Mainwaring's absence in Newfoundland, Spain took the opportunity of turning her attention to the pirates' stronghold at Mamora. The presence of a Dutch squadron in the Straits had no doubt stimulated her to take action, and in the summer of 1614 she gathered together a huge armada, consisting of ninety-nine ships, both large and small, for the purpose of laying

---

[1] Two pardons were granted, one in February and the other in November 1612 (*Cal. S.P. Dom.*).

[2] Whitbourne, pp. 41–2. Easton sailed into Villefranca with fourteen ships in March 1613. He purchased a palace there, and warehoused his booty, which was reputed to be worth two millions of gold. On the eve of the Duke of Savoy's raid on the Duchy of Mantua, Easton was employed in the Duke's siege train. We are told that he covered himself with glory, among his many accomplishments being his skill in laying guns, which was such, ' that a few shots by him produce more effect than most gunners produce with many (*Cal. S.P. Venice*, 1610–13, pref. xxi–xxii.).   [3] Prowse, 102.

siege to that port. The command of this expedition was given to Don Luis Fajardo, and on the 1st of August he sailed from Cadiz. On arriving at his destination, the Spanish admiral suffered the humiliation of finding a Dutch squadron of four ships of war under Admiral Evertsen anchored in the road. Though in possession of the anchorage, the Dutchman had no alternative, in view of the overwhelming force that would be opposed to him, but to make way for Fajardo's ships and salute the Spanish standard. The arrival of the Spanish fleet was at a most opportune time, for, owing to the absence of the principal corsairs, the place was quite unprepared to resist an attack, and the success of the expedition was evident from the first. To the credit of Fajardo, however, it must be said that his plans were carefully matured, and after consulting with Don Pedro de Toledo and the Conde de Elba, general of his galleys, he decided to wait for a calm day in order to land an attacking party, consisting of 2000 men, on a small beach near by. Meanwhile the few defenders that were at Mamora had strengthened their position by sinking two vessels across the mouth of the harbour, and above them had formed a temporary boom with the aid of masts and yards. The port was strongly fortified, and Fajardo bombarded the defences with his heavy guns. The Moors, who had counted on their position as being almost impregnable, were so taken back at the suddenness of the attack, that they abandoned the fort after rendering the guns useless. The Spaniards next turned their attention to the boom, and before long they succeeded in destroying it sufficiently to permit their ships to enter the harbour. The

corsairs, of whom there were some sixteen sail,
now saw that their position was hopeless, and
after setting fire to their ships, they made their
escape as best they could.[1] Fajardo, having thus
accomplished what Spanish gold had failed to
do some few months previously, declared Mamora
to be henceforth under the Spanish crown.

After his successful coup among the Newfoundland fishing fleet, Mainwaring next shaped
his course for the Barbary coast. The news of
Fajardo's victory had also reached him, and
hastened his return to the neighbourhood of
Mamora, where some of the Spanish fleet were
cruising. Though deprived of this port, Villefranca was open to the pirates, and proved a
safe base both for supplies and repairs. In fact,
the downfall of Mamora ushered in the birth
of Villefranca as a pirate rendezvous. As soon
as Mainwaring neared the entrance to the Straits,
he immediately resumed his original plan of
preying on Spanish shipping, a campaign in
which he was ably assisted by a scion of another
famous English family—one Walsingham.[2] It
is even possible that Walsingham was one of
Mainwaring's lieutenants ; at any rate, his success
was pronounced from the first. With six good
ships under his command he was reported to
have taken 500,000 crowns from the Spaniards
within the space of six weeks.[3] The swarms of

---

[1] Fernandez-Duro, *Armada Española*, iii. 332 ; Horozco,
Discorso hist. de presa que del Puerto de la Mamora, 1614
(reprinted in *Rivadeneyra*, xxxvi.) ; Corbett, *England in the
Mediterranean*, i. 58.

[2] Walsingham, like Mainwaring, afterwards gained distinction in the Royal Navy, and in 1622 he was captain of the
Dreadnought.

[3] *Cal. S.P. Dom.*, November 26, 1614. Digby to Winwood.

pirates that infested the Spanish coasts, both
within and without the Mediterranean, at last
stung the King of Spain into action, and in
June 1615 he issued a proclamation permitting
any of his subjects to fit out ships and go privateering.[1] Nor was his action limited to private
enterprise only, and at the same time instructions
were given for five of the royal fleet to be prepared
for sea, to assist in the suppression of Mainwaring
and the like. In the following month (July)
these five ships sailed from Cadiz in search of
any vessel flying the English flag. Their period
of inaction was very brief, for hardly had they
left port when they were encountered by Mainwaring with a squadron of three ships, and
a fierce fight ensued. Of the contest itself, full
details are wanting, but such as are available
show the grim determination with which Mainwaring and his company fought. Though out-
numbered in fighting strength, his superior
seamanship enabled him to inflict a crushing
defeat on the Spanish men-of-war. Through
all that long summer day he clung tenaciously
to his opponents, and it was only under cover
of night that they were enabled to escape. By
this time they had been chased far out of their
course, and as their battered condition would
not permit them to return to Cadiz, they were
forced to make for Lisbon, where the Venetian
Ambassador reported their arrival, adding that
they were glad to withdraw from the contest,
having been ' roughly handled.' [2]

Following on this, Spain, according to Mainwaring, again offered him a pardon, and 20,000

---

[1] *Cal. S.P. Venice*, 1613–15, pref. xliii.
[2] *Ibid.*, July 8, 1615. Morosini to the Doge. See also
Mainwaring's *Discourse of Pirates*.

ducats a year if he would 'go General of that Squadron'; but tempting as the offer was, he refused to enlist his services under the Spanish flag, and this year proved the last but one of his career on the Barbary coast. Like Drake and Raleigh, he was evidently of the opinion that to fight and plunder the Spaniards was in itself a virtue, and in some cases a necessity.

As a typical illustration of the method of engaging a Spaniard on the high seas, the following contemporary account may be read in conjunction with Mainwaring's exploit[1] :

'A sail, how stands she, to windward or leeward, set him by the Compass, he stands right a-head ; or on the weather bow, or lee bow : out with all your sails, a steady man to the helm, sit close to keep her steady. Give chase or fetch him up, he holds his own, no we gather on him, out goeth his flag and pennants or streamers, also his Colours, his waist-cloths and top armings, he furls and slings his main sail, in goes his sprit sail and mizzen, he makes ready his close fights fore and after. Well, we shall reach him by and by.'

'What is all ready ? Yea, yea. Every man to his charge. Dowse your top sail, salute him for the sea : Hail him : whence your ship ? Of Spain. Whence is yours ? Of England. Are you Merchants or Men of War ? We are of the Sea. He waves us to leeward. for the King of Spain, and keeps his luff. Give him a chase piece, a broadside, and run a-head, make ready to tack about, give him your stern pieces, be yare at helm, hail him with a noise of Trumpets.'

'We are shot through and through, and between wind and water, try the pump. Master let us breathe and refresh a little. Sling a man overboard to stop the leak. Done, done. Is all ready again ? Yea, yea : bear up close with him, with all your great and small

[1] Captain John Smith, *An Accidence for all Young Sea-men*, 1626, pp. 18–20.

shot charge him. Board him on his weather quarter, lash fast your grapplins and shear off, then run stemline the mid ships. Board and board, or thwart the hawse. We are foul on each other.'

'The ship's on fire. Cut any thing to get clear, and smother the fire with wet cloths. We are clear, and the fire is out, God be thanked.'

'The day is spent, let us consult. Surgeon look to the wounded. Wind up the slain, with each a weight or bullet at his head and feet, give three pieces for their funerals.'

'Swabber make clean the ship. Purser record their names. Watch be vigilant to keep your berth to windward : and that we loose him not in the night. Gunners spunge your Ordnances. Soldiers scour your pieces. Carpenters about your leaks. Boatswain and the rest, repair the sails and shrouds. Cook see you observe your directions against the morning watch. Boy. Hulloa Master. Hulloa. Is the kettle boiled ? Yea, yea.'

'Boatswain call up the men to Prayer and Breakfast. Boy fetch my cellar of Bottles. A health to you all fore and aft, courage my hearts for a fresh charge. Master lay him aboard luff for luff : Midshipsmen see the tops and yards well manned with stones and brass balls, to enter them in the shrouds, and every squadron else at their best advantage. Sound Drums and Trumpets, and St. George for England.'

'They hang out a flag of truce, stand in with him, hail him amain, abaft or take in his flag, strike their sails and come aboard, with the Captain, Purser, and Gunner, with your Commission, Cocket, or bills of loading.'

'Out goes their Boat, they are launched from the Ship side. Entertain them with a general cry. God save the Captain, and all the Company, with the Trumpets sounding. Examine them in particular ; and then conclude your conditions with feasting, freedom, or punishment as you find occasion.'

After Mainwaring's defeat of the Spanish men-of-war, it was obvious that steps would have to be taken to bring him to book ; and the Spanish and French governments, through their ambassadors in London, lodged reiterated complaints against the depredations committed by him. In one case the French actually issued letters of reprisal to the extent of 15,000l. for the seizure of a French ship, the value of which was stated to be under 1000l.[1] It was evident that James, loth as he may have been to take action in the matter, could not afford to ignore these representations. Sincerely anxious to keep the peace with everyone, he handled the difficulty in a way that was entirely characteristic, and an envoy was despatched to the Barbary coast, offering Mainwaring, on the one hand, a free pardon if he would return and abandon piracy, while on the other it was threatened to send a fleet of sufficient strength that would compel him to surrender, even in the harbours of his ally the Emperor of Morocco.[2] This latter recourse was a length to which Mainwaring did not intend to provoke his natural sovereign. An action against the English fleet was not part of his creed. He bore no malice against his own countrymen, and without hesitation he decided to return and enter into negotiations. With this end in view he passed through the Straits with two ships in his company, reaching the

---

[1] *Cal. S.P. Dom.*, James I. Hill to Brereton, March 1 1624. Probably the *Saint Pierre* captured in 1615 (*S.P. Dom.*, James I, clx. 2 ; Chas. I, dxxvi. 44).

[2] *Chevalier's Journal.*

Irish coast in November 1615.[1] As soon as he
arrived there he sent to his friends in England
to complete the terms of his surrender. The
news of his arrival quickly spread, and such
was his popularity, that while cruising off the
North West coast of Ireland awaiting the result
of these negotiations, no fewer than sixty mariners
came to offer their services to him, while letters
were received from different parts of the country
from adventurous spirits anxious to enlist under
his flag.[2]   To all of these Mainwaring returned
a polite refusal, and finally brought his vessels
into Dover Harbour, where one of them, commanded by Captain Thomas Hill, was ' stayed '
on Christmas eve by the order of Lord Zouch,
the Lord Warden.   This action Mainwaring seems
to have resented, for he immediately afterwards
entered   into   an   agreement   with   Joachim
Wardeman of Lubeck, for the sale of a ship the
Barbary, late the Golden Lion, which was then
lying in Dover Harbour.   She carried ordnance,
and   the   purchase   price   was   settled   at   200*l.*
' of good and lawful money of England,' to be
paid before the 20th of June.   Wardeman, possibly
unaware   of   his   client's   identity,   parted   with
the ship, and was forced to bring an action
against Mainwaring, which was settled by Zouch
on command from the King, the terms of the
settlement being unrecorded.[3]

Mainwaring had now played his last card,
and James, at the request of many of the leading
nobles, consented to grant him a pardon because
he had committed no great wrong,' on condition

[1] *East India Co. Letters,* ed. Foster, ii. 189. Dodsworth
to the East India Co. from aboard the *Hope* in Killybegs
Harbour.

Discourse of Pirates.

S.P. Dom., James I, lxxxvi. 5, 90, 118.

that he would arrange with the interested parties for the damage he had inflicted. The negotiations being brought to a successful issue, it is recorded that on the 9th of June, 1616, ' Captain Mainwaring, the sea captain, was pardoned under the Great Seal of England.' At the same time a general pardon was granted to all those who had served under him, on condition that they returned to England and gave up the ' trade.' [1]

Having received the royal clemency, Mainwaring's atonement seems to have been complete, and as a firstfruits of his gratitude, he proceeded to suppress any pirate that chanced to cross his path. At this period attacks by ' Turkish ' pirates on English shipping trading to the Levant and other parts were frequently reported. In 1616 seven of our ships, while on the homeward voyage from Newfoundland, encountered some thirty sail of them, with the result that two of the English vessels were sunk, and the rest captured. The Mary Anne, of 200 tons burden, belonging to the port of London, was boarded and rifled by them in the Straits of Malaga. Reported to have at their command a fleet of eighty ships, they became such a serious menace to trade, that the Levant Company sought the assistance of James I to suppress them.[2] So daring were they, that Mainwaring reported three of their number actually anchored in the Thames ! According to his own account he found one of the ships ' as high up the river as Leigh.' [3] Knowing how to deal with such rovers,

---

[1] *S.P. Venice,* 1619–21, No. 488 ; *Carew Letters to Roe,* (Camden Soc.), p. 35.   [2] *Carew Letters,* pp. 50, 67.
[3] *Discourse of Pirates* ; *Carew Letters,* p. 51. Leigh in Essex, about two miles from Southend. Camden happily describes it ' as a pretty little town stocked with lusty seamen.'

he promptly boarded the vessel, and released a
number of Christian captives that were on board.
This incident did much to redeem his character,.
and with all Drake's art in smoothing his path
in influential quarters, his next step was to
ingratiate himself with the Lord Warden of the
Cinque Ports, an office which still counted for
much influence in naval affairs. The Warden
was so impressed with Mainwaring's ability,
that he entrusted him with a commission for
the building of a pinnace, which was undertaken
by Phineas Pett, the famous shipwright, who
records that by Mainwaring's order he built

a small pinnace of 40 tons for Lord Zouch, being then
Lord Warden of the Cinque Ports, which pinnace was
launched the 2nd of August, and presently rigged and
fitted, all at my charge.[1]

The pinnace in question was probably the
Silver Falcon, which Zouch, who was a member
of the Council of the Virginia Company, sent
to Virginia early in 1619. On the 6th the vessel
sailed from Woolwich with Mainwaring and Sir
Walter Raleigh on board, and the voyage from
that place to Dover is thus described by Pett :

The first tide we anchored [at] Gravesend ; next night
at the North Foreland ; next tide in the Downs, where
we landed and rode to Dover Castle in the Lord Warden's
coach, sent purposely for us, leaving the pinnace to be
brought in to Dover Pier with the pilot and mariners.[2]

Raleigh was not released from the Tower till
March 1616, and his presence on board suggests
that he may have had an idea of hiring her for

[1] *Phineas Pett*, p. 116. Pett says he lost 100*l.* by the
transaction.
   Ibid., p. 116.

his last expedition, which sailed from Plymouth in June 1617.

During the time that they were the guests of the Lord Warden, many an interesting conversation must have taken place in the rooms over the Constable's Tower. We can picture this curious trio—explorer, pirate, and master shipwright—seated around a bowl of punch, each entertaining their host, a stern old courtier of sixty summers, with their views on men and things in general. Once handsome Raleigh, now careworn and aged from his long confinement in the Tower, would no doubt describe in eulogistic terms his forthcoming voyage to ' El Dorado,' upon the success or failure of which depended his own life. Pett, to whom the secret of the shipwright's profession had descended from father to son, would expound his views on the art of shipbuilding, a discourse which would be taken up with zeal by both Raleigh and Mainwaring. Then there would be Mainwaring, barely thirty years of age and the youngest member of the party, who, despite his years, would thrill his hearers with stories of the sea, and probably inform them of his projected treatise on the suppression of piracy. In the meantime Zouch, on his part, could enliven the conversation with stories of current court scandal and gossip, a subject in which he was kept very well informed by his many correspondents. In this way they would pass many a pleasant hour during their sojourn in the venerable pile. On the 16th of the month their visit came to an end, and as Mainwaring passed through the gateway of Constable's Tower after bidding adieu to his host, little did he dream that a few years hence he would enter that same gateway again,

I.   D

not as a guest, but as the custodian of this—' the key of England.'

Having now the privilege of numbering himself among Zouch's many friends, it was not long before this introduction procured him an opening at court, and he was appointed a gentleman of the royal bedchamber. A scholar of considerable ability, and an agreeable conversationalist, the King was attracted to Mainwaring from the first, and whenever the opportunity occurred, he would freely discuss questions of maritime policy with him. In fact, Mainwaring's foot was now well on the ladder to promotion, but his ingrained love of adventure was soon to lead him to stormier waters that were more akin to his nature than the service of a peace-loving sovereign.

CHAPTER II

1617–19

To Mainwaring the lure of the sea was irresistible, and by a strange turn of the wheel of fate he was destined to play a part in one of the most bewildering of all historical mysteries, the Spanish plot of 1618. This famous conspiracy had for its object the overthrow of the Venetian Republic, and it was so planned that while a powerful Spanish fleet was preying on the commerce of the Republic and threatening her by sea, mysterious strangers in the pay of Spain were crowding her taverns, and conspiring to burn and pillage the city, and massacre the nobles.[1] The principal organiser of this diabolical plot is supposed to have been the Duke of Ossuna, the Spanish viceroy at Naples, and in 1617 he despatched a large squadron to the Gulf of the Adriatic under the command of Francisco de Ribera. To cover up his sinister design various excuses were put forward, and Ribera's fleet he boasted should sail into Venetian waters, 'in spite of the world, in spite of the king, in

---

[1] Corbett, *England in the Mediterranean*, i. 44; *Quarterly Review*, 102, p. 430.

spite of God.'[1]   This outburst of Ossuna's,
followed by the presence of his fleet in the Adriatic,
caused the Venetians to take precautionary
measures for the safety of the Republic.   Gondomar, the Spanish ambassador in England,
had, in the course of a conversation with Mainwaring, concluded with words to the effect that
it would not be long before Spanish was spoken
in Venice, which threat was duly reported to
the Council of Ten.[2]   The Venetians now sought
the assistance of James I, and by the middle
of December 1617 their ambassador in London
had been instructed to ask the King for permission
to levy ships in England, besides 500 infantry.[3]
The English merchant service stood second to
none in the eyes of the Republic, and they
requested the loan of eight or ten ships for the
purpose of defence.   They themselves had prepared a fleet of 100 galleys, and the English
vessels were to act in conjunction with these
and some Dutch ships which had been hired.
No sooner had the news reached the ears of
Gondomar, than he determined to ask a similar
favour of James, but as it was impossible for
him to prove that the ships, if granted, would
be used for purposes other than offence, his
request was refused.   The Venetian demand,
however, was judged to be 'so reasonable,'
that the King could not refuse it, and permission
to levy the ships was granted, on condition
that they were used for defence only.[4]   The
Venetian ambassador having successfully played
his first card, much to the dismay of Gondomar,

---

[1] Pearsall Smith, *Sir H. Wotton,* i. 152–4 ; Romanin,
Venezia, vii. 120.
[2] *Cal. S.P. Venice,* 1617–19, No. 716.
[3] Carleton, *Letters,* 220.   [4] Carleton, 235.

his next difficulty was to find suitable ships,
and for this purpose he naturally sought expert
advice. On Christmas Day, therefore, two
members of the Venetian embassy, Lionello
and Michielini, were sent to interview Mainwaring. Though the real object of their mission
was to solicit his aid in the choice and equipment
of suitable vessels, they vaguely hinted at the
possibility of giving him the command of the
ships in the event of their negotiations proving
successful. They explained that the needs of
the Republic were urgent, and accordingly the
next morning Mainwaring made an inspection
of the various ships then lying in the Thames.
On account of the opposition of the Spanish
ambassador it was necessary to proceed with
the greatest caution, but unfortunately the
Republic's needs occurred at a most unfavourable
time, and nearly all the larger vessels appear
to have been engaged in the East India trade.
In Mainwaring's opinion there were none suitable at the moment for the service required
of them.[1] Dutch vessels could have been hired
at far less cost, but the English were considered
to be better built, and the ambassador having
set his heart on acquiring some of the English
merchantmen, he informed Mainwaring that the
Republic would have to be satisfied with the
best that were available. The English seamen
excelled all others in battle ' that I did not choose
to part with them.' Thus wrote Contarini to
the Doge.[2]

Meanwhile rumours had been circulated that
Mainwaring was to command the merchant

---

[1] *Cal. S.P. Venice,* 1617–19, No. 713. Ed. A. B. Hinds.
I am indebted to Mr. Hinds' *Calendar* for most of the information contained in this chapter. [2] *Ibid.,* pref. xxiv.

ships, and his frequent journeyings to and fro
in search of suitable vessels gave credence to
that report. On this point, however, Contarini
was silent, and when Mainwaring approached
him on the matter, he excused himself from
giving a direct reply by stating that he had no
authority to appoint a commander in chief.[1]
Nevertheless, he sounded the Republic on the
possibility of giving Mainwaring the command,
and on the 31st of January, 1618, he wrote[2]:

> There is here an English gentleman, a certain
> Captain Mainwaring, of yore a most famous pirate,
> who has repeatedly cruised in the Levant and in the
> Indies, and taken a number of vessels, having had as
> many as six or eight of his own ; and for nautical skill,
> for fighting his ship, for his mode of boarding, and
> for resisting the enemy, he is said not to have his superior
> in all England. He did not obtain his pardon from the
> King until two years ago, and is now anxious to be
> employed by the State, and to take out these transports
> with the troops to the Venetian fleet, doing subsequently
> whatsoever may be commanded him by the public
> representatives. Not having orders from your Excel-
> lencies to engage men of this sort, I did not dare
> give him the appointment, although I think he might
> prove very useful, and do good service in the fleet, from
> his great practice and experience in naval warfare.

The Republic were deeply impressed by this
despatch, and the possibility of having such a
distinguished and able commander appealed to
them. They therefore requested Contarini to
endeavour to ascertain whether, in the event
of employing him, they would be doing so with
the King's sanction. The only thing that seems

[1] *Cal. S.P. Venice*, 1617–19, No. 713.
[2] Duffus Hardy, *Report on the Archives of Venice*, 84–5 ;
Cal. S.P. Venice, 1617–19, No. 202.

to have troubled them was whether Mainwaring would receive the necessary support from the other captains, on account of his previous career.

With regard to the captain of whom you write [they replied], we do not seem to have sufficient information about him, or how he stands in the King's favour, whether his Majesty would be pleased at his going, of the fidelity of his service, of his claims, possessions, and credit, so that we cannot say anything definite at this moment. Possibly he would not be readily obeyed by the captains of the other ships, and if the journey is undertaken in conjunction with the Dutch ships, it might give rise to confusion. However, when your replies upon these particulars reach us, he might come by the quick route overland, and our sea-captains would be able to avail themselves of his services.[1]

The possibility of the reappearance of Mainwaring in the Mediterranean, backed by the official sanction of the British Government, was viewed with the liveliest apprehension on the part of Spain,[2] and as soon as Gondomar heard of the proposal, he appeared at the Council table, and strongly objected to Mainwaring enlisting his services in a state that was hostile to his King.[3] It was imperative to Gondomar that Mainwaring should not be allowed to sail with the ships. To this end he approached Mainwaring personally, and sued him for 80,000 ducats, that being the amount he estimated Mainwaring had taken from the subjects of the King of Spain. Finding this useless, he adopted other tactics, offering him a free pardon and a high command if he refused to serve the Venetians; but to all the tempting proposals

---

[1] *Cal. S.P. Venice*, 1617–19, No. 251.
[2] Corbett, vol. i. p. 59.
[3] Pearsall Smith, i. 154 ; *Cal. S.P. Venice*, No. 641.

that Gondomar had to offer, Mainwaring turned
a deaf ear, and the prospect of fighting his old
enemy again made him redouble his exertions to
secure the command of the merchant ships. On
the 21st of March Contarini wrote again [1]:

I have endeavoured to obtain the most precise
information concerning Captain Mainwaring, who offered
his services to the Republic. In like manner as I find
that for nautical experiences and sea-fights, and for a
multitude of daring feats performed afloat when he
was a pirate, he is in high repute, being considered
resolute and courageous, and perfectly suited to that
profession, understanding the management of large
ships [2] better, perhaps, than anyone ; so does the name
of corsair, by its lack of respectability, create a doubt
of his receiving the necessary obedience from other
captains ; besides the small reliance to be placed in any
man of that profession. I understand he has no landed
property of any value, though it is supposed he may have
some treasure secreted from fear of its being claimed by
the owners of his prizes. Only a few days ago the
Spanish ambassador, Gondomar,[3] sued him for 80,000
ducats. He is a gentleman of the bed-chamber to the
King, is in favour at the court, and on this very day his
Majesty sent me a very earnest message in recommendation of him.

[1] Duffus Hardy, 84–5 ; *Cal. S.P. Venice*, 1617–19, No. 286.
[2] In Mr. Hinds' *Calendar* this has been translated as
' first rates.' I have substituted the words ' large ships '
as there is no evidence of ships being classed under rates as
early as this.
[3] Diego de Sarmiento de Acuña was born about 1570.
He landed in England on his first embassy here in August
1613. Four years later he was created Conde de Gondomar.
He exercised a commanding influence over James I, and was
instrumental in bringing about the execution of Raleigh. He
left England on July 15, 1618; but less than two years
elapsed before he was back again, landing at Dover, March 5,
1620. Died at Madrid, October 2, 1626 (Lyon, *El conde
de Gondomar*).

So anxious was the King that Mainwaring should be given the command, that he despatched the Earl of Montgomery to the ambassador to urge his claim. It was pointed out to Contarini that as they were to have landsmen commanded by Sir Henry Peyton, and ships for their convoy to Venice, the King hoped the Republic would allow one of his subjects to command them, and for that purpose his Majesty had thought fit to recommend Captain Mainwaring, 'a gentleman whom he had made special choice of, and who he held most fit for that employment.' [1] The reason for the royal request is not far to seek. James was about to launch out in a new field of naval enterprise, and he was desirous of inaugurating this departure under the flag of a commander whose ability to conduct it successfully was beyond doubt. Hitherto the Mediterranean had always been regarded by England as outside her sphere of action, and now, for the first time in her history, she was despatching an integral portion of her Navy, for such was the mercantile fleet of the time, to a quarter which, in the years to come, was to loom largely in her naval annals. James had granted the ships for the purpose of protecting an ally, and preserving the balance of power in the Mediterranean, and the importance of the sailing of this little fleet cannot be over-estimated. It is also worthy of remembrance that the negotiations which brought about its prompt despatch were simply due to the patriotic impulses of a few merchants backed by the strenuous efforts of Mainwaring acting on behalf of the Venetian government. It is even probable that some of

[1] Finett, *Finetti Philoxensis*, 1656, p. 50.

the ships belonged to Mainwaring ; certainly
one of them, the Anadem, was owned by his
younger brother George.[1]   After having achieved
so much, it must have been a keen disappointment
not to have received the command which he so
earnestly sought ; but, in spite of the King's wish
that Mainwaring should be chosen, Gondomar's
policy prevailed, and Sir Henry Peyton eventually received the commission.[2]   A commander
who had ' no knowledge of naval affairs ' did not
trouble the Spanish ambassador, and Contarini,
writing to the Republic on the 20th of January
regarding Peyton, said :   ' I have concluded the
engagement for a levy of 500 infantry with Sir
Henry Peyton, one of the good soldiers of Flanders.
I find that he enjoys an excellent character, and
is extremely capable of doing the State good
service, but has no knowledge of naval affairs.'
Though the expedition nominally sailed under
the flag of Peyton, it would appear from Contarini's instructions that Captain Daniel Bannister,
of the Royal Exchange, assumed command of
the ships until they reached Venice, when they
were placed under the command of the Venetian
Captain-General at sea, Barbarigo.[3]

----

[1] In the Venetian Archives there is a document giving the
' Articles of Agreement ' made on the 10th of February, 1618,
between George Maynwaring, Esquire, owner of the good ship
Anadem of London, and the Ambassador Contarini, for four
months at 355l. a month (Cal. S.P. Venice, 1617–19, No. 635).

[2] Peyton had already seen service in the Low Countries.
He married in 1607 a daughter of Protector Somerset, and
remained in the Venetian service until his death in 1623
(D.N.B.).

[3] Duffus Hardy, pp. 84–5 ; S.P. Venice, 1617–19, 304.
Sir J. Corbett was unable to trace the name of the actual
commander when writing of this episode (England in the
Mediterranean, i. 86).

The following table gives the names of the vessels that were hired, with their armament and other details, full particulars of which were sent by Gondomar to the King of Spain.[1]

	Tons.	Guns.	Sailors.	Ducats per month.
Centurion	250	26	60	1400
Dragon	270	26	60	1400
Abigail	250	26	70	1600
Devil of Dunkirk (or Anadem)	250	26	60	1400
Hercules	300	28	70	1600
Mathew	330	28	70	1600
Royal Exchange	400	32	80	1800

Disappointed at not receiving the command of the squadron, but nothing daunted, Mainwaring determined to embark 'in a private capacity,' and to apply personally to the Republic in the hope that he would be able to persuade them to enlist his services. The King's belief in Mainwaring's integrity was unshaken, and as a reward for his enterprise in fitting out the merchant ships, he knighted him on the 20th of March, 1617–18, at Woking, Surrey.[2] On the 18th of April, two days before the sailing of Peyton's squadron, Contarini wrote to the Doge and Senate, informing them of Mainwaring's intention.

Sir Henry Mainwaring, of whom I have already sent an account to your Serenity, is so bent on serving the Republic, that as there is no opportunity for him to fill

---

[1] *Documentos Ineditos*, xlvi. p. 374. In Mainwaring's *Memorial* the *Devil of Dunkirk* is not mentioned.

[2] Shaw, *Book of Knights*, i. 167. His patent of knighthood describes him as ' of Surrey.'

any post on board the squadron, now bound for the Gulf (of Venice), he has determined to embark in a private capacity to offer himself in person to the Captain-General, relying that with the good proof he can render of his experience, and with the warm letters given him by the King for your Excellencies, he shall be able to obtain the honour, so earnestly desired of him, of serving the State. I likewise must back his suit by these present letters, both on account of my knowledge of his devoted will and valour, as also by reason of the recommendation intimated to me by a very leading nobleman on behalf of the King, and yet more in the hope that his exertions may prove to the entire satisfaction of your Serenity.[1]

Though Contarini apparently welcomed the idea of Mainwaring seeking a personal interview with the Doge and Senate, it was not to be, and while the ambassador was penning his despatch, Gondomar was seeking an audience of the King, and vehemently protesting against Mainwaring embarking in any capacity whatever. James, who was but a toy in the hands of the wily Spaniard, was easily won over, and, in order 'to give some satisfaction in appearance' to that dignitary, he ordered Mainwaring to postpone his departure until Gondomar had left England. In the meantime Contarini having successfully completed the terms of his agreement, Peyton's fleet sailed from Gravesend on the 20th of April, in spite of Gondomar's bluff that there were forty Spanish vessels laying in wait for them at the entrance to the Straits.[2]

While the ships were nearing Venice, a strange feeling of uneasiness pervaded the city, and the

---

[1] *Cal. S.P. Venice*, 1617-19, 324.

[2] Penn, *Navy under the Early Stuarts*, p. 46. The terms of Peyton's agreement are given in Duffus Hardy, pp. 84-5.

emotion of the populace was intense. Secretly
and silently the Republic were rounding up the
various foreigners that were supposed to be in
the pay of Ossuna, and in the early morning
light of the 18th of May the bodies of two Frenchmen could be discerned on a gibbet in the piazza;
each corpse hung by the leg, thus showing that
their crime was treason. Five days later the
mutilated body of a third was added, and there
were strange rumours that many other con-
spirators had been strangled in prison, and
their bodies tumbled into the canals in the dead
of night. The Venetians could find no explanation for the strange and horrible sight that met
their eyes, and the Government did not enlighten
them. To the populace at large the strangers
had simply disappeared as mysteriously as they
came.[1] Ossuna meanwhile had instructed Ribera
to withdraw his fleet from Brindisi, and the
English merchant vessels arrived in the Adriatic
without molestation towards the end of June.[2]
The active intervention of England had accomplished its object, and all that Peyton and his
ships had to do was to play a watching game.
Though the combined display of naval force had
saved the city, and the Spanish designs had
been frustrated for the time being, the danger,
as we shall see, had not yet passed.

In England, while the Spanish ambassador
was hounding Sir Walter Raleigh to his death,[3]
another of his victims, Sir Henry Mainwaring,
was impatiently kicking his heels at court. The

---

[1] Horatio Brown's *Venetian Studies*, pp. 334–63, where
a full account of the Spanish plot is given.

[2] Corbett, i. p. 64.

[3] Raleigh arrived at Plymouth from his ill-fated expedition
on the 21st of June, 1618.

failure to accompany the fleet had driven him
to seek some other occupation for his ever restless
spirit, and it was during this period of detention
in England that Mainwaring completed his
Discourse on Piracy and its Suppression, the
manuscript of which he presented to the King as
a thank-offering for his own pardon. A human
document of the greatest interest, it is to be
hoped that James profited by the discourse,
especially as he was about to fit out an expedition
against the Barbary corsairs. This treatise of
Mainwaring's affords to the student of English
history a vivid picture of piracy as it flourished
during the early part of the 17th century. The
tactics adopted by the pirates, with an account
of their various haunts when in need of a refit
or victuals, together with advice on their suppression, are all discussed at length in a shrewd
and learned manner by a former follower of
the ' trade.' [1]

Though Gondomar left England on the 15th
of July, some considerable period elapsed before
Mainwaring was enabled to start for Venice, and
even then he was forced to perform the journey
secretly and in disguise.   He had not yet escaped
the clutches of Philip's ambassador, and as
soon as the news of his departure reached Gondomar, he caused Mainwaring's ' portrait' to
be circulated throughout Milan and other places
en route in the hope of having him stopped.
Eventually Mainwaring crossed to Flanders, but
the journey was not without incident, and finding himself in danger there, he was forced to return
to England and adopt a more devious route.
This time he was more successful, and after

---

[1] The MS. is printed in full in Vol. II.

embarking in a small ship from the Isle of Wight, he managed to effect a landing on an obscure part of the coast of Normandy ; and from thence he travelled through France to Savoy.[1] The great secrecy with which Mainwaring started on his second venture is shown by the fact that Contarini himself was unaware that he was on his way to Venice, and actually thought he had gone to Ireland in disguise to resume his former 'trade of pirate.'[2] It is not surprising, therefore, that elaborate as the Spanish ambassador's plans were, his emissaries failed to apprehend Mainwaring, and on the 12th of November the Republic's ambassador at Savoy reported him safe on his way to Venice. While in Savoy he was privately entertained by the Duke, who made him a present, and designated him as the 'foremost and boldest sailor, and sea-captain, that England possessed.'[3] Towards the end of November he ultimately reached Venice, and Sir Henry Wotton, in an audience with the Doge, spoke of him in the following terms : 'Sir Henry Mainwaring, who was once very famous, though his fame was not altogether good, is now in favour with the King, as he has been converted. He is known to be a valiant soldier, and he wishes to serve the Republic. He comes with letters from the ambassadors Contarini and Zen.'[4]

[1] *Cal. S.P. Venice*, 1617–19, No. 716.
[2] *Ibid.*, 532. Contarini wrote on the 14th of September that Mainwaring proceeded, he understood, to Ireland, where he fitted out a vessel, meaning to resume his former trade of pirate.
[3] *Ibid.*, 581, 716.
[4] *Ibid.*, 599. Zen was the ambassador at Savoy, and wrote that the Spaniards would probably do Mainwaring some harm if he fell into their hands.

In December the Council of Ten received information, 'from an individual who has proved trustworthy upon other occasions,' that during the time Mainwaring was negotiating with the Republic, the Spanish ambassador appeared at the Council table in England to protest against his going. Bearing in mind the great losses that Mainwaring had inflicted upon Spanish shipping at various times, Gondomar, as a last resource, informed him that the King of Spain would grant him a free pardon if he refused to serve the Venetians. 'My king will soon have territory in the state of the Venetians,' Gondomar continued, 'and I have orders, like all other ministers of his Majesty, to forward the plans of the Duke of Ossuna.' Though the threatened occupation of Venice was intended to influence Mainwaring's opinion, it would be useless to deny that it was an idle boast. The threat only too plainly revealed the Spanish designs, and Mainwaring, with the idea of drawing from Gondomar further information, asked him bluntly if he thought it 'so easy to catch Venice napping?' to which the ambassador replied that though 'it was a strong city when it was disarmed,' the Spaniards would 'arm under another pretext, and the acquisition would be made in that way.' Such a candid confession, to a man who himself was the victim of Spanish perfidy, and the impression it must have made on his mind, is easier to imagine than to describe. 'Let the Duke of Ossuna alone,' was Gondomar's significant hint as he left,[1] and its effect on Mainwaring was to make him redouble his efforts on behalf of the Venetians. The information

---

[1] *Cal. S.P. Venice,* 1617–19, 641.

naturally caused a profound sensation in Venice, and on the 10th of December the Council of Ten requested their ambassador in England to obtain confirmation, if possible, of Gondomar's conversation.[1] By the end of the month Wotton had a second audience with the Doge concerning Mainwaring, in which he stated that he was a cavalier of high nobility, whose fame in sea-fighting was such that the King freely discussed maritime matters with him, 'for in them, if I may say so, he has no equal.' However, the Republic appear to have been in no haste to settle matters, and the only satisfaction Wotton received in answer, was to the effect that even if Mainwaring's services were not required by the Republic, they would not let him depart without every mark of honour.[2]

In the meantime Donato, their ambassador in England, was busy gleaning what details he could of Gondomar's outburst, and on the 17th of January, 1619, he sent the report of his investigations to the Doge.

With regard to *Sir Henry Mainwaring (Manerino)* [he wrote], and what the *Spanish ambassador of the time* did about his departure, I have heard the following. *The ambassador* did everything in his power to prevent *Mainwaring* from going to Venice, and obtained from the Council that he should not leave with the ships that are in service, some of which belong to *Sir (Henry)*. I have not found any evidence that the *Spanish ambassador* made use before the council of any of the expressions against the Republic such as are described in your Excellencie's letter. It may be that after using every means to prevent the service of this man—who has the reputation of being very courageous, although *a pirate and not trustworthy—the ambassador* said these

---

[1] *Cal. S.P. Venice*, 1617–19, 639.   [2] *Ibid.*, 671.

E

words privately from his heart, as the actions are in conformity, and the Spanish preparations both by sea and land, carried out with such energy, threaten some great undertaking, which may be well feared. The *said ambassador* had a name at this Court for being very loquacious and by no means circumspect.[1]

Sir Henry Wotton was untiring in his efforts to persuade the Republic to take Mainwaring into their service. On the 21st of January, 1619, he had a further audience with the Doge, during which he asked for a speedy decision regarding him. This audience of Wotton's presents a very interesting sidelight on Mainwaring's early career, giving as it does an account of the ' accident ' that led him to adopt the rôle of a pirate. Wotton stated that the manner in which Mainwaring acquired his knowledge of seamanship was perhaps ' not altogether worthy, yet it was very excusable and straightforward.' He informed the Doge that many years ago Mainwaring undertook to go with three ships to the Indies, but owing to the intervention of the Spanish ambassador, the projected voyage did not take place. Disgusted at this treatment, he went off with a number of vessels ; and by way of revenge on the Spaniards, proceeded to capture any of their ships that chanced to cross his path, finally finding himself at the head of thirty or forty sail, mostly taken at the expense of the Spaniards.[2] The Doge replied that the affair was now in the hands of the Signory, and that he believed ' the gentleman would be satisfied.'

[1] *S.P. Venice*, 1617-19, 695. The words printed in italics are in cipher in the original Italian.
[2] *Ibid.*, 699.

As a last resource, Mainwaring himself drew up an account of his endeavours to fit out and command the ships, which he presented to the Doge on the 25th of January. In the ' considerations ' which he advanced, he advocated that three large ships should be employed instead of the seven merchant ships, and that they should be manned with sailors only, and not a mixed crew of soldiers and sailors as was then the case. These ' considerations ' he worked out with mathematical precision, paying the strictest attention to the most minute details. In them he gave the number of guns that would be required for each ship, with the amount of powder and shot necessary for each piece. The number of men to work the sails, the number for each gun, and even the number of powder monkeys were duly noted. The duties of all the officers and non-combatants he set forth in a manner of one thoroughly conversant with all that pertained to the sailing and fighting of a ship. Against three large ships, he stated, the seven merchant-men hired by the Republic would make a very poor show. He concluded by stating that he would undertake to provide efficient seamen, &c., if the Republic would adopt his scheme, which would enable them to effect a saving of over 100,000 ducats a year.

This paper on the relative value of large and small ships in naval warfare, a subject which even in the 20th century continues to evoke discussion,[1] cannot fail to be of interest to all students of naval history, for it throws considerable light on the art of gunnery and maritime warfare as understood by our ancestors in the early Stuart

[1] See Corbett, *Campaign of Trafalgar*, pp. 44-9 : Jane, *Heresies of Sea Power*, pp. 296-309.

period. It is here printed from the original in the
Venetian archives.[1]

Considerations advanced by Sir Henry Mainwaring.

The three ships of 500 and 550 tons burthen are
capable of carrying 20 culverins and 20 half culverins
each, with 200 English sailors. They would defeat seven
ships which were no stronger than those which went
from England, even though manned by Englishmen.
With other nations it would be easier. It is necessary to
consider the difference between the great and the light
galleys. I believe it is admitted that five light galleys
carry the same armament as one large one, and yet
they cannot encounter a large galley because it is easier
to fight, as all the force is concentrated in one unit. I
will try to make my point clear to those who have little
or no experience.[2] I begin with artillery. Everyone
will admit that large pieces which fire heavy shot and
burn more powder produce a greater effect.

Below I have placed in a table the armament of each of
the seven ships [3] :

The Royal Exchange. 28 pieces, that is 6 half culverins
and 22 sakers and lesser pieces.

The Abigail. 26 pieces, that is 4 half culverins and 22
sakers and lesser pieces.

The Thomas Hercules. 22 pieces, that is 4 half culverins
and 18 sakers and lesser pieces.

The Matthew. 24 pieces, that is 2 half culverins and 22
sakers and lesser pieces.

The Adam.[4] 22 pieces, that is 2 half culverins and 20
sakers and lesser pieces.

[1] The original is in Italian, and has been translated by
Mr. Allen Hinds and published in the *Calendars of State
Papers, Venice*, 1617–19, No. 714.

[2] Printed exprience.

[3] The armament differs slightly from Gondomar's list.

[4] Her real name was apparently Ann Adam. Called also
the Anadem.

The Centurion. 22 pieces, that is 2 half culverins and 20 sakers and lesser pieces.

The Dragon. 22 pieces, that is 2 half culverins and 20 sakers and lesser pieces.

A total of 166 pieces, comprising 22 half culverins and 144 sakers and lesser pieces. As they have about as many sakers as minions, I propose to allow 6 pounds of powder for each piece of ordnance.

The quantity for the half culverins at 9 pounds each $22 \times 9 = 198$ pounds.

The quantity for the sakers and minions at 6 pounds each $144 \times 6 = 864$ pounds, making a total of 1062 pounds of powder for the seven ships. The artillery of the three ships of 500 to 550 tons burthen would be as follows :—

In each ship 20 half culverins, 60 in all, and 9 pounds of powder each, gives 540 pounds, also twenty culverins on the lower deck, making sixty in all, at 15 pounds of powder each, gives 900 pounds, or 1445 pounds of powder in all. Deduct 1062, and this leaves 378, or a third less. Although there are three ships for seven, and they carry 120 pieces instead of 166, yet they are one third stronger. This is a great advantage, and I venture to say that no man exists who has given so much consideration to this secret.

The advantage in shot is even greater, as we employ less powder in proportion to an increase in the size of the shot.

Weight of shot.

Culverins [1]	19 pounds
Half culverins . . .	11¾ pounds
Sakers	9 pounds
Minions	5 pounds

[1] A culverin of brass weighed approximately 3761 lbs. ; a demi-culverin of brass, 2894 lbs. ; a saker of brass, 1839 lbs. ; a minion of brass, 1400 lbs. (*Mariner's Mirror*, vi. p. 51).

Thus the seven ships carry in weight [*i.e.* shot] 22 half culverins weighing 258½ pounds, and 144 sakers and minions weighing 1008 pounds, or 1266½ pounds [of shot] in all.   The three ships would carry 60 half culverins, weighing 705, and 60 culverins weighing 19 pounds, making 1845 pounds [of shot] in all, showing a difference of 579 pounds.

The artillery of the seven ships being small can do little damage to large ships, but large ships could do a great deal of harm to them.   These ships also carry land soldiers who are expected to do great execution with their arquebuses.   But the large ships can so damage the upper deck with their artillery that they will not be able to use their artillery or muskets, or very little owing to the smoke, and it is 50 to 1 that they do them no harm. Those who trust so much to a number of land soldiers in sea fights do not know how much they hinder the sailors   In sea fights musketry fire is only useful upon two occasions, if the ship is on fire, to prevent the men from extinguishing it, and if the ship has a gun shot on the water line to keep her steady without pulling her over from the outside.

The amount of space for the men in a large ship is a consideration of great importance as the men are further apart and better able to fight.   If the three ships are as good sailers as the others they would bring more artillery to bear.   I can only prove this by a long discussion in technical terms, and I forbear because I cannot express myself in the language.[1]   If the little ships had to fight in a high wind the big ones would smash them.   What good would they and the Flemish ships of their size be if they met a great galleon, which would fear them as little as a galley would fear as many gondolas.   I hope that I have proved my point that three such ships with English sailors under a good commander would deal with fifteen of the other ships.

Two hundred sailors would suffice to fight each ship, more would be in the way.   Three men to each piece

---

[1] *I e.* the Italian tongue.

of ordnance, not to leave their posts except for extra-ordinary emergencies, that makes 120 men. The following officers and non-combatants : captain, master, helmsman, two barbers, two in the powder magazine, two caulkers, and four powder monkeys, making 133. This leaves 67 men to manage the sails and use their muskets. This number suffices, so that they do not disturb the gunners, and as all are sailors they can be employed in various ways and know where they can hurt the enemy, and can manage the sails. If there were more they would have to go below, as there is no need for land soldiers. Sea fighting consists in two points : orders, which no one can give who does not know the technical terms, and execution, in which a sailor is better than five soldiers, for the latter can only manage their muskets, while the former can work a gun, manage the sails and board the enemy with a decent weapon. Thus when soldiers are on board they should be under the command of the sea captain, or they will get in the way. When two fleets meet, the one best provided with experienced sailors will certainly win.[1]

The seven ships have 500 soldiers and 470 sailors, 970 in all, and the three ships would have 600 sailors or 370 men less. But they would have 130 more sailors than the others, which makes them stronger. To prove this, put the 130 sailors in a ship with 30 pieces of artillery and 1000 soldiers in another, with 40 pieces : the former would take the latter because they would be superior in manipulating the ship and guns. I take the liberty to say that all men experienced in sea fighting are of opinion that the great Galleon of St. Mark and all the ships of the republic would do more service in a fight if two-thirds of these were men sailors and the other troops put on shore.

[1] The Venetian ambassador in England, Foscarini, wrote that the King supplies his ships with sailors only as the soldiers are of little use, and because he will not trust his ships to soldiers (*S.P. Venice*, 1617–19, p. 451).

The cost of the seven English ships is as follows :

	Sailors	Ducats a month.
The Royal Exchange	80	1800
The Abigail . .	70	1600
The Hercules . .	70	1600
The Matthew . .	70	1600
The Anadem . .	60	1400
The Centurion .	60	1400
The Dragon . .	60	1400
Total . .		10,800

The 500 soldiers cost about 4000 ducats a month, 48,000 ducats a year.

Total for the seven ships in the year, 178,320 ducats.

The three ships with their 600 sailors, which could easily beat the others, would cost : 100 fighting men, who must have sufficient food, which is more than is required in merchant ships, 26,400 ducats.

That the Signory may know that it does not pay too dear, the King of Great Britain pays 8*d.* a day to his sailors for food, making 48½ ducats a year, and Sir Henry Peyton pays 10*d.* a day, making 60 ducats, but I will undertake to do it for 44 ducats a year per head.

The wages of the 600 sailors at 6 ducats a month, one ducat more than is given in merchant ships, amount to 43,200 ducats.

The total cost thus comes to 69,600 ducats, a yearly saving of 108,720 ducats.[1]

The Doge and Senate were greatly impressed by the ' considerations ' which Mainwaring propounded, but in spite of the King's wish, and the exertions of Sir Henry Wotton, a post sufficiently worthy of his abilities was not to be found at

[1] Though we know that some of Peyton's soldiers were dissatisfied with their pay, and mutinied soon after their arrival in the Adriatic, history is extraordinarily silent as to the operations of the ships. Apparently their engagement terminated at the end of 1619, but Peyton himself remained in the Venetian service until his death in October 1623.

the time. The Republic, however, realised the possibilities of the ' capital ship ' in naval warfare —four of which in Mainwaring's opinion would have been sufficient to oppose all the galleys that Ossuna possessed[1]—and they were of the opinion, that through Mainwaring's agency, James might be persuaded to lend them some warships. With this end in view they decided to despatch Mainwaring as an envoy to the King, to sound the possibility of such a transaction, and in the event of him being successful, the ships were to be placed under his command. At the same time they issued implicit instructions to their ambassador in England to assist Mainwaring's endeavours both with the King and the Government to obtain the ships.

You will see [they wrote] that Mainwaring obtains, as he promises, the King's promise that he will serve us faithfully. . . . If he complies, and he has made the proposals, you will arrange the rest by the light of his own calculations, for the payment of the sailors and other expenses. We give you power to supply him with 200 crowns a month of 7 lire each for the time that he remains in our service. . . . You must keep to yourself the knowledge that we are thinking of getting rid of the seven English ships, which, to tell the truth, are ill adapted to our needs, if we can obtain the four vessels in question.

The necessity for great secrecy in the matter was impressed upon the ambassador, ' so that Mainwaring, feeling doubtful about our decision, may use the greater efforts to obtain the ships from the King.'[2]

With a gift of six hundred crowns for the expenses of the journey, Mainwaring started on

[1] *Cal. S.P. Venice*, 1617–19, No. 716.
[2] *Ibid.*, 718.

his mission on the 26th of January, Sir Henry
Wotton, who had always held him in high esteem,
entrusting him with two letters, one to the
King explaining his mission, and the other to
Lord Zouch, the Lord Warden of the Cinque
Ports.

The journey overland was one of considerable
difficulty, if we may judge from the accounts
of early 17th century travellers. The roads
were bad, bands of robbers were numerous,
and in the case of Mainwaring there was an
additional anxiety—the possibility of being appre-
hended by the many emissaries of the Spanish
Government. On the way he appears to have
suffered from illness, but otherwise there was
nothing to mar the success of his journey until
he reached the Rhine. In those days the Rhine
was ‘ the great artery of Europe, through which
the life-blood of civilisation flowed.’ Every castle
and fortified village teemed with life and bristled
with arms, and the traveller was frequently stopped
and compelled to pay a heavy toll before he was
able to proceed.[1] At an ‘ Austrian place ’ on
the river, the name of which is not disclosed,
Mainwaring informs us he was detained for a
time, but whether he effected his release by
bribing the authorities or not we do not know.
However, he was eventually able to continue his
journey, reaching England on the 3rd of March,
thirty-six days after leaving Venice.[2] The urgency
of his mission did not permit of any delay, and
Mainwaring, on learning that James was at
Newmarket, immediately set out to interview
him, and deliver Wotton’s letter explaining the

[1] *Quarterly Review*, cii. 403.
[2] The journey in 1617 had occupied Contarini thirty-
seven days.

purport of the Venetian request.[1] The main portion of this letter is here reproduced.[2]

May it please your most Sacred Majesty.

Since the late despatch of my Secretary unto your Majesty I have been called to the Palace, where the Prince by express order of the Senate caused to be read unto me (as their form is) a longer writing, and more solemnly couched, than they had done at any time before, since my last residence : containing a relation of their affairs as they now stand, and thereupon a serious request unto your Majesty, which they besought me to represent unto your gracious will, with those important reasons which did here move it. . . . Now, their suit unto your Majesty hereon grounded, is : That as at other times, you have been pleased, by your Royal goodness to interest your self in their conservation (which they will ever be ready to acknowledge in any of your occasions), so at the present you will be likewise pleased to honour them, and to protect them, with the loan of four of your own vessels, that are otherwise not employed. Wherein, first they consider that your Majesty may do it without any just distaste of any other Prince whosoever : because they require this favour merely (as the Duke expressed unto me) for their own defence, not descending to any Individuum, and therefore it may be shadowed, if your Majesty so please, under the generality of guarding them against the African pirates [3] that swarm in strong number. . . . This is as much, as they have committed to the delivery of my pen, touching their own fears, and their recourse to your Majesty, which I have been the willinger to represent upon considering that your Majesty may do it without any charge to your self ; that your vessels suffer as much with lying still, as with use ; that you may have caution for their restitution, and limit the time at your pleasure. . . . The bearer

[1] *Cal. S.P. Venice*, 1617–19, 769.

[2] Wotton's *Letters* (Roxburghe Club), 1850, pp. 103–7.

[3] An expedition against the Barbary pirates was a favourite excuse to cover up any sinister act in the early 17th century.

of this letter is Sir Henry Mainwaring, who hath been here some weeks. And having had so confident introducement with them, through your Majesty's recommendation of him by my Lord of Montgomery to their Ambassador Contarini, they have taken a singular liking of his person, and have proceeded so far as to communicate with him the purpose of their suit unto your Majesty : and after much conference besides about their own maritime service, they have finally let him return (for he refused any employment, that they could at the present give him) with a thankful recompense, for the charge of his journey, and an honourable testimony of their conceit of him to their ambassador.

And so having discharged the present duty, I humbly commit your Sacred Person and Estates to God's continual guard.   Ever resting,

Your Majesty's most faithful
poor subject and servant,
HENRY WOTTON.

From Venice,
This 22nd of January.
Style of England.   1618.

As already stated, Mainwaring was the bearer of two letters from Sir Henry Wotton, and in his letter to Zouch the ambassador wrote in glowing terms of Mainwaring, on whom he bestowed the not inappropriate epithet of a 'redeemed Neptune.' This letter is here transcribed from the original in the Public Record Office [1] :

I am very glad [Wotton wrote] of this opportunity, that by the hand of a gentleman who doth so entirely honour you, both in his continual speech and in his soul, I may revive also with your Lordship mine own long devotion.

Wotton continues his letter with an account

[1] *S.P. Venice,* xxii. (P.R.O.), February 3, 1619.

of his student days, and sums up the Venetian crisis thus :

For the public affairs we stand here yet very ambiguously. The Land was long since quiet, but the sea, as the more movable element, is still in agitation ; and we are artificially kept at excessive charge by a mad Viceroy and a winking Pope, while the King of Spain, in the meanwhile standeth at the benefit of time and fortune, ready to authorize or disavow the event according to the success, which I take to be the sum of our case. But these things will be more particularly delivered to your Lordship by this redeemed Neptune as I have baptized him : for they here think him more than a man that knows so much more than themselves. And in truth, if any place had been vacant worthy of his sufficiency, there wanted no desire to hold him, as they have expressed by offers to himself, and declared in their letters by him to their ambassador ; and most of all in the confident communication of their affairs and desires with him, which likewise include some hope of their having him again, as your Lordship will perceive by the subject of my despatch to the King; which he carrieth.

I must add hereunto for mine own part that I have been glad of this occasion, which hath given me a better taste of him, and of his fair and clear dispositions, then I could take at a transitory view when I passed my last duty with your Lordship in Canterbury.[1]

From the time that Mainwaring landed in England, the success of his mission does not appear to have been very hopeful. Donato, the Republic's ambassador in England, thought he would have no difficulty in obtaining four or five old ships, though the Archbishop of Canterbury in the course of a conversation with the

[1] This is rather curious. Mainwaring was not officially pardoned till June 1616. Wotton reached England in the autumn of 1615, and left for Venice March 18, 1616.

ambassador regarding the ships, certainly did
not hold out much hope of the Venetian request
being granted. ' Non esse honorificum, non esse
tutum et esse novum committere naves Regias
alieno Principi,' he informed Donato, ' because
if they fell into the hands of an enemy with their
arms and artillery, the King would be bound
to recover them, and it was not becoming to
entrust one's own forces in the hands of others.' [1]

Whatever the private opinion of the Archbishop may have been on the subject, the real
difficulty lay not so much in the propriety of
loaning the ships, as the possibility of being
able to spare them at such a critical time.   The
fact was that James had a card of his own to
play, which demanded the whole of his resources.
The extensive naval preparations of Spain, and
the activity of her ' mad viceroy,' had caused
grave doubts in the mind of the English Government as to what the real intentions of the
Spaniards were, and while Mainwaring was on
his way from Venice, James had actually ordered
six warships and several merchantmen to be
immediately rigged and fitted out for special
service.[2] Of this secret mobilisation, which was
brought about by the alarming news from Spain,
where every dockyard and arsenal in the Empire
was busy equipping a powerful fleet,[3] neither
the Republic nor Mainwaring were of course aware.

---

[1] *Cal. S.P. Venice*, 1617–19, No. 769. Donato to the Doge,
7th March, 1619. Mainwaring became one of Donato's
intimate friends, and being familiar with the Italian tongue,
he acted as Donato's interpreter at court. *Ibid.* 148, 149, 151.

[2] *S.P. Dom.*, James I, cv. 103. In the Bodleian there
is an estimate, dated February 4, 1619, for fitting out sixteen
serviceable ships in the Thames for seven months, with
1440 men (*Cal. of Clarendon State Papers*, i. 13).

[3] Gardiner, *History of England*, iii. 286.

The Spaniards had gathered together a large fleet of galleys, whose rendezvous was stated to be Messina, with the object of forcing a passage through the Gulf of Venice to Trieste. This, however, was believed to be but a cloak for some ulterior design. By some, her objective was thought to be an invasion of England, while our ambassador at the Hague expressed an opinion that the Spanish preparations ' tended to the invasion of some place where assistance is expected from the natives of the country,' which the Dutch believed to be Ireland.[1]

The Venetians, therefore, were not alone in their fear of the Spanish fleet, and throughout England preparations were set on foot to guard against a possible attack. James acted with commendable promptness and showed unusual activity in mobilising a part of the fleet. Ostensibly it was to sail against the pirates of Algiers, as Wotton had suggested, but great secrecy was preserved in its ultimate object and destination. Coke, one of the Navy Commissioners, wrote that ' in this preparation against pirates it may be conceived the state hath some further design,' and therefore it was desirable to carry it out by ' the trust of a few,' instead of by general warrants to all the Navy Commissioners.[2] We now know that the state had some further design, and that secret orders were issued to the fleet to enter the Mediterranean, and in the event of the Spaniards making sail in the direction of the Gulf of Venice they were to attack them.[3] Of the actual composition

[1] Sir Dudley Carleton's *Letters*, p. 342 ; *S.P. Dom.*, James I, cv. 69.

[2] *Hist. MSS. Com.*, 12i, p. 104.

[3] Gardiner, *Relations between England and Germany*, i. xxxii.

of the English fleet contemporary history is extraordinarily silent, but from a naval minute drawn
up nearly fifty years after the event,[1] and hitherto
unnoticed, in connection with an expedition
against Spain, we know that it comprised some
of the most formidable in the English Navy. Of
the royal ships there were the Red Lion and
Vanguard of 650 tons ; the Assurance of 600 tons ;
the Speedwell of 400 tons ; and by a curious irony
of fate, two ships that had originally been built
for Raleigh, the Ark Royal of 800 tons, and the
Destiny of 500 tons, built in 1616.[2] The former
was Nottingham's flagship against the Armada—
'the odd ship in the world for all conditions'—
and the latter the ship in which Raleigh sailed
on his ill-fated expedition to Guiana : a combination of circumstances which the superstitious
might regard as an ill omen for Spain. The
royal ships were manned with 1300 mariners
and gunners, but of the others, consisting of five
of the Cinque Ports and fourteen merchantmen,
we know very little, except that the merchantmen
carried 1200 seamen.[3]

Not only was the English fleet fitted out, but
the troops in Devon and other maritime counties
were mustered, and an effort was made to put
the coast defences—which were in a deplorable
condition—in a state to resist any attempted
invasion of these islands. From Dover it was

[1] Entitled *In the Voyage against ye Pirates of Algiers,
anno* 1618' (*i.e.* 1618–19). Printed in Charnock, ii. 271.
Charnock never knew of the real object of the mobilisation, and
remarks on 'the total silence of historians on the subject
of it.'

[2] At the beginning of 1619 there were only fourteen ships
in the Navy of 400 tons and over.

[3] Charnock, ii. 271.

reported that there was a general fear of the Spaniards in the town, and that the castle and forts were unprovided, while the crippled state of the defences of Plymouth called for urgent measures to be taken by the Government. Money to man the coast defences was therefore called for, and the expense of equipping the fleet, consisting of twenty-five ships, was to be borne by an impost of 2 per cent. on imports and exports.[1]

The financial difficulty that England was confronted with called forth an ingenious suggestion from Mainwaring with regard to the Venetian request. It was addressed to the Marquis of Buckingham, who had just been appointed Lord High Admiral, and was to the effect that the Venetians being willing, at their own expense, to rig out the ships they borrow, the King might save expense by professing that he was no longer suspicious of the Spanish fleet, and would therefore desist in rigging his ships, but, that if the Republic wished they might complete them. The condition on which Mainwaring stated the ships should be lent was that in the event of the Spanish fleet entering the Straits the English ships were to follow them; but on the other hand, if the Spaniards did not sail south the ships would be released by the Venetians, who would then have no further need for them. In the event of the Spanish preparations never maturing, the King, Mainwaring pointed out, would then be free to use his ships against Algiers.[2] Here then was a happy solution

[1] *S.P. Dom.*, James I, cv. 84, 103, 108 ; cvii. 3. Corbett, *England in the Mediterranean*, i. pp. 89–90.
[2] *Cal. S.P. Dom.*, James I, cv. 148. The original document is reprinted in Vol. II.

to the monetary problem, and at the same time
an admirable plan for frustrating whatever move
the Spaniards decided upon. In the event of
their fleet entering the Mediterranean to attack
Venetian territory, it was known that they must
stop at Messina or on the coast of Sardinia in
order to take on board several thousand troops
that they had mustered there.[1] This, as Mainwaring informed Buckingham, would enable the
English ships to reach the Adriatic first. In
the words of Sir Julian Corbett, ' Mainwaring's
suggestion for meeting the whole situation was
as ingenious as his strategy was sound.' [2] Nevertheless, James was loth to abandon a project
which he had set his heart on accomplishing, that
of checking the growing power of the Spaniards
by sea, and at the same time protecting the
interest of the allies in Germany, Venice, and
Bohemia,[3] by a display of naval force in the
Mediterranean. It is no small wonder, therefore, that Mainwaring, though he found the
King ' in a most excellent frame of mind ' towards
the Venetians, and ' used all the arguments in
his power ' to render James favourable, failed
in the object of his mission, and returned from
Newmarket on the 14th of March.[4]

Though the Venetian request was not granted,
their anxiety for the welfare of the Republic
was now allayed. While Mainwaring was

---

[1] *S.P. Dom.*, James I, cv. 148; Gardiner, *England*, iii. 187.

[2] Corbett, *England in the Mediterranean*, i. 94.

[3] Letter of Lord Danvers in the Bodleian, dated Feb. 3,
1618–19 (*Cal. of Clarendon State Papers*, i. p. 13). In
1618 a revolution broke out in Bohemia, which led to the
disastrous European conflagration known as the Thirty Years'
War. In 1619 James' son-in-law Frederick became King
of Bohemia.

[4] Donato to the Doge, *Cal. S.P. Venice*, 1618–19, 784.

negotiating with the King, they became aware of the real destination of our 'secret expedition,' and on the 15th of March, through the agency of Sir Henry Wotton, they expressed their gratitude to James for resolving to send 'sufficient number of your own ships, as likewise other vessels belonging to the merchants of your kingdom, towards the coast of Spain to invigilate for the common safety over the preparations and designs of that King.' [1]

James found his policy crowned with success. By the end of the month there were signs that the Spanish preparations were abating, and at the beginning of April the English ships were in consequence stayed. On the 18th the Council informed the Lord Warden of the Cinque Ports that the King, for reasons best known to himself, 'had decided to postpone the expedition against the pirates.' [2]

It therefore stands to the credit of James, that by his prompt action in ordering the fleet to be prepared for sea, he had shattered whatever ambitions the Spaniards may have had, and although the ships that were to constitute the English fleet never actually left home waters, they proved to the world that 'besides being a fighting machine, a powerful navy is also a powerful diplomatic asset.' [3] To cut Venice off from supplies and reinforcements by land did not present serious difficulties to Spain, but she

[1] Gardiner, *Letters, &c.,* i. 49.
[2] *Cal. S.P. Dom.,* James I, cviii. 15, 53. Curiously enough, the Spaniards themselves declared their preparations were for an attack on Algiers, and had 'no manner of reference to our quarters' (Letter dated Feb. 16, 1618–19, in Bishop Goodman's *Memoirs,* ii. 177).
[3] Corbett, i. 4.

could never have hoped for a like success on sea while the English fleet were acting against her and keeping the sea routes open.

On the 30th of April the Doge thanked Wotton for his own and Mainwaring's efforts on behalf of the Republic, and with this episode all hope of adventure and distinction in the Venetian service came to an end.

CHAPTER III

1620–23

THE CINQUE PORTS

ON Mainwaring's return from Venice, it was obvious that some post worthy of his acceptance would have to be found for him in England. A man of his adventurous spirit could not be expected to play the idle rôle of a courtier, and fortunately soon after his return an employment in which he could do service to the state happened to present itself—that of Lieutenant of Dover Castle and Deputy Warden of the Cinque Ports.

The early history of the Cinque Ports is closely allied with that of the Royal Navy : being the nearest harbours to the continent the state depended on their support in times of national peril, and in reward for their services in ships and men granted them certain privileges and honours. Though the position they occupied was originally of great importance, their status had considerably deteriorated by the beginning of the 17th century. Their decline was simultaneous with that of the Navy, and the office of Lord Warden was conducted with scarcely more zeal and honesty than that of the Lord High Admiral. Patriots like Raleigh had drawn attention to the 'beggary and decay' of the Ports, and Mainwaring had advocated the employment of some of the maritime population in repairing 'the castles and forts on the sea-coast,' which were ' miserably ruined and decayed.'

Lord Zouch, who had held the office of Lord Warden since 1615, was old and infirm, and most of his time seems to have been passed at his country seat in Hampshire. Prior to his appointment he had already seen considerable service under the crown, and, to relieve himself of the irksome duties of the Wardenship, he was on the look-out for a suitable person as his deputy at Dover. Mainwaring having been strongly recommended to him by Sir Henry Wotton, he decided to offer him the post, an offer which was gladly accepted. By the middle of February Mainwaring was installed in his new position, and on the 21st of the month he wrote to Zouch thanking him for the appointment.' [1]

I know your Lordship doth expect that it is fit that my works not words should express my dutiful thankfulness to your Lordship in the careful and diligent following and performing of your Lordship's directions and commands. I will therefore spare your Lordship the labour of reading, and myself of writing in that theme, and strive to expel most devices of this age in sining, and doing according to the doctrine of love profest unto your Lordship. Wherein though I doubt not that my actions shall ever justify me in your good opinion and favour, and believe that all my works cannot merit the loss of your Lordship's so many noble, kind, and truly noble favours. . . . Let me beg leave of your Lordship to make this protestation from the bottom of my heart, and most sincere assertion of my soul, that no man shall serve your Lordship with more diligence, more love, or more honesty. And for those errors I may now at my first entrance commit (which yet I hope

[1] *S.P. Dom.*, James I, cxii. 96.

shall not be gross) for want of experience, I doubt not of your Lordship's pardon and patience, till a little time spent in diligent observation hath made me more able to do your Lordship service.

He also gave particulars about the Boder [1] and Gunners of the Castle, and concluded his letter by asking Zouch to send ' as soon as conveniently may be, my companions and most beloved friends the books and instruments which your Lordship promised me.'

What the duties of the Lieutenant were during the 17th century is uncertain, but, as his title indicates, he was the deputy of the Constable, and acted under his instructions. In an ancient code of laws drawn up for regulating the duties of the various officers of the Castle, the Lieutenant, the Clerk of the Exchequer, the Marshal, and others, were at stated times to survey the works and walls of the Castle, both within and without, and order any repairs that were necessary. It was also customary for the Lieutenant, when he came to reside in the Castle, to show the authority which had been exercised by his predecessors in office, by having the keys of the gates brought to him every night after the mounting of the guard. It is also interesting to note, that if the King came unexpectedly in the night, the great gates were not to be opened to him, but he was to go to the postern, called the King's gate, where he would gain admittance with some of his suite, the rest being admitted at sunrise. The porters at the gates were not to suffer any persons to enter until they had taken particular notice of them, and in the event of their being

[1] A very ancient office in the Castle; the Boder's chief duty seems to have consisted in executing the warrants of the Warden and Constable's courts (Statham, *Dover*, p. 305).

strangers, the Constable or his Lieutenant was to be called.[1]

During the reign of James I the corporation of Dover surrendered to the crown all their claims upon 'the duties, droits, and waste lands belonging to the pier,' which the King vested in a special board consisting of the Lord Warden, his Lieutenant, and several others called assistants.[2] Full of zeal for his new post, one of Mainwaring's first efforts on taking up his residence at the Castle was to endeavour to put the defences on a sounder footing. The mounting of the guard was also unsatisfactory, and he asked leave to have two men to watch by night, and four by day.[3] At this period there were sworn watchmen, who had to keep ward in turns, and at the end of a month they were allowed to return to their houses, to attend to their lands, and to enjoy the rural amusements with their families and friends during the vacation.[4]

As a sign of the condition into which the national defences had sunk, it is worthy of note that the forts of the Castle were reported unprovided for ; the guns were without gunpowder, and in lieu of it ashes and sand were substituted ![5] Nor were the other castles of the Cinque Ports in a less lamentable condition, and the captains of three of them informed the Lord Treasurer that they had long petitioned for a supply of ordnance, and money for repairs, but without success. In consequence they were neither able to defend the coast from attacks of ships of war, nor defend their own merchantmen who sought

[1] Lyon, *Dover*, ii. 125, 134.
[2] Statham, *Dover*, p. 115.
[3] *S.P. Dom.*, James I, cxii. 109.
[4] Lyon, *Dover*, ii. 113.
[5] *S.P. Dom.*, James I, cv. 108 ; cvii. 29.

refuge there.[1] Although guns and powder were badly wanted in most of the forts throughout the kingdom, the Spanish ambassador was allowed to export a great quantity of powder at a time when there were rumours of a Spanish invasion of England. Had the Spaniards come, a contemporary wrote, ' the English would have had their throats cut.'[2] Although this expresses the feeling of the time, the nation was happily spared such a catastrophe, even supposing it to have been possible. At the moment, however, Spanish policy did not favour a war with England. The state of affairs in Bohemia, and the recent blow to her prestige in the Mediterranean, had forced her more than ever to seek the friendship of England, and early in 1620 Gondomar was once again despatched on a mission to James, with the Spanish marriage treaty in his pocket.

On the 5th of March the ambassador landed at Dover, and the following letter announcing his arrival was immediately sent by Mainwaring to Zouch :[3]

Right Honourable—The Spanish ambassador with his train landed at Dover this Sunday after dinner about two of the clock in the afternoon, being the 5th of this month. I understand 'tis the custom to acquaint your Lordship in post of such men's arrival, and therefore I have instantly despatched this away. News I know none, nor do I think it fit to attend the knowing of any, lest (your) Lordship should not have the first knowledge of his arrival. Humbly taking my leave I rest

Your Lordships most humble
and faithful servant,
H. MAINWARING.

Dover Castle, this 5 of March, 1619.[4]

---

[1] *S.P. Dom.*, James I, cxxviii. 109.
[2] *Ibid.*, cv. 103, 140 ; cvii. 31.   [3] *Ibid.*, cxiii. 8.
[4] *I.e.* Old Style, really 1619–20.

The ambassador's arrival in a small vessel
which lacked ordnance did not permit of a salute
being fired in his honour.   The town also extended
a very cold welcome to him, and the resources
of the corporation would not admit of a banquet.
Mainwaring, ever suspicious of his old enemy,
went down to the beach to meet him, for which
courtesy Gondomar offered to forgive him twelve
crowns out of the million that he had taken
from the subjects of the King of Spain, provided
Mainwaring would make good the rest.

I gave him no pieces at his landing [Mainwaring
wrote], because he came in a little ship which had no
ordnance to salute or give notice to the Castle.   Therefore
I took no notice of him, but afterwards I went down to
present myself unto him.   He received me very kindly,
and being merry with me so was willing now to come
to a composition with me for the million of crowns
which he said I owed the Spaniards, and that he would,
for the favour I did him in coming, rebate me 12 crowns
if I would pay him the rest.[1]

In spite of Gondomar's courtly jest, it is to be
presumed that they parted on good terms, for
Mainwaring records that he ordered a salute of
nine pieces to be fired on the ambassador's
departure for London.
    Though thoroughly taken up with his work
at the Castle, Mainwaring still found time to pursue
his mathematical studies.   In consequence of a
hurried return from Venice, his books and instruments had been left behind, the loss of which
prompted him to inquire again if Zouch would
supply the deficiency.   ' I pray you,' he wrote
to Nicholas, [2] ' put my Lord in mind of my books,

---

[1] *S.P. Dom.*, James I, cxiii. 10.
[2] *Ibid.*, cxiii. 25.   Edward Nicholas, born 1593.   In
December 1618 he was appointed secretary to Lord Zouch,

also of his rules or any mathematical instruments. My own are all left in my trunk at Venice.'

Every precaution was taken during the reign of James I to guard against foreign spies and Jesuit emissaries landing in England. In the State Papers of the period are to be found many incidents connected with this watching of the coast. The guns being all dismounted at Dover Castle, one of the first things Mainwaring did was to exclude all foreigners from the gun-yard.[1] The same vigilance was kept up in the other ports, and a recusant named Anthony Lynch was arrested on landing at Folkestone. He was sent to Dover Castle by the Mayor, and on the 3rd of April, 1620, Mainwaring reported the result of his examination to Zouch. It showed that Lynch was a native of Galway, who had been to Rouen while on his way to England. According to his own statement he had not conversed with Jesuit or other priests. When asked to take the oath of allegiance he professed not to understand it, but was finally prevailed upon to take the oath of supremacy.[2] Another recusant was Robert Whitmore who had been detained at Dover, and afterwards kept a close prisoner in the Castle. He excited the pity of Gondomar when he landed at Dover, and the

and when Buckingham took over the Wardenship in 1624, he was continued in that office. In 1625 he was made Secretary to the Admiralty. During 1627–8 he represented Dover in Parliament. He was knighted 26th November 1641, and appointed principal Secretary of State. He died in 1669 (*D.N.B.*).

[1] *S.P. Dom.*, cxii. 96. In 1623 the brass ordnance in Dover Castle consisted of : Basilisco, 1 ; Canon per. 2 ; Sakers, 6 ; Mynions, 2 ; Fawcons, 5 ; Fawconetts, 2 (*Add. MSS.*, 9294, f. 247).

[2] *Ibid.*, cxiii. 81.

ambassador begged Mainwaring that Whitmore might be allowed to exercise on the beach for the benefit of his health.[1]

Whatever the occasion demanded, whether it was the examination of strangers landing at Dover, or necessary repairs to the Castle, or anything that concerned the welfare of the Ports generally, nothing seems to have escaped Mainwaring's vigilance.

His activity, however, by no means excluded his older interests, and about this time he obtained leave to come to London in connection with the business of the Virginia Company.[2] Two of his brothers were also connected with the enterprise at this period—Sir Arthur,[3] and his younger brother Thomas. In a contemporary tract entitled : ' A declaration of the affairs of Virginia, with the names of the adventurers,' the former is shown as holding shares to the value of £25.[4] Mainwaring's transactions with the Company show that on the 15th of May 1620 he received ' one bill of Adventure of 10 shares ' from the Earl of Dorset, and at ' an extraordinary Court,' held on the 23rd of the month, he assigned over 5 shares of land to Sir Edward Sackville, which the court ratified and confirmed.   A Mr. Englebert had devised an ' engine ' for preserving the plantation of Virginia from force of arms, and on the 31st of May the invention was submitted

[1] S.P. Dom., James I, cxiii. 30.

[2] This band of adventurers had; in 1606, been granted a charter by James I, 'to reduce a colony of sundry of our people into that part of America commonly called Virginia,' with power to occupy islands within 100 miles of the coast. (Neill, *Virginia Co.*, p. 3).

[3] Sir Arthur was also one of the original incorporators of the North-west Passage Company in 1612.

[4] Published 22 July, 1620 (Force's *Tracts*, iii.).

to a committee, which had Mainwaring for one of its members.[1]

On his return he found that the Mayor of Dover had been abusing his office by selling licences to certain French fishing-vessels to fish at the Sowe, whereas the only persons authorised to grant them were the Warden or his Lieutenant.[2] From the time of his appointment, Mainwaring was incessant in his demands regarding the improvements that were necessary at the Castle. His energy was untiring, but his endeavours met with little encouragement. On the 12th of June he informed Zouch that after much trouble he had obtained £117 towards the platforms, but was unable to obtain a like sum for the gun carriages and munitions. The contract to supply stone for the platforms had been given to a ' quarry man of Fowlston.'[3]

Among the old friends who took an early opportunity of visiting him at Dover was Sir Henry Wotton, and on the 12th of June 1620 Mainwaring wrote to Zouch regarding Sir Henry, enclosing at the same time a copy of a sonnet, written by the latter in honour of the Queen of Bohemia, the daughter of James I.

I expect Sir Henry Wotton at Dover towards the latter end of this week. From him I brought letters to my Lord and Lady Wotton. He goes (ambassador) extraordinary to the Duke of Saxony, the Duke of Bavaria, the United Princes, and the King of Bohemia, and Venice. Being in Greenwich Park he made a sonnet of the Queen of Bohemia which he sent by me to the

---

[1] *Virginia Co. of London Records,* ed. Kingsbury, 1906, i. 344, 364, 365. On 22 May 1622 Mainwaring passed over two shares to his brother Thomas.

[2] *S.P. Dom.,* James I, cxiii. 81.

[3] *Ibid.,* cxv. 69. *I.e.* Folkestone.

Lady Wotton ; the copy I have sent your Lordship.
'Twill be a good exercise for your Lordship's two choristers,
Mr. Fookes and Mr. North, to set it to a sound.[1]

Unfortunately the copy which Mainwaring speaks
of is not to be found among the State Papers
in the Public Record Office. The poem in question,
' On his Mistress, the Queen of Bohemia,' is
familiar to all lovers of English poetry, but the
date of its composition has hitherto been open
to doubt. By Mainwaring's letter we are now
able to fix definitely the year of its composition,
and incidentally to note the interesting fact that
it was written in Greenwich Park. One of the
earliest versions of the poem is that printed in the
' Reliquiae Wottonianae,' 1651, which the Rev.
Alexander Dyce has reprinted with notes in his
edition of Wotton's poems.   It is here given [2] :

> You meaner beauties of the night,
>   That poorly satisfy our eyes
> More by your number than your light,
>   You common people of the skies,
>   What are you when the moon shall rise ?
>
> You curious chanters of the wood,
>   That warble forth dame Nature's lays,
> Thinking your passions understood
>   By your weak accents, what's your praise
>   When Philomel her voice shall raise ?

---

[1] *S.P. Dom.*, James I, cxv. 69.

[2] Wotton, *Poems*, 1843 (Percy Soc.).   It has been a
favourite theme for imitators. Allan Ramsay printed a
version of it, with three additional stanzas, in his *Tea-table
Miscellany*, 1763, pp. 403–4, stating that ' The following song
is said to be made in honour of Mary Queen of Scots.'   Robert
Chalmers, also ignorant of the authorship, printed it in his
Scottish Songs, 1829, ii. 631, as if ' written by Lord Darnley
in praise of the beauty of Queen Mary, before their marriage.'
He omitted the last stanza, but printed three additional.

You violets that first appear,
  By your pure purple mantles known,
Like the proud virgins of the year,
  As if the spring were all your own,
  What are you when the rose is blown ?

So when my mistress shall be seen
  In form and beauty of her mind,
By virtue first, then choice, a queen,
  Tell me, if she were not designed
  Th' eclipse and glory of her kind ?

This beautiful little poem [1] is probably without equal for its elegance and simplicity, and Sir Henry Wotton at the time of its composition was fifty-two years of age. He was about to be employed by the Queen on a mission to Germany, and the poem really proceeded from the feeling of chivalrous loyalty that he felt towards her. Sir Henry seems to have formed an extraordinary attachment to her merit and fortunes ; and it is recorded that on one occasion he gave away a jewel worth £1000 that had been presented to him, because the giver was an enemy to his royal mistress.

In the July following Mainwaring was again in London interviewing the various officials of the Exchequer and Ordnance ' concerning the provision of Dover Castle.' On the 15th of the month he wrote to Zouch from Clerkenwell, stating that he had hoped to have called on him ' this Saturday at Bramshill,' but that his attendance concerning the provision of Dover Castle was

---

[1] The poem was set to music by Michael Est, and published in 1624, in his ' Sixt Set of Bookes Wherein are Anthemes for Versus and Chorus of 5 and 6 parts, apt for Violls and Voyces. Newly composed by Michael Est, Batchelar of Musicke and Master of the Choristers of the Cathedral Church in Litchfield ' (Rimbault, *Bibl. Madrigaliana*, p. 48).

'so tedious that I shall not have fully despatched it before Monday night, so that Thursday after, being the Court day at Dover, I shall not have time betwixt those days to wait on your Lordship otherwise than by letter.'[1] Two days later, however, he is found back at Dover, where, during his absence, he reported to Zouch that one Ned Kemp of Dover had challenged a native of Canterbury, Fotherby by name, to go over to Gravelines to fight a duel. The continuance of the Mayor of Dover's opposition to Zouch's and his own authority had caused him to inflict a fine of £5 on the master of a vessel belonging to the Mayor, for refusing to lower her flag to the Castle.[2]

In 1620 an expedition was fitted out to operate against the pirates, and Zouch was commanded by the King to impress 100 mariners in Kent. Each of the Cinque Ports failed to provide the number required of them, and the expedition, which was to have sailed on the 1st of August, was in consequence delayed. Eight days later the necessary men had not been impressed, and Zouch gave instructions for a search to be made throughout the county for mariners who had fled inland.[3]

Though Mainwaring had been Lieutenant of Dover Castle for less than a year, he had filled his position so well that the Corporation proposed to mark their appreciation of his services by nominating him as one of their Burgesses for the Parliament summoned to meet at Westminster on the 16th of January 1621. Before, however, he could be nominated as a Burgess, it was necessary for the Common Council to make him a Freeman.

---

[1] *S.P. Dom.*, James I, cxvi. 31.

[2] *Ibid.*, cxvi. 32, 43.

[3] *Archaeologia Cantiana*, 10, cxxiv.

On the 7th of December he informed Zouch of the proposed honour.

> The Mayor of Dover told me that they have purposed to elect me for their Burgess, but I cannot be chosen unless first they call a Common Council to make me a Freeman, which they would willingly do altogether, therefore I would humbly beseech your Lordship, if it may stand with your Lordship's good liking, that they may receive their summons for electing the Burgesses before I come up, which I purpose shall be when my Lord Wotton comes. They tell me I cannot take my oath of a Freeman but before the Common Council of the Town, and so must the other Burgess whom your Lordship shall nominate.[1]

Sir Richard Young was the burgess nominated by Zouch, and both he and Mainwaring were returned for Dover on the 9th of January.[2] This Parliament, the third of James I, was destined to be shortlived, and there is no evidence that Mainwaring took an active part in its proceedings, before it was dissolved on the 8th of February 1622. In the March following his election, he reported the wreck of a large vessel, the Ark Noah, on the Goodwins. Coming from Hamburg she carried a very valuable cargo, which included £4000 in coin. This, Mainwaring complained, was saved from the wreck, and kept at Deal Castle by Thomas Fulnetby, Serjeant of the Admiralty of the Cinque Ports, who refused to

---

[1] *S.P. Dom.*, James I, cxviii. 14. A copy of the oath taken by a Freeman of the Cinque Ports is given in Oldfield's *Parliamentary History of Great Britain*, v. 361. On the 1st of January 1621, the Mayor of Dover wrote to Zouch that he would gladly spare Sir R. Young the trouble of coming to Dover to take his oath as a freeman, but there was no precedent for taking the oath by commission (*S.P. Dom.*, James I, cxix. 2).

[2] Return of Members of Parliament.

I.

G

have it conveyed to Dover as was then the custom. At this insubordination, Mainwaring was very indignant, and he enclosed to his 'very worthy friend Mr. Edward Nicholas' the following letter, which he requested should be delivered to Lord Zouch with all speed.[1] Zouch was on a bed of sickness at the time, and Mainwaring seems to have thought that the sight of the money bags would have revived his drooping spirits.

RIGHT HONOURABLE AND MY MOST HONOURABLE LORD,—I arrived at Deal by 9 of the clock at night being Wednesday night, where I find Thomas Fulnetby safely guarded and his watch all awake, which I think was not usual, but I believe he is more afraid of losing the money than the Castle. For the quantity of it, there are 80 bags, among which I know are bags of 100*l.* or more, some of 30*l.* or thereabout; we suppose it in all to be about the matter of 4000*l.* I am instantly carrying it away to Dover Castle according to your Lordship's direction. Also, there were saved 40 casks of cinnamon . . . the casks are commonly worth 7*l.* or 8*l.* a piece, and pepper, 4 bags. I will stay at Dover till I receive your Lordship's further directions concerning the money which I now wish in your Lordship's Chamber, the sight of which I think would do your Lordship more good than a draught of the doctor's aurum potabile,[2] so humbly kissing your Lordship's hand I rest,

Your Lordship's most humble servant,

H. MAINWARING.

Deal this 15 *of March.*

Written up the left-hand side of the letter is this hurried postscript :

MY LORD,—After I had sealed you this packet, Fulnetby asked me if I had any warrant from your

---

[1] *S.P. Dom.*, James I, cxx. 22.

[2] Aurum potabile, 'drinkable gold, that is gold held in a state of minute subdivision in some volatile oil. It was formerly in repute as cordial' (*Oxf. Eng. Dict.*).

Lordship to have it from him, and told me he had command from your Lordship not to deliver any without your Lordship's special warrant. It hath been ever certified that the serjeant was subordinate to the Lieutenant and I hope your Lordship will ever let it be so, for else it will much take off from my reputation in particular. He is your Lordship's servant, but shall never prove the more faithful than I am myself. I am not willing to oppose him, but humbly beseech your Lordship's warrant that he may see I come not without command, and that he may know from your Lordship that I am to command the money, therefore now I shall rest at Deal till I hear from your Lordship.

What eventually became of the money is not recorded, but the incident was the beginning of one of the many quarrels between Mainwaring and Fulnetby.

At the beginning of April Mainwaring again journeyed to London to consult with the various officials of the ordnance, endeavouring to hasten the much delayed supplies for Dover Castle. These interviews were far from satisfactory, and he wrote that Lord Carew would not give out the necessary stores without Zouch's warrant. At the time he happened to be in London an attack was made on 'Old Don Diego,' as he dubbed the Ambassador Gondomar, an account of which he forwarded to Zouch.[1]

RIGHT HONOURABLE AND MY MOST HONOURABLE LORD,—I had made use of your Lordship's leave to go to my friends in the country, but that I knew it was my duty to despatch such business as does belong to my place wherein it hath pleased your Lordship to make me your Lordship's servant. I attended therefore the delivery and the expedition for our store at the Castle which till yesterday I could get no answer of, for my Lord Carew

[1] *S.P. Dom.*, James I, cxx. 69.

hath kept his chamber and taken physic, so that I could not till then speak with any. And now he says I must, according to the direction in his letter from the Lords to him, have an assignment from your Lordship. And then I must apply for them at the Tower, so that I cannot go by any means till that be despatched, it being now so convenient and necessary to be performed. I humbly expect your Lordship's answer and according to my duty will ever prefer your Lordship's service before any private occasions of my own.

On Easter day Old Don Diego went to see the Ambassador of Pole. In Fenchurch Street, he being in his horse litter, divers prentices and men did come to his litter with stones in their hands and shaked them at him (but did not fling any) and called Dog and Devil. The King is much offended with them who did it and swears they shall be severely punished.[1]

Yesterday the Prince and the Lords tilted but the King saw it not. The Prince and my Lord of Dorset did best, the Prince broke 11 staves [2] and Dorset 12.

This is all the news I can advertise your Lordship of, saving that on Easter day it was much noted that the King sent no meat from his table to the Marquis,[3] which is the strangest news of all. The Marquis is gone to Lincoln to a horse race.

I dined on Monday with my Lord of Canterbury,[4]

---

[1] Gondomar was not slow in informing James of the affront. Three of the offenders were whipped through the streets at a cart's tail, as a result of which one of their number died (Nichols, *Progresses of James I*, iv. 661).

[2] This word is illegible in the original; but is probably staves.

[3] George Villiers, Marquis (afterwards Duke) of Buckingham.

[4] George Abbot, Archbishop of Canterbury. He was the cause of an unfortunate accident when he did visit Zouch. On the 24th of July in this year, while shooting at a buck with a crossbow in Bramshill Park, he had the misfortune to kill one of the keepers. Abbot was greatly distressed at the occurrence, and prescribed a monthly fast for himself on the day of the accident, besides settling £20 a year on the

who commands his best love unto your Lordship. He means to visit your Lordship this summer.

I shall ever be glad to hear of your Lordship's good health, which I daily pray for as the greatest blessing that can befall myself. And therefore most humbly recommending your Lordship to the protection of the Almighty, I humbly kiss your Lordship's hand and rest,

> Your Lordship's most humble servant,
> H. MAINWARING.

London the 6 April, 1621.

I humbly beseech your Lordship to be pleased to return the Lord's letter with the assignity.

On receipt of this letter Zouch despatched the necessary warrant to his Lieutenant. Armed with this, Mainwaring obtained a further interview with the authorities, and impressed upon them the necessity for prompt action. The 9th of July 1621 he informed Zouch how far he had been successful in his endeavours to obtain supplies for the Castle.

I went to my Lord Treasurer in your Lordship's name for a supply for the reparations of the Castle, acquainting him with the necessity of some reparations for those parts, that thereafter it might not lay on your Lordship's servants if any fault should be found. He told me that after the King was gone to his progress he would have me come to him and he would do what he could, and told me that he had purposed to pull down 20 castles to save the King charges.[1]

Mainwaring then continues his letter with an account of the assizes at Maidstone, and also gives us an interesting sidelight on the French

man's widow (*D.N.B.*). A copy of Mainwaring's *Seaman's Dictionary* in manuscript, dedicated to the Archbishop, is in Lambeth Palace Library.

[1] *S.P. Dom.,* James I, cxxii. 8.

refugees that were settled in Dover. They are
first heard of at Dover on the 4th of June, when
John Reading, the rector of St. Mary's Church,
wrote to Zouch asking permission for them ' on
certain days to use our church.' [1] That this
request was granted is shown by the extract
from Mainwaring's letter given below.

The Wednesday after your Lordship's departure
I set forward to Maidstone, where the Assizes began on
the Thursday.[2]   There were divers in for manslaughter.
Two women indicted for murdering their own children
at the birth, but all cleared by favourable jury.   Two
men condemned for burglary by day and one for a
felony who is this day to be executed with the other.
Saturday night I came to Canterbury and stayed all
Sunday with my Lord Wotton,[3] who with my Lady doth
remember his service unto your Lordship, and was
much joyed to hear that your Lordship means to come
into his parts the next summer. . . . This Monday

    [1] In 1621 the Protestants of France rose in revolt, but
their appeal to arms proved very disastrous, and within a
few months refugees began to arrive in this country.   There
is a return furnished by the French Church at Dover of the
number of refugees in the town, October 26, 1621, also a
similar list for 1622 (*Huguenot Soc. Proc.*, iii. pp. 129–132,
162, 165).
    [2] From the beginning of the 17th century the Kent
assizes were generally held at Maidstone.   There is a curious
sketch of the Upper and Lower Court Houses at Maidstone
in 1623, showing them supported on pillars, in J. M. Russell's
History of Maidstone, p. 280.
    [3] Edward, First Baron Wotton (1548–1626), half brother
to Sir Henry Wotton.   In 1597 he was an unsuccessful
candidate for the Wardenship of the Cinque Ports.   During
the early years of James I he was Lord Lieutenant of Kent.
His residence, ' The Ruins, Canterbury,' was on the site of
the old St. Augustine's monastery.   A spacious mansion, with
beautiful grounds and gardens, was made up of the old
structure which came into the possession of the Wotton family
in the early part of the 17th century.

morning I arrived at Dover, where I find Omnia et omnes bene. Here are some hundred French or thereabouts in all. They have here two ministers which preach twice on Sundays in St. Mary's Church before and after Mr. Reading, and once on the Thursday. They live well here without any charge to the town, and some are of good quality, but as yet I have not seen any of them.

The influx of these Protestant refugees into Dover stirred the sympathies of the townspeople, and besides providing them with a place to worship in, they did everything in their power to help them. By October of this year their community had grown to 272 persons. A census of all the refugees in the Ports was afterwards ordered, and Mainwaring requested the Mayor and Jurats of Hythe to furnish him with a return of the strangers there. On the 28th of April 1622 they sent Mainwaring the following letter, giving the required information.

RIGHT WORSHIPFUL,—We received your letter whereby you require to be speedily certified what strangers are resident and inhabiting here amongst us, in performance whereof these are to certify you that here are inhabiting and resident in this town the strangers hereafter named (and none other), viz. :

John Jacob alias van de Stat who professeth practise in physick, planting, and gardening ; also he occupyeth some marshland in Romney Marsh, and manureth the same with sheep, and some other land he soweth with flax : he had a stranger father and (as he saith) was born in Flanders. Philip van de Walle, who is by trade a woolcomer and professeth the same : he sometimes deals in merchandise and keeps a shop of small wares here ; he was born of strangers parents at Sandwich : And these two have inhabited here by the space of seven years together last past.

Peter Morter, who is by trade a cooper and (as he saith) was born in Flanders, and about nine years of his age came over into England, and he hath dwelt here about twenty-two years together last past.

To all which persons we have imparted the tenure of your letter, and also of the copy of Sir Robert Heath's [1] letter, and so remembering our duties unto you we remain

Your assured loving friends,

THE MAYOR AND JURATS OF HYTHE.

Hythe, 28 April, 1622.

To the Right Worshipful Sir Henry Mainwaring, Knight, Lieutenant of Dover Castle. [2]

A similar request was also sent to the Mayor and Jurats of Rye, who on the 3rd of May informed Mainwaring that two Dutchmen, three Frenchmen, twenty women, and thirty children were the only strangers resident there.[3]

In the May of this year, 1622, there were signs of the rebellion in France coming to an end, and most of the fugitives seemed to have returned to their own country, only 91 remaining in Dover.[4]

The post of Lieutenant of Dover Castle was by no means a sinecure, and in order to keep in touch with the happenings at the various ports and their members, it was necessary for Mainwaring to make frequent journeys from the Castle. In the September of 1621, in company with the Mayor of Dover, Robert Garrett, he paid a visit to Margate in order to ascertain the extent of the damage done there by the encroachment

---

[1] Recorder of London, and afterwards Solicitor-General.

[2] *S.P. Dom.*, James I, cxxix. 66 (cited in *Huguenot Soc. Proc.*, iii. 134).

[3] *Ibid.*, cxxx. 11. A list of the Protestant refugees in the Cinque Ports at this period will be found in Mr. W. D. Cooper's *List of Foreign Protestants*, pp. 12–17.

[4] *Huguenot Soc. Proc.*, iii. 134.

of the sea. Eighteen houses had been washed away, while seventy-four others and some 350 acres of land were in the same danger. In their report they informed Zouch that the jetty built adjoining the pier was the cause of the danger. To remedy the evil it was proposed to erect two jetties, and Zouch expressed an opinion that the profits of the pier should go towards defraying the cost of the work. This somewhat alarmed the pier wardens, who petitioned him, stating that the pier was poor, and as the two previous ones had been washed away, whatever profits accrued they needed for its upkeep. It was necessary to hurry the work on before the winter storms, and Mainwaring stated that the pier wardens, though unwilling, should be made to bear the charge. Accordingly, a tax of 223*l*. 0*s*. 6*d*. was levied on the pier and the houses endangered, but as this sum proved inadequate, a further levy was eventually made.[1]

One of the great difficulties encountered in the administration of the Cinque Ports was that of finding sufficient seamen for the King's service. Though formerly the ports had responded nobly to whatever calls were made upon them, the same sentiment seems to have been lacking during the seventeenth century. A typical case was that of the Constable of Sandwich, Henry Foster, who strenuously refused to assist in impressing mariners for the King's ships, and in consequence was arrested. While being conveyed to Dover Castle he managed to escape from his escort, who spent several days in an unsuccessful attempt to capture him. Main-

---

[1] *S.P. Dom.*, James I, cxxii. 57, 105, 119 ; cxxix. 4.

waring thereupon wrote to the Mayor of Sandwich reproving him for allowing the Constable to escape, and cautioned him to amend his ways, 'lest evil construction be put on his conduct.' [1]

Numerous instances are to be found in the State Papers at this period of the conviction of French fishing vessels, who had been caught fishing at the Sowe, without licences and with unlawful nets. In the February of 1622, Zouch commissioned Mainwaring, with the Mayor and Jurats of Rye, to try some of these cases, and in the event of finding the fishermen guilty, they were to inflict a fine of 'ten French crowns the master of each boat, two crowns French every servant in the boats.' [2] The fishery was under the direct jurisdiction of the Lord Warden, and Mainwaring was fully aware of the disadvantages of allowing the French to fish there. In 1630 he presented a discourse on the subject to Sir John Coke, pointing out how the prosperity of the town of Rye had suffered from the intrusion of the French on its fishing-ground. [3]

[1] *S.P. Dom.*, James I, cxxii. 120, 143.

[2] *Ibid.*, cxxvii. 143. A French crown was the common English name in the 17th century for the French écu, equivalent to about 4s. 6d. (*Mundy Travels*, i. 120, note). A licence to fish at the Sowe is printed verbatim in Fulton's *Sovereignty of the Sea*, 749–50.

[3] It is printed for the first time in Vol. II.

CHAPTER IV

1623

THE SPANISH MATCH

DURING 1623 negotiations for the Spanish match, which had been laboured for many years, were reopened, and the intended betrothal of Prince Charles to the Infanta of Spain became the one topic of discussion.[1] In the February of that year Mainwaring, by the King's request, was sent to Calais to bring over the Infanta's ambassador, Boischot,[2] and while fulfilling this little diplomatic mission he was one of the chief actors in an amusing episode, which is worth relating in full. Early in the year the Prince and Buckingham had announced their intention to James of making a journey incognito to Madrid. On the 17th of February, after binding the King to secrecy, they started, the Prince giving out that he was going to hunt at Theobalds, and the Duke that he was about to 'take physic at Chelsea.'[3] That same night they proceeded to Buckingham's

---

[1] James' son-in-law, Frederick, after a crushing defeat before Prague in 1620, had been driven out of Bohemia, and before the end of 1622 the whole of the Palatinate was in the hands of the Spaniards. James hoped by marrying his son to the Infanta that the Spaniards would restore the Palatinate.

[2] S.P. Dom., James I, cxliii. 64.

[3] Aikin, James I, ii. 322.

seat at Newhall in Essex. The following morning
they were astir early, and after disguising themselves with false beards, and assuming the names
of John and Tom Smith, they rode through
Kent, attended by Buckingham's Master of the
Horse, Sir Richard Graham. The only others
who were aware of the identity of the masqueraders
were two of the Prince's suite, Sir Francis Cottington and Endymion Porter, who were instructed
to have a vessel in readiness at Dover to carry the
Prince to France. On reaching Gravesend, Charles
and his companions were imprudent enough to
bestow a gold piece of two and twenty shillings
on the man who ferried them across. This
unheard-of generosity 'struck the. poor fellow
into such a melting tenderness,' that out of
consideration for their persons, he informed
the authorities of what he believed to be duellists
who were crossing the Channel to settle an affair
of honour.[1] Their fair riding cloaks, and the
temporary loss of one of their false beards added
to the suspicion, and in consequence messengers
were sent to detain them at Rochester, but
before the information arrived, Charles and
Buckingham had passed through the town.[2]
On the brow of the hill beyond Rochester a
royal equipage and a cavalcade of horsemen
were seen approaching. Here was an unlooked-
for danger, for the royal coach contained no
less a dignitary than the Ambassador Boischot,
whom Mainwaring and Sir Lewis Lewkenor,
Master of the Ceremonies, were escorting from
Calais to London. There was no time to be lost,
and Charles and his companions, fully realising
the possibility of detention, put spurs to their

---

[1] Wotton, *Reliquae*, 1685, 212.
[2] *S.P. Dom.*, James I, cxxxviii. 59.

horses and fled, which situation, as Sir Henry
Wotton humorously records, 'made them baulk
the beaten road, and teach post hackneys to
leap hedges.' [1]   Such a spectacle can better be
imagined than described, and Mainwaring, be-
lieving them to be two of Barneveldt's sons,
who had been involved in the attempted assassina-
tion of the Prince of Orange, sent with all speed
after them to Canterbury, where they were
detained by the mayor.[2]   Mainwaring's own
account of the adventure is given in his despatch
to Zouch, written from London on the 22nd of
February, in which he says :

> Coming towards London hoping to have seen your
> Lordship there to despatch some business which I left,
> we meet three disguised with hoods and false beards,
> and presently after followed one from Gravesend to tell
> Sir Lewis Lewkener and myself that they came out of
> Essex, and would not leave at the ordinary bridge, and
> had false beards and pistols, which suspicious fashion
> made me send a packet after them to stay them.   We
> have not got any answer of the Prince's landing.[3]

It was not until Buckingham had removed
his disguise, and assured the Mayor of Canterbury
that he was going to Dover in his capacity of
Lord High Admiral to make a private inspection of the fleet, that they were allowed to proceed.
The night of the 18th was spent at Dover, where
Cottington and Porter had a ship in readiness,
and early next morning they set sail for Boulogne.[4]

---

[1] Wotton, *Reliquae*, 213.

[2] *S.P. Dom.*, James I, cxxxviii. 51.

[3] *Ibid.*, cxxxviii. 51.   Mainwaring's name figures largely
in Ainsworth's *Spanish Match*, i. pp. 100-12.

[4] On the 21st they arrived in Paris, and on the following
evening Charles and Buckingham gained admittance to a
masque in which the Queen and Princess Henrietta Maria

No sooner was the Prince's escapade known than its danger was realised. The condition in which our relations with Spain were at the time made it obviously highly detrimental to the British position that such hostages should be placed in Spanish hands, for mediæval methods of diplomacy were not yet obsolete. Something clearly had to be done at once, not only to secure the truants' speedy return, but also to deter Spain from taking advantage of their indiscretion. Accordingly preparations for fitting out a fleet were at once set on foot. Ostensibly, of course, it was to fetch the Prince home in due state, but in reality this was but a thinly veiled disguise for a formidable naval demonstration, such as that with which James had forced the King of Spain's hand four years earlier. Its significance is shown in the estimate prepared by the Navy Commissioners, in which they required a sum of 17,434*l*. 10s. for setting forth eight ships and two pinnaces 'in a warlike manner' to the coast of Spain for five months.[1] As we see, it was to go in considerable force, and Mainwaring, on account of his ' abilities for such a service,' was strongly recommended for the post of flag-captain to the admiral. James had informed the Venetian republic, when recommending Mainwaring to their service in 1618, that if any similar naval command occurred at home, he would employ Mainwaring before others, and he was now about to fulfil that promise.

(whom Charles eventually married) were taking part. The next morning before daybreak the Prince and Buckingham set out on their way to Bayonne ; and about 8 o'clock in the evening of March 7th they arrived at Madrid.

[1] *S.P. Dom.*, James I, cxxxviii. 50.

On the 28th of February Sir Robert Naunton sent the following letter to Sir Edward Conway, 'one of his Majesty's principal Secretaries,' in favour of Mainwaring being given the appointment'[1]:

This gentleman, Sir Henry Mainwaring, hath a desire to go Captain in the Admiral that is to go for Spain. My Lord of Rutland tells him he shall be very willing and glad to rest upon him for the execution of that charge, so far as it shall lie in him to dispose of it. But because the choice of so important a Minister to such a trust is fittest to be made by his Majesty's own person, so hath earnestly requested to be recommended to your noble favour by my mediation, out of the notice which he hath taken of my many obligations to you. Which office I have taken the rather, upon the assurance I have long had of his abilities for such a service, and withal out of my privity to those extraordinary testimonies with which his Majesty was pleased to grace and recommend him to a place of important command and charge to the State of Venice by my pen, wherein he gave me this particular instruction to assure that State, that he would have committed any like employment by sea unto his performance before others, if any occasion had been offered him of that nature. My due zeal to the public service hath likewise concurred in my making you this motion, which I hope his Majestie will consider graciously of and thank you for putting him in mind of so able and worthy a gentleman.

On the 3rd of March, Mainwaring himself wrote to Conway to the effect that the Earl of Rutland had promised him the captain's place.[2] This information he begged might not reach the ears of Lord Zouch, whose displeasure he had incurred, as the following letter written from

[1] *S.P. Dom.*, James I, cxxxviii. 113.
[2] *Ibid.*, cxxxix. 20,

Bramshill clearly shows.[1]   In it Zouch requested him to resign his post as Lieutenant of Dover Castle, accusing him of going to Canterbury without leave ; sleeping in the town instead of the Castle ; and assaulting a man in the street.

Mr. Lieutenant,—I received a letter from you from Dover, but presently after I received another from one who signified you were gone to Canterbury.   I am sorry Dover doth please you so little.   When I placed you there I purposed to make it a comfort both to you and myself ; but to me I find it not, neither do I think you do, but sith you do not, me thinketh in good nature you should consigne it to me againe that I might take more comfort therein than now I do.

I have not heard of a Lieutenant of Dover Castle that hath made all Kent talk of him for women's matters ; nor that after he had such a place would go to cuffs, nor leave the Castle to lie in the Town.   These disorders trouble me much but not you, otherwise it would make a change either of the place or of you in the place ; but sith it doth not I pray you resign the place to me again, or else I must press you to your promise, for I assure you I would have been there myself in these troublesome times ; which I cannot do (as I found the last summer) by reason of my often removing and especially of my stuff, but if you will remove I will presently send stuff down and not tarry long after. I pray you therefore accept of my kind desire to part fair, for (unless you change much) I must take another

---

[1] *S.P. Dom.*, James I, cxxxix. 121.   Bramshill House in the parish of Eversley, Hants.   The original house was built by Thomas Foxley between 1351 and 1360.   It was purchased by Lord Zouche in 1605.   He rebuilt it and entertained James I there in 1620.   This noble example of Stuart architecture is in existence at the present day.   Several letters written to Mainwaring from Bramshill are among the State Papers.   The History of Bramshill has been written by Sir W. H. Cope, in whose family the mansion has been since the 18th century.

course, and therefore hoping you will accordingly both
think of this, and your promises to me, I rest
Your loving friend,
(————[1]).

From my house in Bramshill Park, 17 Martii, 1622.[2]

These alleged misdemeanours, trivial though
they are, appear to have been the outcome of
jealousy. The charges were brought against him
by those to whom his strict discipline was ever
apparent, and Richard Marsh, the Clerk of Dover
Castle, seems to have been one of that number,
who seized on any incident that would be likely to
injure the Lieutenant in the eyes of the Warden.
On the 3rd of March he wrote[3] :

When I arrived at Gravesend to come homeward l
found Mr. Lieutenant thither come with the Ambassador
of the Archduchess. The next day after I was gone
Mr. Hemsley here in the street met with Mr. Lieutenant,
and after some difference between them they fell together
(without weapons) tumbling in the street. And on their
parting, in came Mr. Lieutenant with his weapon and
gave Hemsley a wound on the head.

On the 9th of April Mainwaring replied to
Zouch's letter and defended himself from these
accusations.[4] He writes :

Your Lordship's first letter did so much amaze me
that I know not well what I have done ever since, much
less I could not settle or compose myself in any order
to write unto your Lordship, but now having since had
your command for the pressing of seamen I shall humbly
crave your Lordship's pardon if I make a short answer

---

[1] Unsigned, but endorsed by Nicholas ' Lo. Zouch, a
copy of my Lord's letter to Sir Hen. Mainwaring to resign up
his place of Lieutenant of Dover Castle. Sat. 17 Martii 1622.'
[2] Old Style, really 1623.
[3] *S.P. Dom.*, James I, cxxxix. 24.
[4] *Ibid.*, cxlii. 49.

I.   H

to those things which have misdirected your Lordship
against me by the information of those busy and very
good friends (whom I must leave as myself to your Lordship). For my going to Canterbury . . . I had not been
near it before the date of your Lordship's letter, but
that Friday after I went to Sir George Newman,[1] being
occasioned thereunto by the letter sent to Mr. Marsh,
as also by speeches he used to Mr. Fulnetby that he would
not come to try the prisoners without a special warrant
from your Lordship. The day was appointed and for
that cause I went thither. I should not have held it
for an offence to your Lordship to have gone thither or
anywhere else as long as I neglect not your Lordship's
affairs. And then within one hour or two riding of the
Castle if any occasion should be offered.

For the second, I was assaulted. I never struck blow or
drew sword, he drew upon me. . . . I walked to my
lodgings and scarce spake ten words to him. Witnesses
can testify that I spoke but twenty or I will answer to
God and your Lordship. The greatest persons in
the world are not free from assaults, and the Law of
Nature and Nations allows a man to defend himself;
besides I asked your Lordship's leave which you granted
me. As for women I know of no more save those which
your Lordship knew of before. . . . I am sure the world
cannot tax me for keeping any woman or frequenting
their companies. . . . For the last, which was lying
in town, 'tis true that instantly on my coming to Dover
My Lord of Rochford[2] came. I had been at the pier,
winning some timber; going up to the Castle I called
at Capt. Wilsford, my Lord sent earnestly to speak with
me. He desired me to sup with him, to stay with him,
having no company, which I was very willing to do,
having not any thing special for me at the Castle. He
coursed the next day, and I anciently known to him,
desired most to stay that night with him. I did so not

[1] Admiralty judge of the Cinque Ports.
[2] Henry Carey, Baron Hunsdon, created Viscount Rochford
on 6 July 1621, and afterwards Earl of Dover on 8 March
1628. He was attached to the Prince's suite in Spain.

knowing that it could be any prejudice to your Lordship's affairs.

Mainwaring then continues his letter with an account of the means he had adopted regarding the impressment of mariners for the expedition to Spain, and states that he had succeeded in pressing the finest lot of men that were ever sent out of the Cinque Ports, some of whom rather than be forced to serve, would have given him large sums, ' for I assure your Lordship,' he writes, ' I could safely have gained 200*l*. by this business.' [1] He concludes by asking Zouch to suspend his judgment ' till you hear my answer,' and stated that he would feel the loss of his post ten times more than if he had never enjoyed it.

Mainwaring, as we see, was already busy in providing men for the fleet of which he hoped to have the practical direction, and the following day he reported the presence of a Dutch vessel in the Downs, which had many English sailors aboard, bound for the West Indies. By his instructions the Mayor of Sandwich was ordered to detain such of the crew as came on shore, because, in spite of the King's proclamation, many entered foreign service, owing to the higher rate of remuneration. ' It is endless toil,' he wrote, ' to supply the King's ships with fit men.' Mainwaring eventually had the Dutchman brought into Dover Harbour, and was ordered to attend the council thereon, but after waiting four days in vain, he went to Windsor, to discuss with the

---

[1] On the 25th of March, Mainwaring wrote to the Mayors and Jurats of the Ports, 'to attend diligently to the King's orders for the pressing of seamen.' For the fleet preparing for Spain, 150 men were required from the Cinque Ports, and efficient men were to be chosen with discretion, ' so as to injure trade as little as possible' (*S.P. Dom.*, cxl. 34).

King the question of impressing seamen.[1] On
the 26th of April Conway, in a letter to Zouch,
requested that Mainwaring might be granted
leave of absence to go as captain under the Earl
of Rutland. This he advised Zouch not to with-
stand, 'being a point on which the King is much
set.'[2] To which Zouch replied that he had already
sent Mainwaring a friendly dismissal, and that he
only held the Lieutenancy on condition that he
gave it up when required.[3]

Whatever the real reason was that caused
Mainwaring's dismissal, it failed to lower his
prestige with the King, and he was duly made
flag-captain to Rutland. On the fleet where he
held this important command it may be said the
hopes of the country were fixed. As the danger
of the Prince's escapade became realised, the
anxiety displayed by James for the return of his
son was shared in no less a degree by his subjects.
There was a rooted opinion among all classes
that the Prince would never come back. Spain
was looked upon as an implacable and ruthless
enemy, and the Inquisition had graven in the
public imagination a picture of cruelty and
oppression. There is a story told of Archie, the
King's jester, which shows the state of feeling in
England at the time. He approached James
one day and offered to exchange his fool's cap
with him. On the King asking the reason, he
explained that the Prince had been given leave

---

[1] *S.P. Dom.*, James I, cxlii. 50, 64.

[2] *Ibid.*, cxliii. 70.

[3] *Ibid.*, cxliii. 71. The Venetian ambassador informed
the Doge that the Earl of Rutland was to command the ten
ships for Spain, and that 'Sir Henry Mainwaring may have
the first place, being an experienced seaman, well known to
your Serenity' (*S.P. Venice*, 1623–25, No. 14).

to go into Spain, and would never return. But, replied James, suppose that he does return. Then, retorted the Jester, I will take my fool's cap from off your Majesty's head, and place it on the King of Spain's![1] Be this as it may, the powerful fleet that was fitting out to proceed to Spain was no doubt intended to make a demonstration, had the Spaniards any such desire to detain the Prince. Though Rutland was appointed Admiral of the fleet, the real seaman commander was Mainwaring. It is no small testimony to the position he held at this time that he should have been chosen to conduct an enterprise, on the success of which was set the heart, not only of the King, but of the whole nation, and the honour of the appointment remained to the end of his career one of his most cherished memories.

'I send you now,' wrote James to his 'Sweet Boys' in Spain, 'the first Sea-Captain of our Admiral's choice, who I hope shall ever prove worthy of such a Patron.'[2]

The Prince Royal, which remained the largest ship in the Navy until 1637, was chosen as the flagship of the fleet, and she was fitted up with a gorgeously decorated cabin 'as if to receive a goddess,' in the hope that the Prince would return with the Infanta to England; a hope which was never realised.[3]

The following is a list of the ships that composed Rutland's squadron,[4] the strength of which greatly impressed the Venetian ambassador. 'God

---

[1] Chancellor, *Life of Charles I*, p. 112 n.
[2] Nicholls, *Progresses of James I*, iv. 844.
[3] *S.P. Dom.*, James I, cxliv. 11.
[4] *Ibid.*, July 29, 1623; Clowes, ii. p. 56, erroneously states that the fleet was under the command of the Earl of Denbigh.

grant,' he wrote, ' that this great preparation be not in vain, or may not serve the wishes of the Spaniards except in bringing back the Prince.[1]

		Tons	Guns
Prince Royal .	Admiral, the Earl of Rutland	1200	55
	Captain, Sir Henry Mainwaring		
St. Andrew .	Vice-Admiral, Lord Morley	895	42
Swiftsure .	Rear-Admiral, Lord Windsor	700	42
Defiance .	Sir Sackville Trevor	700	40
St. George .	Sir F. Steward	895	42
Bonaventure .	Sir W. St. Leger	674	34
Rainbow .	Sir H. Palmer	650	40
Antelope .	Captain Thomas Love	450	34
Charles .	Captain Harris	140	14
Seven Stars	? ?	140	14

The anxiety of the King was displayed in the keen personal interest he took in the victualling and equipment of the ships, and on the 10th of April he wrote to the Prince and Buckingham informing them of the readiness in which he found the fleet.[2]

SWEET BOYS,—As for the fleet, that should, with God's grace, bring my Baby home ; they are in far greater readiness than you could have believed, for they will be ready to make sail before the first of May, if need

[1] *Cal. S.P. Venice*, 1623–25, No. 51. Neither Rutland, Morley, nor Windsor had held a naval command before, but the other captains were all experienced seamen. Trevor was in command of a royal ship in 1602 ; Love commanded the *Convertive* in the Algiers expedition of 1620 ; and Harris is undoubtedly the Christopher Harris who commanded the *Samuel* in the same expedition, while Palmer was captain of the *Antelope*.

[2] *Hardwicke State Papers*, i. 413–14.

were ; and the smallest of six, besides the two that go for Steenie, are between five and six hundred tons, their names and burden, Dick Grame shall bring you, who is to follow two days hence ; it is therefore now your promise to advertise by the next post, how soon ye would have them to sail, for the charge and trouble will be infinite, if their equipage stay long aboard, consuming victuals, and making the ships to stink.

On the 2nd of May the Prince Royal was brought from her moorings to St. Mary's Creek, where she was inspected by the Commissioners of the Navy, who had travelled down from London for that purpose. By the 20th of the month the repairs that were necessary had been completed, and she sailed down the river to Queenborough, anchoring in the Downs five days later.[1] As soon as she joined the rest of the fleet in the Downs, Rutland came on board and assumed command. First and foremost a courtier, he was fully conscious of his unfitness for such an high office. ' His Majesty,' he wrote, ' never had so poor an Admiral,' and in truth he might say so, for he had never held a naval command before. The sea service had apparently little attraction for him, and the humble fare of the seamen, ' poor john and ling,' did not appeal to his sensitive palate, as the following letter written to Conway clearly shows [2] :

SIR,—I would intreat you to do me the favour as to let his Majesty know that I am now aboard the Prince Royal in the Downs, where I thank God I find all the fleet in very good trim, and withal I pray acquaint his Majesty that he never had so poor an Admiral, for I do assure that I am a plain dealing man and have no

[1] *Phineas Pett* (N.R.S.), p. 126. Pett was appointed to the *Prince Royal* on February 17.

[2] Brit. Museum, *Add. MSS.*, 9294, f. 317.

shift, besides here is not a spit to roast a piece of flesh on, therefore we must feed on poor john and ling, a dish his Majesty I know loves so well that he will not pity us, therefore I must needs intreat you to be a means unto his Majesty that he will be pleased to give us leave to stay here till our things come aboard, and then none shall be more ready to obey his commands then we his poor fishermen, so praying sweet Jesus to bless him with long life, I wish you farewell from aboard the Prince, and rest

Your most affectionate friend,
F. RUTLAND.

From the Downs, 28 May.

The following day in response to an urgent message from the King to get under way, Rutland was forced to send a certificate under the hands of Mainwaring and others, to the effect that it was impossible to set sail ' with the wind in the present quarter.' On the 4th of June he informed Conway that he was still detained by contrary winds, ' tied by the leg in this floating and tottering prison of the sea,' as he quaintly put it.[1] After several unsuccessful efforts the fleet weighed on the 28th, and succeeded in getting ' as high ' as Fairlight near Hastings, where, Pett records, ' we anchored all the flood, and so plyed to windward all the ebbs, being fair weather.'[2] Finally, on the 1st of July, they anchored in Stokes Bay, near Portsmouth. Here the victualling of the ships was vigorously pushed forward, and Mainwaring assumed command in the absence of Rutland, who had not yet found his sea-legs, and had been slightly injured by a fall. Mainwaring

---

[1] *S.P. Dom.*, James I, cxlvi. 11. The fleet lying in the Downs was costing £300 a day, and to meet the expense the knighting of a thousand gentlemen at £100 a head was recommended. *Ibid.*, cxlvii. 80.

[2] *Phineas Pett*, p. 126.

was a strict disciplinarian, and on this occasion
we get a glimpse of the man and the method he
employed in keeping order on board the fleet.
In one of his despatches he reported that a man
who had stolen a jerkin had been summarily dealt
with, and that he had been forced to put the
coxswain in the bilboes for being drunk. His
letter, which is directed ' To the Right Honourable
and my most Honoured Lord the Earl of Rutland,
Lord General of his Majesty's Fleet now bound
for the Coast of Spain, at his house in the Strand
called Bedford House,' is here reproduced [1] :

RIGHT HONOURABLE AND MY MOST HONOURED
LORD,—Though I know no news, yet I know it is my
duty not to omit any occasion, wherein I may give your
Lordship assurance, that I forget not my duty towards
your Lordship in any thing. All things were here so
well settled in a fair and quiet government by your
Lordship, that they cannot now have suffered any
sudden alteration since your Lordship's departure, but
rest well still. We have no disorders aboard, no complaints from the shore of any misdemeanours there, a
thing I do believe not heard of before, in so great a fleet.
One fellow, a West Country man (a foremast man), I
caught who had stolen a jerkin, and ducked him at
the yard arm, and so towed him ashore in the water at a
boats-stern, and turned him away. My Lord Windsor
carries himself very discreetly, and worthily amongst us,
so as he is commonly beloved and respected of us all.
Some fellows :—two of the Stars, one of the Charles,
and a coxswain, made three fires ashore the other night,
which we thought had been for our packet from your
Lordship. My Lord Windsor (as I think he had reason)
took it ill complaining to me of the coxswain. I put
him in the bilboes [2] for being drunk ; but for the fires

---

[1] *S.P. Dom.*, James I, cxlviii. 105.

[2] The most usual modes of correction at sea during the
early part of the 17th century appear to have been the capstan,

I think he will go clear. We live here expecting news
of our departure, and most desirous of your Lordship's
safe return to us, and especially to myself, who for so
many great testimonies of your Lordship's favour, and
good opinion of me, am for ever bound to live or die
Your Lordship's most humble
and most affectionate servant,
H. Mainwaring.

From aboard the Prince Royal, this 12 *July,* 1623.

There was a considerable amount of sickness
among the crews of Rutland's fleet, and besides
this, it was estimated that 300 men at least
had deserted since the ships were at Portsmouth.[1]
The Prince and Buckingham, like James, were
anxious that the fleet should reach them at the
earliest possible moment, and on the 29th of

the bilboes and ducking. The capstan :—' A capstan bar thrust
through the hole of the barrel, the offender's arms are extended
to the full length, and so made fast unto the bar crosswise,
having sometimes a basket of bullets or some other the like
weight, hanging about his neck.'   The bilboes :—The offender
' is put in irons, or in a kind of stocks used for that purpose, the
which are more or less heavy and pinching, as the quality of
the offence is proved against the delinquent.'   Ducking ' at
the main yard arm is, when a malefactor by having a rope
fastened under his arms and about his middle, and under
his breech, is thus hoised up to the end of the yard ; from
whence he is again violently let fall into the sea, sometimes
twice, sometimes three several times one after another ; and
if the offence be very foul, he is also drawn under the very
keel of the ship, and whilst he is under the water a great gun
is given fire right over his head.'   In the event of a sailor
stealing ' he was to be thrice ducked at the boltsprit and then
to be dragged at the boat stern, and set on shore upon the
next land with a loaf of bread and a can of beer.' (' Dialogical
Discourse of Marine affairs.' *Harleian MSS.* 1341. By
Nathaniel Boteler, printed in 1685, but composed during the
reign of James I.)

[1] *S.P. Dom.,* James I, cxlix. 73.

July they wrote to the King beseeching him, if the ships were not already on the way, ' to use all the speed' he could to hasten them.[1] On receipt of this letter James became both excited and alarmed, and expressed his displeasure to the Navy Commissioners that the victualling of the ships was so backward. ' Either these ships were not furnished with fresh victual to spare their seasoned and ship store, or that seasoned victual was not bespoken out of other ships,' wrote Conway at the request of the King. ' Give me leave to tell you,' he warned the Commissioners, ' the King is in earnest, for he verily believes that the Prince will be ready to come away before the fleet come thither to meet them.'[2] Two days later, on August the 8th, they stated that all the victuals would be aboard on the morrow, so that there would be no need to take provisions from merchant ships.[3] However, their promise does not seem to have been fulfilled, and Rutland came up to London to interview the Commissioners. In his absence Mainwaring again assumed command, and on the 19th of the month he wrote to Conway informing him that he had been left Superintendent of the fleet.[4] While visiting some of his sick men he had unfortunately caught the infection himself, and had been forced to stop on shore for a few days, but had now recovered.

RIGHT HONOURABLE,—My Lord General's care to satisfy his Majesty's earnest desire in hastening away the fleet caused him (with his own great pains of toil)

---

[1] Hardwicke, *State Papers*, i. 433.
[2] *Hist. MSS. Com.* 12 i, p. 146.
[3] Hardwicke, i. 447.
[4] *S.P. Dom.*, James I, cli. 16.

to post up to London to see those necessaries of victuals and other provisions (without which the fleet cannot proceed) despatched away, which he understood went on but slowly or not with as much expedition as he desired.

In his absence as when he was last at Court, it pleased my Lord General to depute me his Superintendent over the fleet, and did authorise me to open such letters as might come from your Honour or the State concerning the fleet, and to make such answer as should be required. And therefore to the particulars of your Honour's letter. That my Lord General is in good health I understood last night from my Lord Windsor, who came late to Portsmouth, and parted yesterday morning from him, by whom my Lord sent me word that this afternoon without fail he would be aboard the ships. For being provided to take the first wind, I understand that by my Lord's extraordinary care and solicitation the victuals are in the Downs, for which only we shall attend, being a consideration of so great importance, as without which it will be very dangerous to adventure the fleet to sea. Upon my Lord's arrival I know he will instantly make a despatch to your Honour, who I assure myself will be ready with all diligence, and hazard that his Majesty shall enjoin him to set sail the first wind. More I cannot acquaint your Honour in my Lord's absence, but that all things belonging to the ships shall be ready in an hour's warning, victuals only excepted, which let me [be] bold to answer your Honour was not well advised to be provided at London, for here at Portsmouth, Hampton, and the Isle of Wight all provisions are better, and better cheap, and upon all occasions and winds, been instantly put aboard. Sir, I must humbly crave his Majesty's, my Lord General's, and your Honour's pardon that I, who never before had night out of the ship, have lain this few days ashore, by reason I took an infection from some sick men whom I visited aboard, all which I sent ashore, and are excepting two or three recovered, so am I myself, who purpose (God willing) to be this night aboard, where as in all other places, I shall be ready to wait upon your Honour's commands, and strive to express myself that, which I am most truly,

Your Honour's most humble servant,

H. MAINWARING.

Portsmouth, this 19 *August* 1623.

The following day the King, who was staying at Beaulieu in the New Forest, paid a surprise visit to the fleet. After inspecting the ships, he dined on board the Prince Royal, where, in Rutland's absence, Mainwaring received His Majesty.

The 20th of August [Pett records],[1] His Majesty, then lying in the New Forest at Beaulieu House, embarked himself and train and came on board the Prince, then riding in Stokes Bay, accompanied with Marquis of Hamilton, the Lord Chamberlain (Pembroke), Holderness, Kelly, Carlisle, Montgomery, and divers other attendants, who all dined on board the Prince, our Admiral, the Earl of Rutland, being absent in London.

James was delighted with his reception and the smartness of the fleet. After dinner he embarked in the royal barge, and while it hovered in the midst of the fleet all the ships discharged their great ordnance in honour of the visit.

On Rutland's return instructions were received from the King to set sail, and on the 25th of the month the Earl reported that he had done so, though the wind was not very favourable, and they were still in need of men and provisions. Pett states, 'the wind taking us short put us into the grass at Weymouth, where we rode till the 26th.' On the night of the 26th, with the wind easterly, they left Weymouth, and two days later came to an anchor in Plymouth Sound.

[1] *Phineas Pett*, pp. 126–7.

Here they were again detained by contrary winds, and it was not until the 2nd of September that they were able to leave for Santander.[1] This port had been decided on instead of Corunna, being nearer England, though the Venetian ambassador feared that the entrance to Santander, being very narrow, might lead to some treachery, and the Spaniards, by ' placing some impediment, which might be made to look fortuitous,' would succeed in ' shutting in such powerful ships for ever.' With the departure of the fleet he wrote, ' All the best things of England would be in Spain, the best ships, the richest jewels, the King's sole favourite and his only son.'[2]

[1] *Phineas Pett*, pp. 127–8.
[2] *Cal. S.P. Venice*, 1623–25, Nos. 115, 120.

CHAPTER V

1623–24

THE VOYAGE TO SPAIN

THE history and negotiations concerning the Spanish marriage treaty have been fully gone into by Dr. Gardiner,[1] and do not come within the scope of this work. Suffice it to say, that nothing short of the conversion of the Prince would have allowed the Spanish and Papal authorities to sanction the marriage. Both Charles and Buckingham offended Spanish propriety during their sojourn in Madrid. Buckingham had quarrelled with Olivares, the Prime Minister, and the Prince had permitted his wooing to break down all the bounds of Spanish etiquette.

On the 2nd of September, Charles left the Escurial after an affectionate parting with Philip, Buckingham having departed on horseback earlier in the day, leaving the Prince to follow in a royal coach that had been provided.[2]

In the meantime the English fleet, which had been so long delayed, was crossing the Bay towards the coast of Spain. A week after having left Plymouth Sound they made Cape

[1] *Prince Charles and the Spanish Marriage*, 2 v., 1869.
[2] Gardiner, *England*, v. pp. 115–16.

Ortegal bearing south-west, but it was not till
the 11th of the month, 'about 2 of the clock in
the forenoon,' that Rutland's squadron anchored
in the Port of Santander, having accomplished
the journey without opposition from friend or
foe, in spite of the rumour of 'great fleets
abroad.'[1] Sir John Finett, who was on board
the Prince Royal, had received instructions to
inform the Prince immediately on the fleet's
arrival, and having an assurance that Charles
and his suite were within two days' journey of
the port, he set out to welcome them. Accompanied by Sir Thomas Somerset, he was rowed
ashore from the Prince Royal, and, as he informs
us, riding hard that night 'over the mountains
in most dark and tempestuous weather,' encountered the Prince early next morning about
six leagues inland. So delighted was Charles
at the news of the fleet's arrival, that Finett
records the Prince 'looked upon him as one
that had the face of an angel.' Buckingham,
in his gratitude and pleasure, kissed Finett,
and taking a ring off his finger worth above
100*l.*, bestowed it upon him.[2] On entering Santander, bells were rung, and the cannon of the
fort were discharged in the Prince's honour.
Charles, however, failed to respond to these
signs of welcome ; his whole thoughts were
centred on the fleet that flew the English flag.
Though late in the afternoon, he decided to
board the Prince Royal in order to greet the
Admiral and learn the latest news from court.
On returning to the shore in his barge after
nightfall, the freshening of the wind made it
impossible for the royal seamen to make headway,

[1] *S.P. Dom.*, James I, cxlv. 32.
[2] Finett, *Finetti Philoxensis*, 1656, pp. 120–1.

the tide sweeping them out of their course. What might have been a catastrophe was promptly averted by the ingenuity of Sir Sackville Trevor in the Defiance, who, seeing the danger that was threatening the barge, threw out ropes attached to buoys, on which were affixed lanterns. One of the ropes was seized by the sailors, and Charles passed the night on Trevor's ship.[1]

For some days the fleet remained weatherbound at Santander, and on the 14th, Charles entertained his Spanish retinue on board the Prince Royal. At the royal table, placed across one end of the cabin, were seated Sir Walter Aston, Cardinal Zapata, and the ambassadors Gondomar and Hurtado de Mendoza, while the other persons of rank were seated at a table placed lengthways. The feast consisted, according to Phineas Pett, 'of no other than we had brought from England with us.' Stalled oxen, fatted sheep, venison, and all manner of fowl were presented, and the Spaniards returned to the shore delighted with the festivities.

At last, on the 18th of September, the wind being favourable, the fleet were ordered to weigh anchor, which news was received 'with much joy, elevation of voices, thundering of drums and trumpets, and that excellent musical tumult of mariners nimbly running up and down to set forward so royal a business.'[2] The story of the homeward voyage has been fully chronicled by Pett. 'On Thursday, being the 18th of

[1] *Phineas Pett*, p. 129.

[2] In the Queen's presence chamber at Hampton Court is a picture of the fleet leaving Santander. First on the right leading the squadron is the *Prince Royal* ; then the *Defiance*, followed by the *St. Andrew*, and the *Bonaventure* and the others (Law, *Hampton Court Gallery*, 1898, pp. 297-8).

September,' he writes, ' we set sail out of Santander River, the wind somewhat southerly ;
from whence we beat it to and fro with contrary
winds till the 26th day after, being Friday, at
which time a little before noon we had sight of
Scilly, which bore north-east of us, about eight
leagues off.'[1] On this day four Dunkirk men-of-war
were encountered who were being chased by seven
Hollanders.   Before leaving England Rutland
had received instructions that in the event of
finding a Spaniard and a Hollander fighting
' upon our coast, or within the Narrow Seas,'
he was to use all endeavours to separate them,[2]
and therefore the Seven Stars and the Rainbow,
being the foremost ships in the fleet, were ordered
to fire a shot and hail the combatants.   Upon
this signal both the Dunkirkers and Hollanders
came up, and were then ' bidden to go to the
leeward and speak to the Prince of England.'
On nearing the Prince Royal, the admirals of
the rival squadrons were invited on board, and
Charles ' laboured to have them accept a peace-
able course.'   The Hollander, however, refused
to be bound, and Charles endeavoured to settle
the matter by allowing the Dunkirkers ' to have
the start of the Hollanders.'[3]

The following day the English fleet were
within four leagues of the Scilly Islands, ' the
wind at north-east, but fair weather.'   The next
day, Sunday, a Council of War was held on the
Prince Royal, at which the possibility of landing
the Prince on one of the Islands in a ketch was
discussed.   For this purpose several pilots had
put off from the Islands, but by the time they

[1] *Phineas Pett*, p. 130.
[2] *S.P. Dom.*, James I, cxlv. 33.
[3] Somers, *Tracts*, ii. 548 ; *Phineas Pett*, p. 130.

reached the flagship, the idea had been post-poned. However, after supper the matter was again debated, and, 'beyond expectation, order was given to make ready the long-boat, and to call the ketch,' and the Prince made choice of the company that were to accompany him on shore, Mainwaring being one of them.

About one of the clock after midnight, with great danger to his Highness' person and to the Lord Duke of Buckingham, they were put into our long boat, which was veered astern by a long warp, where the ketch, laying the long boat on board, and the sea going somewhat high, they entered the ketch disorderly, without regard to any, but everyone shifting for themselves. Being all shipped, the ketch was so overburdened as she could make but little way, so that after we had taken farewell with a discharge of a volley of our great ordnance, we tacked into the sea.

After six hours' buffeting the ketch succeeded in reaching St. Mary's Island, where the Prince and his retinue landed. The flagship being now temporary bereft of the services of her Captain, and also the Master, Walter Whiting, the Earl held a council on board to decide what course it would be advisable to take. After serious consultation with two pilots of the Island, it was agreed that the Prince Royal might go into the roadstead without danger, and

after two or three boards, we laid it in quarter winds, and came to anchor in the best of the road about two of the clock afternoon ; the Prince and all his train standing upon the lower point of the land, and welcomed us in as we passed close by with much expression of joy and heaving up their hats.[1]

Charles remained on the Island four nights,

---

[1] *Phineas Pett*, pp. 131–2.

and was taken aboard again on the 3rd of October, when, to continue Pett's narrative,

we set sail out of Scilly, and on Sunday following, being the 5th day, we came into St. Helen's and anchored on No Man's Land, and shipped the Prince and his train into our long boat, and other ships' boats, who were safely landed at Portsmouth about 11 of the clock ; we taking our farewell with discharge of all our great ordnance, seconded by all the Fleet, with general thanksgiving to God for our safe arrival, to the joy and comfort of all true hearted subjects.[1]

Commenting on the return of the fleet, the Venetian ambassador wrote that the ships had ' proved as excellent ' as they were ' fine in appearance.' [2] Soon after their arrival in the Downs the ships were paid off, Rutland being remunerated at the rate of 3*l.* 6*s.* 8*d.* a day ; Vice-Admiral Lord Morley at 1*l.* 3*s.* 4*d.* ; Mainwaring at 1*l.* ; and Lord Windsor, Rear-Admiral, at 16*s.* 8*d.*[3]

The Prince, who was in feverish haste to see his father, hurried on to London, reaching York House early the following morning.

The news of his home-coming had preceded him, and such were the acclamations of joy with which he was received, that the streets were spread with tables of provisions and hogsheads of wine by the wealthy citizens of the metropolis. A cartload of offenders on their way to Tyburn were set at liberty, and bonfires were lighted all along the Prince's route.[4] At Cambridge, a contemporary records, ' every college had a speech, and one dish more at supper, and bonfires and

[1] *Phineas Pett*, p. 132.
[2] *S.P. Venice*, 1623–25, No. 184.
[3] Charnock, *Marine Architecture*, ii. 209.
[4] *S.P. Dom.*, James I, cliii. 44 ; Gardiner, v. 129.

squibs in their courts. . . . The close, at night, was with bonfires, drums, guns, fireworks, till past midnight all the town about.'[1] Never within living memory had such stirring scenes been witnessed in England.

The rejoicings of the people at the return of the Prince had scarcely died away, when we find him labouring on Mainwaring's behalf for his reappointment to Dover Castle. The good work that Mainwaring had rendered in the voyage to and from Spain merited some recognition, and the Prince wrote to Zouch that it was owing to

the late service he hath done us in our journey out of Spain, we are glad of any occasion to let him see that we do esteem of his person, and do therefore hereby earnestly pray your Lordship to let him know how valuable this our recommendation is with you, and to seal him again in that Lieutenancy which we shall esteem as a respect unto ourself.

In the meantime Zouch had informed both the Prince and Buckingham of his reasons for dismissing Mainwaring, and the latter had undertaken to procure all the gentlemen of Kent to certify against Zouch's damaging statements. On the other side, Sir Edward Zouch, 'a courtier and drolling favourite of James,'[2] had promised to influence all the judges on his cousin's behalf, while Zouch himself stated he would vacate the Wardenship on condition that 1000*l*. a year were settled on him.[3] A reply that Zouch sent the Prince in answer to one of his letters so displeased him, that he promptly burnt it. On the 20th of November, Zouch wrote a letter to Con-

[1] Ellis, *Orig. Letters*, iii. 160.
[2] Aubrey, *Brief Lives*, 1898, ii. p. 203.
[3] *S.P. Dom.*, James I, cliii. 81, 82.

way to the effect that he hoped the Prince would
not urge him to receive Sir Henry Mainwaring
again. Owing to bodily infirmity, he stated, he
was unable to go fully into the matter, and being
so ill, he expected to end his days at the Castle,
but if the Prince persisted, he would be carried
in his litter to London, to give his reasons against
Mainwaring's restoration.[1] The Prince, however,
was persistent, and on the 25th of the month,
Zouch had a full account prepared of the charges
brought against his former Lieutenant. Various
statements were recorded in this document,
amongst others being reports from Richard Marsh,
Clerk of Dover Castle, and Thomas Fulnetby.
That of the latter, who was Sergeant of the
Admiralty Court of the Cinque Ports, is without
doubt the most audacious, and in its way
amusing.[2] In his report he stated that Mainwaring tried hard to gain possession of some
8000*l*. or 9000*l*. of merchants' money, belonging
to a ship wrecked within the jurisdiction of the
Cinque Ports, which he (Fulnetby) had deposited
at Deal Castle, pending its return to the rightful
owners. He alleged that Mainwaring, being unsuccessful in his efforts to obtain the money,
persuaded him to rip up the bags, and tumble
the contents together, so that when the claimants
put in an appearance they would be unable to
prove how much belonged to them! How Mainwaring would have benefited by this elaborate
plot, one fails to see. The incident probably
refers to the wreck of the Ark Noah on the
Goodwins in the March of 1621.[3] These

---

[1] *S.P. Dom.*, James I, cliv. 10, 23, 38, 52.
[2] *Ibid.*, clv. 4.
[3] See Mainwaring's Despatch to Zouch, 15 March, 1621,
ante p. 81. It was the custom for all recovery from wreckage

accusations failed to injure Mainwaring's reputation in the eyes of the Prince, and in his reply to the indictment prepared by Zouch, he stated that he saw no cause whatever in the allegations produced, and thought Mainwaring 'a discreet and able gentleman worthy of some good employment.'[1] His letter is here reproduced :

To our right trusty and well beloved Lord Zouch, Lord Warden of the Cinque Ports.

RIGHT TRUSTY AND WELL BeLOVED,—Howsoever we thought it not necessary to have given any answer unto those papers which you sent by your Secretary concerning Sir Henry Mainwaring, seeing you are resolved not to give way unto the request we made you on his behalf for the admitting him again unto the Lieutenancy of Dover Castle, yet least to his prejudice and disreputation, it should be conceived that in these accusations, you have given cause to conceive unworthiness or demerit of Sir Henry Mainwaring, we have thought fitting hereby to declare that in those papers and allegations so delivered us by your Secretary we found no cause at all, why you might not very well have admitted him into that place without any inconvenience unto the service of his Majesty. We never doubted but that the place is merely in your Lordship's disposition, nor do we enquire the cause of any particular distaste or dislike that you may have unto the person of Sir Henry, but certainly for anything that hath yet appeared unto us, he is both a discreet and an able gentleman, and in every way worthy of some good employment from his Majesty. And so we bid your Lordship farewell.

Your friend,
CHARLES P.

From our Court at St. James'
This 23 day of January, 1623.[2]

within the jurisdiction of the Cinque Ports to be conveyed to Dover Castle.

[1] *S.P. Dom.*, James I, clviii. 41.   [2] *I.e.* 1623–4.

The royal recommendation, however, failed to move Zouch, who, to the end of his life, remained Mainwaring's bitterest enemy, and wrote that rather than have him restored to Dover, he would gladly suffer execution.[1] The character of Zouch, unfortunately, is not without blemish. It is known that he was a most difficult personage to work under. He had an absolute command over the Cinque Ports and a great part of the Admiralty, and would brook no rival in the administration of his office. Prior to his appointment as Lord Warden, he had been President of Wales, and from one of his contemporaries we are able to glean a few details of the man and his methods. During the time he held this important post, we are informed that he played ' Rex both with the Council and justices, and with the poor Welshmen,' [2] and in consequence many complaints were lodged against him that his conduct brought disgrace upon the office. It is not surprising, therefore, that he failed to agree with Mainwaring, who with his many suggestions for improving the condition of the Cinque Ports, tended rather to overshadow, as Zouch probably thought, the dignity of the Lord Warden. Whether this was the reason or not for the particular ' distaste or dislike' that Zouch had for Mainwaring, it is difficult to see how he could have been guilty of the many misdemeanours of which Zouch accused him. As we have seen, under Mainwaring's Lieutenancy the defences of Dover Castle had been put on a sounder basis, and foreigners had been prohibited from viewing the fortifications. A like care and consideration had been bestowed

---

[1] *S.P. Dom.*, James I, cliv. 79. He eventually appointed Sir John Hippisley to the post in December 1624 (*S.P. Dom.*, clxxvi. 50).   [2] *S.P. Dom.*, cclxxxv. 32.

on the rest of the ports. The accusation that he had absented himself from the Castle, and that his subordinates had in consequence been forced to transact the duties of his post, is extremely difficult to substantiate.[1] In considering the evidence that is available, it is necessary to take into consideration that Mainwaring was a voluminous correspondent, and a considerable number of his letters to Zouch and other eminent personages, written from Dover, are still preserved in the Public Record Office. Also, it is interesting to note that the whole of the ' Seaman's Dictionary,' which Mainwaring dedicated to Zouch,[2] was written within the precincts of the Castle, a combination of circumstances which does not point to him having neglected his office.

Mainwaring himself stated he was dismissed for affecting ' Buckingham's desires,' [3] and there is probably some truth in this statement, when we consider that Buckingham was Lord High Admiral, and that his office frequently clashed with that of the Lord Warden of the Cinque Ports. Buckingham's jurisdiction was claimed for the Narrow Seas, and the Lord Warden claimed all ' flotsam, wrecks, &c.,' to belong to him from ' Shoe beacon in Essex to the Red Nore in Sussex, half seas over,' denying that the Lord Admiral had any power to exercise his jurisdiction in that limit, which was an encroachment upon the Warden's right and privilege. The Cinque Ports claimed exemption from having men pressed out of their ships for the King's

---

[1] Fulnetby, one of his accusers, was himself accused of negligence in his office by Richard Marsh, the Clerk of the Castle (Marsh to Mainwaring, *S.P. Dom.*, cxviii. 51).

[2] See Volume II, where the dedication is given in full.

[3] *S.P. Dom.*, James I, cliv. 23.

service, but the Lord Admiral's officers pressed them when necessary. If the mayors, or in fact any of the officers of the Cinque Ports, refused to execute the Lord Admiral's warrant, they were punished : the same fate awaited them at the hands of the Warden if they gave way to the Lord Admiral. On account of these, and many other inconveniences, a movement was set on foot for securing unity in the administration of the sea forces by vesting both offices in one and the same individual, and this was eventually carried through in 1624, on the eve of the war, by Buckingham purchasing the Lord Wardenship from Lord Zouch.[1] The jurisdiction of the Lord Warden is clearly defined in a statute of George III, in which it states,[2]

whereas doubts have arisen, as to the exact boundaries of the jurisdiction of the Lord High Admiral, and the Lord Warden of the Cinque Ports . . . now it is hereby declared and enacted, that the boundaries of the jurisdiction of the Lord Warden of the Cinque Ports shall be from a point to the westward of Seaford in Sussex, called Red Cliff, including the same ; thence passing in a line 1 mile without the sand or shoal called the Horse of Willingdon, and continuing the same distance, without the Ridge and New Shoals, and thence in a line within 5 miles of Cape Grisnez, on the coast of France ; thence round the shoal called the Overfalls, 2 miles distant of the same ; thence in a line without, and the same distance along the Eastern side of the Galloper Sand, until the N. end bears W.N.W., true bearing : from thence it runs, in a direct line, across the shoal called Thwart Middle, till it reaches the shore underneath the Mase Tower ; thence following the

[1] *S.P. Dom.*, cliv. 23, and ' Argument in Favour of the Amalgamation of both Offices ' (in Gardiner's *Docs. Rel. to Impeachment of Buckingham*, pp. 3–8).
[2] 48 Geo. III, clause 20 (cited in Lyon *Dover*, i. 284–5).

shore, up to St. Osyth, Co. Essex; and following the shore up to the River Colne, to the landing place nearest Brightlinsea; from thence to the Shoe Beacon; thence to the point of Shellness, I. of Sheppey; thence across the waters to Faversham; thence round the N. and S. Forelands and Beachy Head, till it reaches the said Red Cliff; including all the waters, creeks, and havens comprehended between them.

There still exists in a neatly written document preserved at the Public Record Office, the instructions drawn up by Mainwaring, for the observance of the Lord Warden's droit gatherers, which is here printed for the first time [1]:

First if any wreck doth happen, or any goods flotsam be found, or are brought into any port, the Droit gatherers of the place shall presently take some inventory and note of the business of the ship or vessel, anchors, cables, tackle, furniture, loading, and goods in every particular, and of the place where, and time when it happened, or was found. And with all convenient speed make certificate thereof unto your Lordship or your Lordship's Lieutenant at Dover Castle.

2. Item, when any ship or vessel groundeth on any coast or place within your Lordship's Admiralty, which doth afterwards float off again, the Droit gatherer shall not only pass to your Lordship's use the best Cable and Anchor of the vessel according to the custom in that case used, but shall also make like certificate unto your Lordship, or your Lieutenant, of the time and place it happened, and of the burthen of the vessel with all speed convenient.

3. Item, when any Anchor, Cable, or goods wrecked, shall be apprised, such assignment shall be always made by four persons at the least, of the most ancient and substantial habitants of the place, in the presence of the Mayor, or Bailiff of the town, or his Deputy, and the

---

[1] *S.P. Dom.*, James I, lxxxi. 26. The MS. is undated, but has been wrongly calendared under the date of 1615.

same so made, being signed under the hands of the Mayor
and the Apprisors, shall be presently certified unto your
Lordship, or your Lordship's Lieutenant at Dover Castle.

4. Item, no Droit gatherer shall sell or do away or
compound for any Anchor, Cable, or your Lordship's
part of any wrecked goods until such time as he shall
receive warrant so to do, under your Lordship's hand
or your Lordship's Lieutenant.

5. Item, every Droit gatherer (within one Month or
what time it shall please your Lordship to nominate
after sale made of any such goods aforesaid) shall make
a full and perfect accompt in writing of the goods sold,
and to inform together with payment of the moneys
for which it shall be sold, unto your Lordship or your
Lieutenant at Dover Castle.

These, or the like conditions to be kept and insisted
upon by the Serjeant of the Admiralty, by which means
things passing in so open and fair a way, it will not be
possible for any whosoever to beguile your Lordship of
your right.

Not only did Zouch remove his Lieutenant
from Dover Castle, but he was determined that
Mainwaring should be debarred from holding any
position connected with the Cinque Ports. Therefore for the last Parliament of James I, which
was summoned to meet at Westminster on the 12th
of February 1624, he nominated for Dover, Sir
Richard Young, the late member, and in place
of Mainwaring, Sir Edward Cecil. Such was
the corruption of the ports at this time, and such
the arrogance of the Lord Warden, that he
assumed to himself the power of nominating one,
and occasionally both parliamentary representatives.[1] Nothing daunted, however, Mainwaring

---

[1] Oldfield, *Repr. Hist. of Gt. Britain*, v. 355–6. This
usurpation was quietly submitted to till the Revolution,
after which date an Act was passed declaring such procedure
contrary to the laws and constitution of the Realm (*ibid.*).

with Sir Thomas Wilsford, a native of Kent, took
the field in opposition to Cecil and Young, stating
that he wished to prove the respect with which
he was held by the townspeople.[1] Whether the
inhabitants had any respect or not for Mainwaring
is difficult to determine, because the freemen of
the town on this occasion had no voice in the
election, and Zouch's nominees in consequence
were returned. Nevertheless, there was an un-
pleasant surprise in store for them. The session
was barely a month old when Mainwaring was
reported 'wandering about Westminster,' an
ominous sign that he was trying to enlist the
sympathies of Parliament in his cause. A petition
was drawn up against the return of Cecil and
Young on the ground that the freemen inhabitants
of Dover had no voice in their election. Young
wrote to Zouch that he had received certain
papers about Mainwaring's petition, and requested
more time to falsify witnesses to it, but feared
that it would not be granted, 'as the House is
violent for free elections.' 'If witnesses were
present,' Young wrote, 'to prove that the summons
for election was public ; that none were nominated
but Sir Edward Cecil, himself, and Mainwaring,
and that no other freemen pressed to vote ' ;
then, as the court of election was of long standing,
he thought there was a chance of the petition
being overthrown.[2]

Eventually two petitions were presented to
the Commons on the 24th of March ; one by the

---

[1] *S.P. Dom.*, James I, clxi. 38. Up till the early 19th
century the elections always took place in the parish church
of St. Mary's, while the local Court of Chancery and the
Admiralty Court of the Cinque Ports were usually held in
St. James' church (*Huguenot Soc. Proceedings*, iii. 132).

[2] *Ibid.*, clx. 94.

inhabitants at large, the other by the Mayor, Jurats and Common Council.[1] The question was as to the right of election, and the Committee of Privileges were of the opinion, that the freemen inhabitants of Dover ought to have a voice in the election of their members. It was resolved upon question, ' that the freemen and free burgesses, inhabitants of Dover, ought to have voice in the election of their barons to serve in Parliament.' Upon a second question it was resolved, ' that the election of Sir Edward Cecil and Sir Richard Young is void, and that a new warrant go out for a new choice with expedition.'[2] By the aid of Sir Richard Young we are enabled to get a passing glimpse of the proceedings. ' General Cecil,' he informed Zouch, went away at the very beginning of the debate, without speaking a word, when he saw how things were likely to turn, stating ' that Count Maurice[3] had sent for him, and he could not be turned out of the House at a better time.' Mainwaring was also there, but did not take any part in the debate. On the other hand the Mayor of Dover spoke hesitatingly as to whether the right of election should be general or not, ' thus implying,' wrote Young, ' the right of the freemen,' and when pressed on the point, he admitted that the freemen should be allowed to vote.[4] Both Cecil and Young complained bitterly to Zouch at their having been unseated, and Young wrote to the effect

---

[1] *House of Commons Journal*, 24 March, 1624; *Cal. S.P. Dom.*, Young to Zouch, 23 March 1624.

[2] Oldfield, v. p. 368. It was a common occurrence at this period for elections to be declared void, owing to some flaw in the member's election.

[3] Count Maurice of Nassau.

[4] *S.P. Dom.*, James I, clxi. 32.

'that he hoped to be chosen again, the rather
because the House expressed approbation of their
persons, with an implied intimation to the freemen
to choose them.'[1] Cecil attributed his being
'put out of the House' to the malice of Mainwaring, and his letter to Zouch, with its curious
phraseology, is given below.[2]

MY VERY GOOD LORD,—As your Lordship may
understand by the malice of Sir Henry Mainwaring to
your Lordship your two Burgesses are put out of the
House, upon the general opinion that the House hath
given, that is no Burgess to be chosen without the
choice of the Commons by an Ancient law of Parliament, and if this law were so generally followed, as it
hath been against us there, there would be but few sit
in Parliament, yet a blot is no blot till it be hit, so
now it is hit, therefore if there be any means for us to
recover the honour, I humbly beseech your Lordship
to take it into your consideration, for that no man is
more your Lordship's humble servant than is

This 25 [*of March*] *in great hast.*   ED. CECIL.

A new writ was forthwith issued, and the
cause of Mainwaring and Wilsford was stoutly
championed by Sir Edwin Sandys, a prominent
member of the Virginia Company, and others.
Whatever their united efforts may have been,
and whatever arguments were propounded on
their behalf, they proved fruitless, and Zouch,
who was all powerful in Dover, had the satisfaction of seeing his 'two Burgesses' re-elected.[3]
Perhaps the secret of Young's success lies in
the fact that he was a wealthy London merchant,
and had acted the part of a money-lender to

[1] *S.P. Dom.*, James. I, clxi. 51.
[2] *Ibid.*, clxi. 39 ; cited in Dalton's *Life of Cecil*, ii. 55.
[3] Return of Members of Parliament.

Zouch. Just about the time of the election he had advanced 2000*l.* to him, besides becoming his tenant at Odiham House.[1]

Having dismissed Mainwaring, Zouch himself was anxious to be rid of a post in which he had incurred the royal displeasure, and on the 17th of July he made an agreement with Buckingham for the surrender of the Lord Wardenship of the Cinque Ports. The conditions were, that Zouch should receive 1000*l.* in ready money, and a settlement of 500*l.* a year for life. Even this goodly offer would not permit him to depart from his post in peace, and he thought fit to frame two stipulations, one to the effect that Buckingham should not re-instate Mainwaring, and the other that Marsh and Fulnetby, Mainwaring's accusers, should retain their respective offices. The part of the agreement that concerns Mainwaring and the others reads as follows :

Item it is agreed (in respect of true and faithful service done to the Lord Zouch) that Marsh, the Clerk of the Castle, shall hold his place ; Fulnetby, Serjeant of the Admiralty, shall hold his place ; and Captain Hill, Muster Master, shall hold his place, during their natural lives, if they carry themselves justly and truly, or that George Duke of Buckingham shall not otherwise prefer them or give them content.

Item it is agreed that Sir Henry Mainwaring shall have no place or command in the Cinque Ports during the Duke of Buckingham's time in respect of his ungrateful labouring the Lord Zouch's disgrace both at the Court and Parliament, and threatening of revenge on those poor men who did certify truths of his misdemeanours.[2]

[1] *S.P. Dom.*, James I, clxi. 51 ; clxiv. 43.
[2] *Ibid.*, clxx. 16 ; cited in Gardiner's *Docs. Rel. to the Impeachment of Buckingham,* p. 2.

On the 2nd of September following, the agreement was signed and sealed, and Zouch, in accordance with the custom of the time, sold his office.[1] Soon after Zouch's vacation, a rumour gained credence that Buckingham intended parting with the Wardenship to the Earl of Warwick. Naturally somewhat alarmed at the news, Zouch wrote to Nicholas for information, fearing that the Earl, who held Mainwaring in high esteem, might appoint him as his Lieutenant.[2]

Though deprived of his office, it must have afforded some consolation to Mainwaring to know that his labours on behalf of Dover Castle had not been in vain, for at the end of 1624 the sum of 40*l.* was paid to Bernard Johnson for surveying and directing the repairs at Dover Castle, upon which 1000*l.* was expended.[3]

[1] *S.P. Dom.*, James I, clxxii. 2.

[2] *Ibid.*, clxxv. 15. This report was unfounded, and Buckingham held office till his death, 23 Aug. 1628. Zouch died in the following year, 1625.

[3] *Lords MSS.* (*Hist. MSS. Com.*, iii. p. 35). Johnson was the King's engineer, and is sometimes styled 'Engineer of the Tower of London.' He took part in the expedition to Rhé, 1627, and was one of those killed at the landing. His widow was granted an annuity of 100*l.* during pleasure (*S.P. Dom.*, Charles I, lxxvii. 29 ; xciii. 61).

CHAPTER VI

1624–27

THE NAVY DURING BUCKINGHAM'S REGIME

ALL connection in an official capacity with the Cinque Ports having come to an end, Mainwaring's career from now onwards is closely bound up with the history of the Royal Navy, and the period of maritime expansion that was ushered in during the last seven years of the reign of James the First. Prior to 1618, although the King had expended more money on the Navy than in former years, its strength and efficiency was seriously undermined by the employment of inefficient officials and the corruption of the age.[1] It was not until the Naval Commission of 1618 got to work that any serious effort to place the fleet on a sound basis was attempted, and the fraudulent officials, who for years had filled their pockets at the nation's expense, were removed. After

---

[1] A flagrant example is given in Bishop Goodman's *Memoirs*. Walking one day with a friend in Chatham where the King's ships were, his friend remarked, ' I will tell you a wonder. All these goodly houses that you see— houses fit for knights to dwell in—they are all made of chips.' His meaning was that the officers of the Navy took all the best timber which was intended for repairing the ships for the building of their own houses (i. pp. 53–4).

a full investigation by the Commissioners who were entrusted with the task of regenerating the naval service, the Surveyor and the Controller of the Navy were both ' sequestered from their posts,' and their duties entrusted to a Board of Commissioners.[1] Of the forty-three vessels that were on the navy list at the time, nearly one-half on examination were found to be practically useless, and it was resolved that, in order to bring the Navy up to its former strength, ten new ships should be built within the next five years. The Commissioners suggested that in future warships ' should have the length treble to the breadth, and breadth in like proportion answerable to the depth, but not to draw above 16 foot water,' because, they stated in their report, ' deeper ships are seldom good sailers.' They must be ' somewhat snug built,' they advised, ' with double galleries, and not too lofty upper works, which overcharge many ships,' as was the case with those constructed during the Elizabethan period.[2] Not only did they advise, but they saw their programme carried through, with a precision and punctuality that, to say the least of it, was remarkable, and by the end of 1623 the ten ships that they had proposed had been added to the Navy. Their names are given in the table on the following page.[3]

Thanks to the energy of the Commission, it is to this period that a definite revival in England's maritime interests can be traced. Following on their report, Buckingham was appointed Lord High Admiral in 1619, and the members of the Commission themselves were constituted as a

[1] *S.P. Dom.*, James I, cv. 93.
[2] Charnock, *Marine Architecture*, ii. p. 249.
[3] *S.P. Dom.*, James I, clvi. 12. The details of the ships are taken from Mr. Oppenheim's *Naval Administrations*, p. 202.

permanent Naval Board in that year.[1]   Although
Buckingham did not bring to his high office the
requisite knowledge of seamanship, his zeal in
the administration of it stamped him as a man
of indefatigable energy.   In order to become
thoroughly acquainted with every branch of the
naval service, he surrounded himself with a group
of able and experienced seamen, whose advice
he sought, and whose suggestions for the improvement of the Navy he encouraged.[2]   Prominent

Ship.	Year.	Tons.	Length of Keel.	Beam.	Depth.	Guns.
			Ft.	Ft. Ins.	Ft. Ins.	
Constant Reformation .	1619	752	106	35 6	15 0	42
Happy Entrance . .	1619	582	96	32 6	14 0	32
Victory : . .	1620	875	108	35 9	17 0	42
Garland . . .	1620	683	93	33 0	16 0	34
Swiftsure . . .	1621	887	106	36 10	16 8	42
Bonaventure . .	1621	675	98	33 0	15 8	34
St. George . . .	1622	895	110	37 0	16 6	42
St. Andrew . . .	1622	895	110	37 0	16 6	42
Triumph . . .	1623	922	110	37 0	17 0	42
Mary Rose . . .	1623	394	83	27 0	13 0	26

among this little circle was Sir Henry Mainwaring,
and from the time of Buckingham's appointment
until his death in 1628, Mainwaring was continually advising him on naval matters.

[1] They were Sir Thomas Smith, Sir Lionel Cranfield, Sir
Richard Weston, Sir J. Wolstenholme, Nicholas Fortescue,
John Osborne, Francis Gofton, Richard Sutton, William Pitt,
John Coke, Thomas Norreys, and William Burrell (Charnock,
ii. 204).

[2] James, in his speech at the opening of Parliament in
1621, was enthusiastic over his ' young Admiral's ' abilities.
' Though he be young,' he informed Parliament, ' yet I find
him true in faith, and an honest man . . . He took under
himself divers Commissioners, as a young commander should
do, the better to preserve him from error ' (*Parl. Hist.*, vol. i.
p. 1178).

Though the services of the fleet had not been seriously requisitioned during the reign of James I, with the exception of Mansell's expedition to Algiers in 1620–21, and Rutland's voyage to Spain two years later, the Commissioners had accomplished their work so well, that by 1619 the Navy, as we have seen, was ready to spring into being as England's first arm of defence. To no continental power was this more apparent than to Spain, and Gondomar, in his secret report on England in that year, emphasised the importance of keeping the peace with James on that account. The English nation was very rich, he informed Philip; in a few weeks a powerful fleet could be manned and equipped, the sea would swarm with privateers, and, he added wisely, ' whoever was master at sea, would soon be master on shore.'[1]

Spain had certainly occasion to view the English naval reforms with alarm, for side by side with Buckingham's interest in the Navy, and in no less a degree pronounced, was the enthusiasm displayed by the King. ' The wooden walls of the kingdom,' the Lord Keeper informed Parliament in 1621, were ' his Majesty's special care.'[2] The same sentiment was shown in the King's speech to a deputation of both houses which waited on him at Theobalds in the March of 1624, when he struck the true keynote of British naval policy— that was, the importance of having an ample margin in ships over our continental rivals. Though the Navy was in a better state than it had ever been before, he informed them, ' yet more must be done, before it can be prepared as it ought to be.' For that purpose ' a new charge '

---

[1] From a document in the Simancas archives. Cited in Gardiner's *England*, iii. 283.
[2] *Parl. Hist.*, vol. i. p. 1382.

was necessary, ' as well for its own strength as
for securing of the coasts.'[1]   As a proof of his
sincerity, within three months he decided to
mobilize a fleet of twelve royal ships and thirty
merchantmen for the defence of the realm,[2] and
on his death in the following year the Navy
bequeathed to his son consisted of the undermentioned ships (see Table opposite).[3]

It was during the reign of James that a school
of professional seamen were beginning to assert
themselves.   As a shipbuilder Phineas Pett stands
out head and shoulders above his contemporaries ;
while Mainwaring, towards the end of the reign,
had compiled a treatise on seamanship, which he
presented to Buckingham, whom he describes as
' my most honoured Lord and Patron.'[4]   Prior
to this, numerous works had appeared on navigation, but until Mainwaring committed pen to paper
there ' was not so much as a means thought of,
to inform any one of the practice of mechanical
working of ships, with the proper terms belonging
to them.'   The fact was that hitherto seamen
had preserved a sort of freemasonry concerning
their profession, though probably an inability to
express themselves in writing was responsible
for a dearth of literature on the subject.

Mainwaring, in writing of the Navy of the time,
gives the following rules for fixing the lengths
of masts and yards, which prior to the reign of
James do not seem to have been governed by any

---

[1] *Parl. Hist.*, vol. i. p. 1390.
[2] *S.P. Venice;* 1623–25, No. 410.
[3] *Oppenheim*, pp. 207, 251.
[4] It remained in manuscript some twenty years, but was
freely circulated among the naval commanders of the time.
It was printed in 1644 under the title of *The Seaman's
Dictionary*.

proportion.[1] With the aid of this table, and the

Ship.	Built.	Rebuilt.	Tonnage.	Guns.
Prince	1610	..	1200	55
Bear	..	1599	900	51
Merhonour	..	1611–14	800	44
Ann Royal	..	1608	800	44
Repulse	..	1610	700	40
Defiance	..	1611–14	700	40
Triumph	1623	..	921	42
St. George	1622	..	880	42
St. Andrew	1622	..	880	42
Swiftsure	1621	..	876	42
Victory	1620	..	870	42
Constant Reformation . .	1619	..	750	42
Warspite	1596	..	650	38
Vanguard	..	1615	651	40
Rainbow	..	1618	650	40
Red Lion	..	1609	650	38
Assurance	..	1603	600	38
Nonsuch	..	1603	600	38
Bonaventure	1621	..	674	34
Garland	1620	..	680	32
Happy Entrance . . .	1619	..	580	32
Convertive	1616	..	500	34
Dreadnought	..	1611–14	450	32
Antelope	..	1618	450	34
Adventure	1594	..	350	26
Mary Rose	1623	..	388	26
Phoenix	1612	..	250	20
Moon [2]	1590	..	140	..
Seven Stars	1615	..	140	14
Charles	..	..	140	14
Desire	1616	..	60	6

regulations propounded by the Naval Commission in 1618 as to building, we are able to gain some

[1] Charnock, ii. 196.

[2] The pinnace *Moon* is not mentioned in Mr. Oppenheim's list. That she was on the active list is shown by the report of the Naval Commission of 1626.

idea of the structure and appearance of warships of the period.[1]

Main-mast . . $\frac{4}{5}$ of the breadth of the ship multiplied by 3.
Fore-mast . . $\frac{4}{5}$ of the main-mast.
Mizzen-mast . $\frac{1}{2}$ the length of the main-mast.
Bow-sprit . . $\frac{4}{5}$ the length of the main-mast.
Top-masts . . $\frac{1}{2}$ the length of the lower masts.

'The bigness (of all masts) to be one inch to a yard in length.'

Main-yard . . $\frac{5}{6}$ the length of the keel
Fore-yard . . $\frac{4}{5}$ of the main-yard.
Top-sail-yard . $\frac{3}{7}$ of the main-yard.
Cross-jack-yard . $\frac{4}{5}$ of the main-yard
Sprit-sail-yard . $\frac{4}{5}$ of the main-yard.

'The bigness (of all yards) to be $\frac{1}{4}$ of an inch for a yard in length.'

While on the subject of ship-building it is interesting to note that the dockyards which were available for the purpose were at Deptford, Woolwich, and Chatham, the latter being the most used. Strange as it may seem, Portsmouth is hardly mentioned till 1623, when it was decided to fill up the great dock there, and ram the mouth of it with stones for the better preservation of the yard against the violence of the sea.[2] Two years later, when Buckingham had persuaded Charles to declare war against Spain, and despatch a large fleet to Cadiz, Mainwaring came forward with a remarkable proposition to the Lord High Admiral, regarding the use of Portsmouth as a permanent naval base. In the paper which he

[1] *Seaman's Dictionary*, pp. 64-7, 117.
[2] Oppenheim, p. 210. This was the end of the first dry dock in England.

presented to Buckingham on the subject, Mainwaring set forth his reasons why some of the King's ships should be stationed at Portsmouth, and not all at Chatham, as was then the case. Raleigh had also held similar views, and in his ' Observations on the Navy and Sea Service ' had dwelt on the inconvenience of Rochester and Chatham as a base for the fleet.

It had long been pointed out that for a fleet to get round from the Thames to Portsmouth, entailed as much time and trouble as it did to get from that place to the Mediterranean.[1] As Mainwaring remarked, the difference between Chatham and Portsmouth was ' as much as for one to have his sword drawn in his hand, whilst the other is rusty in his scabbard.' His paper, which is preserved in the Public Record Office, is entitled, ' Reasons to have some of the King's ships at Portsmouth rather than to be all at Chatham. By Sir Hen. Mainwaring.'[2] The following is a full transcript of the original document, which cannot fail to be of interest, in view of the important position that Portsmouth occupies in the naval world to-day.

The going into the harbour deep and broad enough, and the narrowing not long, so that though there be no convenient breadth to turn in with a contrary wind, yet every small spurt of a fair wind will serve to bring a ship into the harbour, or else they may quickly warp in.

The harbour within is roomy enough for more than 100 sail of great ships, depth of water sufficient, the ground very good, the tide not so strong. The gust of wind not so violent as at Chatham, and therefore the

---

[1] Oppenheim, p. 296.
[2] *S.P. Dom.*, Charles I, xiii. 62. Endorsed ' Reasons expressing the fitness and necessity to have some of his Majesty's ships at Portsmouth . . . especially in this time of war.'

mooring will not be so chargeable, and the ships ride safer.

The outlet very good for all northerly wind to go for the southward, and westerly wind to go for the northward, and if it do not overblow, the great ships may warp out all winds, and the less may kedge out. By reason whereof, taking the winds as they commonly fall, a fleet, especially of great ships, shall arrive sooner in Spain from Portsmouth than come from Chatham to the Isle of Wight, and so upon the matter in all such voyages a six weeks' pay of wages and charge of victuals might be saved to the King in every voyage, which is a great profit.

Also, ships may be much sooner in the Downs from hence, and with less danger than from Chatham, whence the great ships going through the sand are in great danger of storms, and the lesser (I mean the middle sort) of calms going over the flat, in case they should not fetch over in one tide, but be forced to anchor. Within the harbour it haines[1] enough to grave all such ships as either for build of mould under water, or charge of weight overhead, are fit to lie with the ground, and the graving place very firm and good ground.

It is a very convenient place if need require to careen a ship in ; beside, the river of Hamble [2] is within two or three hours' sail, where ships may ride safely and careen with great ease and convenience. For the greater ships, it haines[1] sufficient to make a dock for the biggest ship in England, which dock I suppose will be made for less than £3,000, wherein it will be a fit consideration to examine on which side the harbour it will be most convenient to make it ; I took no great notice of it, but I suppose that Gosport side will be the fitter. By reason that the breach doth set in on Portsmouth side, and the charge of this dock will be saved in the surplusaged charge in

---

[1] Hain = to raise, heighten, set up. (*New English Dictionary*.)

[2] The river Hamble, which empties itself into Southampton Water. At the mouth of the river is Hamble creek. In the 15th century it was a favourite roadstead for the Royal ships.

transporting the ships about to Chatham in one year's voyage. And the dock for perpetual use, either in building, graving, or repairing of shipping, a consideration of greater importance, in respect there is not any dock in all the western parts of England.

The harbour not given to mussels and foulness so much as at Chatham, by reason whereof, and the good outlet, ships may go much cleaner to sea than now they do, which is a great commodity, especially in time of war.

The bay without so good that ships may ride securely all winds, to attend either the proceeding or determining of a voyage. The ships safe by reason of the fort, and for less than half the charge of Gillingham Boom.[1] One may be made here to stop all manner of merchant ships from going so high as the King's, or in case this fort were not sufficient, a small charge will raise new platforms to plant more ordnance on them. In case it were possible to practise any treachery upon the King's Navy it is much safer to have them divided. The ships lying here it will be a great strength and security to the kingdom, either in offensive or defensive war, and most ready for other ordinary service, by reason they will be so ready to set sail. Where the difference between this and Chatham is as much as for one to have his sword drawn in his hand, whilst the other is rusty in his scabbard.

All materials for building and repairing of shipping much cheaper, timber being much cheaper and sooner supplied than it is at Chatham, and iron better somewhat.

All kinds of victuals better, and both cheap and more convenient to be boarded than at Chatham.

A greater commodity for all seafaring men that are pressed out of the western ports, and profit to the King in saving so much conduct money to bring them to Chatham. And to them in respect they may bring their clothes and necessaries by boat, for want of which many perish in the King's ships.

---

[1] A chain was placed across the Medway at Upnor by Hawkins in 1585. It was replaced in 1623 by a boom made of 16 masts, 43 hundredweight of iron, and the hulls of two ships and two pinnaces (Oppenheim, p. 211).

To have one-half or one-third part of the King's ships here would be a means to enrich one of the choicest ports and forts of the kingdom, which now decays for lack of trade and money.

There are store-houses very convenient already built.

There are many things concerning the managing of this design for the best advantage, wherein I shall be ready to deliver my weak opinion to your Grace if you please to command my further service, or think me worthy to be advised with.

That Mainwaring's advice was acted upon is proved by the fact that in 1627 Buckingham caused estimates to be drawn up for the construction of a dock at Portsmouth ' on Gosport side,' as Mainwaring had proposed. This suggestion seems to have met with general approval, and Captain Giffard, a prominent naval official, wrote to the effect that he was very glad Buckingham had determined to build a new dock at Portsmouth, which procedure would be ' much to his honour, profitable to the King, and the only way for the good government of the Navy.' [1]

In the State Papers, under the date of September 10, 1627, is a draft of the instructions issued to the Commissioners that were appointed to see into the matter. [2] Earlier in the year it was ordered that Robert Tranckmore and Jonas Day should be allowed the sum of £972 16s. 0d. for making the dry dock there, with wharf, crane,

---

[1] *S.P. Dom.*, Charles I, lxvi. 55.   Among the Addit. MSS. in the British Museum (9294, ff. 315–19) is a paper entitled, *Observations touching the Harbour at Portsmouth*.   It is fuller than Mainwaring's paper, but is unsigned.   Though of a somewhat later date, it was evidently copied from Mainwaring's, as parts of it are identical.   Sir W. Monson was of the opinion that Chatham was the best and safest place for the fleet, and for his views on the subject the reader is referred to his *Naval Tracts*, Book V.   [2] *Ibid.*, lxxvii. 29.

saw-house, and two new lighters.[1] A further sum of £500 was estimated in September for the work, and prominent among the Commissioners were William Burrell and the Mayor of Portsmouth; 'Sir Hen. Mainwaring, Kt., to be Controller.'[2]

As no further steps appear to have been taken in the matter, it is to be assumed that Buckingham's death in the following year deferred the project. In 1630 Pett and Sir Thomas Aylesbury among others were sent down to Portsmouth, with instructions to report on its adaptabilities as a station for the fleet. They were, however, adverse in their opinions regarding the construction of a dry dock, thinking the rise and fall of the tide too little, and they reported 'there is no use of any there.'[3]

One reason why Portsmouth was not adopted earlier as a permanent naval station was owing to the diverse opinions that were expressed as to the existence of a particular worm in the harbour, which played havoc with ships both sheathed and unsheathed.[4] In August 1630 a commission consisting of all the principal officers of the Navy, with six of the chief masters of the Trinity House, was sent down to Portsmouth to report on the existence or not of this maritime pest. Phineas Pett, who was one of the commission, records that 'there was much dispute and contrariety about the business,' and in the November following he was again sent down 'to search and inquire about the worm.' Several master shipwrights

---

[1] *S.P. Dom.*, Charles I, lxii. 54.
[2] *Ibid.*, lxvii. 29.
[3] Oppenheim, pp. 296–7.
[4] For an account of this worm, the *Teredo Navalis*, see *Hawkin's Voyages*, 1878 (Hakluyt Soc.), p. 202.

accompanied Pett, and they found, ' upon oath,' that the existence of the pest was only ' a rumour raised to hinder the keeping of any of his Majesty's ships in that harbour.'[1]   Nevertheless, from this time onwards some of the Royal Navy were always stationed there, but it was not until eight years later that a master shipwright entered into permanent residence.[2]   The dry-dock, however, was not started till 1656, when the first Dutch war proved both the wisdom and the necessity of a base at Portsmouth.

As previously stated, at the time of Mainwaring's proposal concerning Portsmouth, England had declared war against Spain, and a fleet consisting of 9 royal ships, and about 80 other vessels, which conveyed a land force of 10,000 men, was despatched to Cadiz under the command of Sir Edward Cecil.   The King's ships and their commanders were[3] :

Anne Royal .	Admiral, Sir Edward Cecil. Sir Thomas Love, Captain
Swiftsure .	Vice-Admiral, the Earl of Essex. Sir S. Argall, Captain.
St. Andrew .	Rear-Admiral, the Earl of Denbigh. Sir John Watts, Captain.
Reformation.	Viscount Valentia. Raleigh Gilbert, Captain.
Rainbow .	Sir John Chudleigh.
Convertive .	Sir W. St. Leger. Captain Porter.
St. George .	Lord Delaware. Sir M. Geere, Captain.
Bonaventure	Lord Cromwell. Captain Collins.
Dreadnought	Sir Beverly Newcome.

[1] *Phineas Pett*, p. 145.
[2] Oppenheim, p. 297.
[3] *Glanville's Journal*, pp. 125-7.

Cecil, it will be remembered, had been Mainwaring's opponent in the Dover election of 1624, and although he had achieved fame as a soldier in the Low Countries, he was entirely ignorant of naval warfare. The fleet, which was divided into three squadrons, eventually left Plymouth on the 8th of October, 1625, and arrived off Cadiz a fortnight later. It is not within the scope of this book to give an account of the subsequent operations there of the English fleet.[1] Suffice it to say that Cadiz was ' considered too strong to assault,' and by the 29th Cecil had withdrawn his troops, and the fleet thereupon directed its attention to the Spanish treasure ships which were due to arrive from America. On the 4th of November, while the English commander was lying in wait off Cape St. Vincent, the Spanish ships, by taking a southerly route, reached Cadiz two days after Cecil's squadron had left.

By the end of November the English ships ' were driven home in scattered groups, with no semblance of discipline or cohesion left.'[2] The expedition, which owed its origin to the Duke of Buckingham, proved a complete failure, and some of the chief causes of this are not difficult to ascertain. The old abuses, which the Naval Commission of 1618 had attempted to reform, had crept into the service again. Fraudulent officials had supplied the fleet with rotten cordage ; the ships themselves were unseaworthy and leaky ; while the unwholesome food that had been shipped aboard had stricken the crews with sickness.

---

[1] For a detailed account, the reader is referred to *Glanville's Journal*, published by the Camden Society ; Penn's *Navy under the Early Stuarts* ; and Dalton's *Life of Sir E. Cecil.*   [2] Corbett, *England in the Mediterranean*, i. 160.

Cecil informed Coke that there was ' hardly a ship of the whole fleet clean enough for the chase of a prize,' and there was ' a crying out of leaks and dangers of the King's ships,' which were old and unfit for those seas. This statement was borne out by his flag-captain, Sir Thomas Love, who wrote to Buckingham that the men ' fell sick so fast ; our victuals proved bad, and drink scant, and many ships, especially the King's ships, so weak and leak.'[1] In Sir Michael Geere's ship, the St. George, ' one shift of sails were the old Triumph's in '88,' and the other suit of sails were those discarded from the Ann Royal. ' Our fore shrouds,' he wrote, ' were the old Garland's ; our store of new ropes, when we came to open the coils, were of divers pieces, and the best of them stark rotten, but fairly tarred over.'[2] On his return Cecil was subjected to severe criticism, and an inquiry was held into his conduct of the expedition. Such a procedure might have been beneficial to the service generally if it had involved also the examination of the Victualler of the Navy, and the various dockyard officials who were certainly deserving of censure, but it did not. These individuals escaped punishment, and Charles immediately set his heart on the preparation of another fleet, which was to sail in the summer of 1626, to retrieve Cecil's failure of the previous autumn.

Though money to equip the expedition was only found with the utmost difficulty, and the seamen deserted daily, a fleet of 39 sail, including the Triumph, Vanguard, Swiftsure, Red Lion, Bonaventure, and Convertive, eventually left Stokes Bay towards the end of September, under

[1] Dalton's *Life of Cecil*, ii. pp. 216, 230.
[2] *Ibid.*, p. 226.

the command of Lord Willoughby, another professional soldier.[1] By the time the fleet had
reached Torbay, several ships were found to be
leaky, and in consequence had to be sent back.[2]
On the 12th of October, while crossing the Bay of
Biscay, a storm, which raged for two days, so
severely buffeted his already unseaworthy squadron,
that Willoughby was forced to return to England.
His ships had proved 'so leaky,' and 'so weak
under the weight of their ordnance,' that a contemporary records, had they been 'but a hundred
leagues further at sea' they would have probably foundered. The Triumph, Willoughby's flagship, built in 1623, on this her first voyage, proved
the weakest of the squadron, and spent her bow-
sprit, foremast, and mainyard, besides springing
'a principal knee forward on.'[3]

Both Cecil's and Willoughby's crews were in a
state of mutiny, and earlier in the year it had been
brought to the notice of the King that a debt of
£4,000 a month was being incurred for want of
£14,000 to pay off the seamen, who were forced
to steal in order to supply themselves with clothing
and food.[4] Neither were the officers in some cases
better provided for, and several of them petitioned
Buckingham for their discharge, stating that
neither pay nor food was forthcoming, and but
for the hospitality of their friends they would
have starved.[5]

Towards the end of November the temper of
the seamen was unmistakable, and 300 of them

[1] *S.P. Dom.*, Charles I, xxxii. 74. The Earl of Denbigh
was his vice-admiral, and Capt. John Pennington his rear-
admiral (*Court and Times of Charles I*, i. 139).

[2] *Ibid.*, xxxvii. 20.

[3] *Court and Times of Charles I*, i. 160.

[4] Oppenheim, p. 227.   [5] *Ibid.*, 224.

marched to London to demand their pay. On reaching the residence of Sir William Russell, the Treasurer of the Navy, they broke open the gates, and would have 'plucked' that dignity 'by the ears, had he not given them fair words.'[1]

The sudden and unexpected return of Willoughby's fleet, and the growing spirit of discontent among the seamen, at last stung Charles into action. It was obvious that he could no longer delay an inquiry into his maritime affairs, the state of which, as revealed in the two last expeditions, threatened the safety of the realm. On the 12th of December, therefore, he appointed a Special Commission, consisting of the Duke of Buckingham; the Earls of Bridgewater, Pembroke, Totnes, Denbigh, and Marlborough the Lord Treasurer; Sir Edward Cecil and Lord Willoughby, who, in spite of their failures, had now been created Viscount Wimbledon and Earl of Lindsey respectively; William, Lord Hervey, and Edward, Lord Herbert; Sir John Coke, Mainwaring, Sir Sackville Trevor, Sir Robert Cotton, Sir Thomas Love, Sir William Heydon, Sir John Watts, Sir John Trevor, and Captains John Pennington, Richard Giffard, and Phineas Pett.[2] 'His Majesty,' so runs the original warrant, 'having entered into a resolution of a speedy reformation, to prevent all inconveniency and dangers which may grow by the negligence, corruption, or abuse of officers, or other undue means crept in, to the weakening or impairing of the Navy, or the means provided for the maintenance thereof, and to take order in all other defects, and to provide for payment of such sums as are

---

[1] *Court and Times of Charles I*, i. 175.

[2] *S.P. Dom.*, Charles I, xlii. 11. The other Commissioners were Sir John Savile, Thomas Aylesbury, and Sackville Crow.

due.'[1] In the choice of his ' Council of the Sea,' as it is called by a contemporary,[2] Charles showed considerable tact and judgment. Unlike his father's commission of 1618, he placed a leavening of practical seamen on it, in the hope that their presence and suggestions would enable him to convince Parliament of the Navy's urgent need of supplies. Pennington had acted as Raleigh's Vice-Admiral in the expedition to the Orinoco, and had been constantly afloat since. Pett had served as a carpenter's mate as early as 1592, and had, besides his professional duties, taken part in the expeditions of 1620 and 1623. Giffard had been engaged by the East India Company in 1614 for a voyage to the Straits of Magellan, having the ' courage, art, and knowledge to attempt such an enterprise,' and was in command of one of the royal ships in 1626. Lord Hervey was an Elizabethan veteran who had distinguished himself against the Armada, and in the attack on Cadiz in 1596. Sir Sackville Trevor had held naval commands since 1602, and his elder brother, Sir John, had acted as Surveyor of the Navy from 1598 to 1611. Watts was the son of a wealthy merchant and ship-owner, who had fought against the Armada. He himself had been knighted for his services in the Cadiz expedition of 1625, and at the time of his appointment was adjudged one of the best seamen in England. Love appears to have been in the service of the East India Company prior to 1620, when he took part in Mansell's expedition to Algiers. As Cecil's flag-captain in the Cadiz expedition he ' played the Captain, Master, and all other offices in the ship.'[3] Mainwaring,

[1] *S.P. Dom.*, Charles I, xli. 84.
[2] *Court and Times of Charles I*, i. 182.
[3] Dalton's *Life of Cecil*, ii. 244.

at the time of his appointment to this ' Council
of the Sea,' was Surveyor of the Navy, according
to the statement of Sir John Oglander, the Deputy
Governor of the Isle of Wight.[1]   This is the only
record we have that Mainwaring was ever Surveyor,
though in effect it is probably true.   When the
officers of the Navy were ' sequestered from their
posts ' in 1619, their duties were entrusted to a
Board of Naval Commissioners for five years, and
one of their number, Thomas Norreys, acted as
Surveyor.   When this commission was renewed,
it is not known who acted in Norrey's place, but
it was probably Mainwaring.   Certainly most of
his work was well within the functions of that
office.   The ' Council of the Sea' appears to have
acted a good deal by committees, and when such
a committee was constituted for surveyor's duties,
Mainwaring appears as its first member.   Thus
on December 13th, the day following the appointment of the Special Commission, a warrant was
given ' to our loving friends Sir Henry Mainwaring,
Knight, Captain Pennington, and Phineas Pett,'
authorising them to repair to Rochester, Chatham,
and Gillingham, and prepare the King's ships there
for a survey.[2]   The undermentioned list gives
the names of the ships that were in the Medway
and in dry dock at Chatham.   It is of particular
interest, as being a very early instance of ships
classed under rates.[3]

[1] *Oglander Memoirs :* ed. W. H. Long, p. 15.   Oglander
was a relation by marriage, and he styles Mainwaring as
' that quondam famous pirate,' who on sea ' had not many
equals.'
[2] *S.P. Dom.*, Charles I, xlii. 12.
[3] *Ibid.*, xlii. 127.   In some cases the names of the Commissioners who surveyed a particular ship are given in the
margin.   The *Vanguard, Merhonor, Victory,* and *Reformation*
have 'Sir H. Mainwaring.'

1. Prince Royal.
   Merhonor.
   Bear.
   Anne Royal.

2. Dieu Repulse.
   Defiance.
   Red Lion.
   Vanguard.
   Nonsuch.
   Assurance.
   Victory.
   Reformation.
   Mary Rose.

3. Dreadnought.
   Adventure.
   Moon.
   Henrietta, pinnace.
   George, drumler.
   Eagle, lighter.
   Desire, pinnace new re-
       turned from sea.

   Esperance ⎫
   George   ⎬ Prizes.
             ⎭

By the 20th of December Mainwaring and his colleagues had finished their business at Chatham, and were present at a meeting of the Commission at the Star Chamber two days later.[1] On Mainwaring's suggestion it was decided that the Victory and the Rainbow, then in dry dock, should be repaired and launched to give place to the Vanguard and Reformation. A suggestion of William Burrell, the Master shipwright, that the Bonaventure should be cut down a deck lower in order to 'make her sail as well as any ships in Dunkirk,' was also agreed to, as was his proposal to girdle the Victory. On the 27th of the month, several of the Commissioners, including Mainwaring, were authorised to 'view the defects of his Majesty's Navy and the stores thereof' at Chatham, Woolwich, and Deptford.

[1] Except where otherwise stated, the information in this chapter is taken from the minutes of the proceedings of the Special Commissioners from Dec. 12, 1626, to May 17, 1627, entitled, *Book of the Orders and Entries about the Survey of his Majesty's Navy*, 1626 (*S.P. Dom.*, Charles I, vol. xlv.).

Early in the new year the Commissioners assembled at Chatham for that purpose, and a general survey of the hulls, masts, yards, tops, and rigging of the various ships was commenced under their direction. As an illustration of the deplorable condition into which the royal ships had been allowed to drift, two instances may be sighted, that of the Swiftsure and Triumph, built in 1621 and 1623 respectively. On examination, the former was found to have her bowsprit sprung in two places ; the bolts of the cross-pillars in the hold broken ; the cook room so decayed that the sailors were afraid of firing the ship ; while her bows were ' very leaky under the lining of the hawse.' It was reported that in a storm she shipped so much water that the crew ' pumped 200 stroke a watch,' with their main-pump in order to keep her afloat. The catalogue of the defects in the Triumph was no less serious. Owing to her rudder being too small, she would not steer properly ; the main knee of her beak-head was broken, as was also her bow-sprit. Of her masts, the foremast was cracked, the main-mast weak, and the main-mizzen mast broken. From these two instances we may judge the amount of work that the Commissioners were confronted with. Not only did they note the defects, but they took full particulars of the dimensions of each ship. From Chatham they proceeded to Rochester, and on the 7th of January the Earl of Denbigh, Mainwaring, and Sir John Watts surveyed the Merhonour, while their colleagues examined the Assurance and the Rainbow. On the following day they were back at Chatham, where a letter was received from Buckingham regretting his inability to be present, and requesting them to prepare a fleet for immediate

service. ' I desire you,' he wrote, ' to be pleased
to take a speedy and effectual course for
the present surveying, repairing, and making
ready of about twenty or so of the most serviceable ships of his Majesty's Navy as may be
made ready for service by the end of February.'
To this end the Commissioners made an almost
superhuman effort to supply the Lord Admiral's
demand, but their appeals to the shipwrights
and others employed at Chatham dockyard to
hurry on the necessary repairs were futile. It
was not that the men were unpatriotic. They
had genuine grievances, and until they were
rectified they refused to render any further
service. In answer to the Commissioner's request, they took the opportunity to present
a petition to the effect that for twelve months
they had been ' without one penny pay, neither
having any allowance for meat or drink, by
which many of them, having pawned all they can,
others turned out of doors for non-payment of
rent, which with the cries of their wives and
children for food and necessaries, doth heavily
dishearten them.' [1] Nor were the crews of the
various ships, when approached, in a happier
frame of mind, or more ready to carry out
Buckingham's wishes. Those of the Lion, Vanguard, and Reformation, numbering in all about
750 men, stated that they had neither clothes
on their backs, shoes on their feet, nor credit on
shore.[2] The seamen of the Vanguard drew up a
petition stating that by reason of the ill-
providing and bad meat, want of firing, lodging,
clothing, and other necessaries, they were forced
to lie on the open deck, which with the non-

[1] Oppenheim, p. 230.
[2] *S.P. Dom.*, Charles I, xlix. 68.

payment of their wages, and the inclemency of the
weather, would force them to take some very
'prejudicial courses,' unless their 'insupportable
distresses' were attended to.[1] Thus, from these
touching appeals, we may see the difficulties
that the Commissioners had to contend with,
and the chaos, to say nothing of fraud, that
existed in the administrative departments of
the Navy. It was not within the power of the
Commissioners to afford the petitioners any relief,
though they wrote to Buckingham on the 16th
of January and informed him of the true condition of things. 'The carpenters and workmen
here,' they wrote, 'have complained unto us,
that for one whole year and upwards they were
behind hand of their wages, and that they are
no longer able to continue their service without
some present relief.' In the meantime, as no
satisfaction was forthcoming at Chatham, the
workmen left the dockyard in a body and marched
to London, to lay their grievances before Buckingham and the Treasurer of the Navy.[2]

By the end of the month the Commissioners
had completed the survey and returned to
London. The result of their labours was dis-
cussed at a special meeting held in the Star
Chamber on the 1st of February, 1626–7, at which
there were present the Earl of Denbigh, Viscount
Wimbledon, Lord Hervey, Lord Herbert, Sir
Sackville Trevor, Sir Henry Mainwaring, Sir
John Watts, Captain Giffard and Captain Pett.
It was then resolved that an account of the sur-
veys of the ships at Chatham should be digested

---

[1] *S.P. Dom.*, Charles I, xlix. 71.

[2] In the following April their position was laid before the
Council by Buckingham, but what was done in the matter is
not recorded (*S.P. Dom.*, lxi. 78).

in brief, and for that purpose the following table was afterwards drawn up[1]:

Names of the Ships.	Their ranks.	Estimate of reparations.			Time for repairs.	Service for which they are able.	Continuance with ordinary reparations.
		£	s.	d.			
Prince Royal	First	469	11	4	8 weeks	Southward upon the coast	3 yrs. or more
Merhonour	First	546	0	0	6 weeks	Southward	Many yrs.
Anne Royal	First	973	6	0	3 weeks	Southward for only summer's voyage	6 or 7 yrs.
White Bear	First	(Unserviceable)					
Rainbow	Second	268	15	0	Presently	Southward	Many yrs.
Vanguard	Second	903	2	5	7 weeks	Southward	Many yrs.
Dieu Repulse	Second	213	10	0	4 weeks	Southward for a summer's voyage	4 or 5 yrs.
Warspite	Second	221	2	0	7 weeks	Southward	2 or 3 yrs.
Red Lion	Second	347	10	8	6 weeks	Southward	Many yrs.
Defiance	Second	790	5	9	6 weeks	Southward	Many yrs.
Victory	Second	582	17	0	7 weeks	Southward	Many yrs.
Nonsuch	Second	248	0	4	5 weeks	Southward	4 or 5 yrs.
Constant Reformation	Second	543	9	0	10 weeks	Southward	Many yrs.
Assurance	Second	242	15	6	7 or 8 weeks	On the coast	2 or 3 yrs.
Dreadnought	Third	687	6	6	5 weeks	Southward	Many yrs.
Mary Rose	Fourth	88	9	0	7 or 8	Southward	Many yrs.
Adventure	Fourth	142	18	0	7 or 8 weeks	Southward	3 yrs. at least
Moon, pinnace		54	12	9	2 weeks	Any service	A long time
		£ 7,323	11	3			

The most striking point revealed by the survey was that out of thirty ships on the active list at the death of James, no less than nineteen (including the Swiftsure and Triumph at Woolwich, not included in the above list) were in need of substantial repairs, and one had become unserviceable. It is almost incredible, but never-

[1] *S.P. Dom.*, Charles I, xlv.

theless a fact, that in the short space of three years since the Navy Commissioners had finished their programme, two-thirds of the Navy should have become unseaworthy. The prime causes of this astonishing decay were no doubt the financial straits in which the Government found themselves, and the corruption and peculation of the various officials employed in the dockyards and elsewhere. Although in this respect the Commissioners summoned before them and examined William Burrell, the Master ship-wright ; Kenrick Edisbury, the Paymaster of the Navy ; Roger Parr, the Clerk to the Navy Commissioners ; and John Wells, keeper of naval stores, among others, no steps appear to have been taken to prevent a recurrence of the evils that existed. Phineas Pett, one of the Special Commissioners, stated that the Commission ' trenched so far upon some great personages that it was let fall, and nothing to any purpose done in it,'[1] and herein probably lies the secret of the reluctance of the Government to punish the offenders.

Strange as it may seem, the ' great personages ' were certainly some of the Navy Commissioners of 1619, who in a few years had become parties to the very abuses and frauds that they had been appointed to check and reform. Four years after they assumed office, Sir John Coke, probably the most honest and scrupulous of their number, wrote, that although he had laboured to have a frame of government that would discover errors in their accounts, his plan had been overruled. ' All kept right until the Algiers voyage,' Coke reported in August, 1623, ' when

---

[1] *Phineas Pett*, p. 137.

there was dealing on the part of some Commissioners in passing off their own wares amongst the provisions then laid in, which has continued occasionally since.' One of his colleagues, William Burrell, Coke accused of buying provisions wholesale and selling them to the Service retail ; while another, Thomas Norreys, Surveyor, 'instead of limiting the faults' of the boatswains and others, was a party to their waste of government stores.[1] The keeper of naval stores, John Wells, when examined before the Special Commissioners, presented a petition, stating that seven and a half years' pay was due to him, and suggested that in order to compensate him for his labours, the Commissioners should allow him to sell such stores at Deptford and Chatham as were unserviceable![2] In this he was probably already an adept, for, as Mr. Oppenheim shrewdly remarks, unless he was more honest than his fellows, the crown, if it did not pay him directly, had to do so indirectly.[3]

The most damaging evidence brought before the Commission was that preferred against Burrell, who in 1619 had been appointed by his fellow commissioners to be in charge of all ship-building and repairs at a salary of £300 a year.[4]

The ten ships that he had been entrusted to build for the Navy between that date and 1623 had not come up to expectations in the late expedition, and on being docked and surveyed they were found to be very defective. The following catalogue of their defects as drawn

[1] *S.P. Dom.*, Charles I, cli. 35.

[2] *Ibid.*, xliii. 47.

[3] *Administrations of the Navy*, p. 230.

[4] In 1624 Burrell was accused of behaving 'most foully and corruptly' (*Hist. MSS. Com.*, 12 i, 176).

up by the Special Commissioners, which has not been printed before, proves that his work was not up to the level of his contemporary, Phineas Pett.[1]

Reformation.—For materials sufficient. Well bound within and without board ; warlike and well countenanced. Bears a good sail, and worketh well at sea, saving that the beams of the false orlop have but one standing knee upon the end of the beams, whereas there should be two small knees ' wyned ' with them, all well bolted. The main orlop is laid so low, as there can be no use made of her lower tier of ordnance in any reasonable gale of wind.

Victory.—Well sized in her timbers, but footwales fewer. So weak and tender sided that she is ordered to be girdled with 4 inch plank between the wales. To have two more wales without, more beams, knees, and iron work. Spar deck to be cut down.

Entrance.—At sea, and not yet surveyed.[2]

Garland.—Sufficiently sized in her scantlings, but wanting strength in her inner bindings. Very tender sided. Held an imperfect ship, and reported a slug of sail. To be girdled with 4 inch plank, with addition of main knee in her binding of timber, and standing knees upon the orlop.

Swiftsure.—A very weak ship. Undersized in the scantling of her whole frame in comparison of the former. Her main binding of footwales but 6 inch or little more, too few in number and too thin in substance, all ill-nailed. The keelson insufficient. All her inner binding but 4 inch plank, her main beams 11 and 12 foot asunder.

Bonaventure.—In the self same manner, a weak, very tender sided, and a labouring ship. To be girdled, etc.

---

[1] ' Defects of his Majesty's ten new ships built by Mr. Burrell ' (*S.P. Dom.*, Charles I, lii. 52).

[2] There is no evidence that she was ever surveyed by the Special Commissioners.

St. George.—Sufficient for sizes and scantlings,[1] but her bindings of footwales[2] and clamps[3] too few and too thin. Her keelson not broad and deep enough for a ship of her burthen. Her main beams sufficient for substance and kneeing, but slenderly bolted. The beams[4] also of the false orlop having but two knees at an end. She wanteth a wale of timber in the place of her chainwale, which is but 4 inch plank. A well-conditioned ship, but thought somewhat leeward.

St. Andrew.—Scantlings, timber, and frame sufficient, but binding not sufficient, having but 4 strakes of foot-waling upon the rest in the floors. Slender clamped under the beams of the main orlop. Binding between the clamps of footwales but 4 inch plank. The beams and knees of both orlops ill fayed, and wanting much iron work within and without board. Reported a very good conditioned ship.

Triumph.—Sufficient for sizes and scantlings of her frame, but wanting within board bindings of iron work; wales and chainwales without board. All her great masts unserviceable.

Mary Rose.—Tender sided, hard of steering, and said a slug of a sail. She hath been furred and girdled, and lengthened abaft with a false post and false keel.

When it is remembered that with such warships as these—weak and tender sided, supplied with rotten cordage and old sails—both Cecil and Willoughby had been expected to deal a vital blow to Spanish sea power, it is no small

---

[1] The dimension of any piece of timber with regard to its breadth and thickness (Falconer).

[2] The inside planking or lining of a ship over the floor-timbers.

[3] Clamps were thick timbers placed fore and aft, close under the beams of the first orlop or deck.

[4] Cross timbers which kept the ship's sides asunder, and supported the decks or orlops.

wonder that they failed.   In discussing the failure, historians with one or two exceptions have shown an inclination to ascribe the cause of it to the incompetence of the commanders and the decadence of English seamanship ; but it is doubtful whether, even in the hands of the Elizabethan sailors, such vessels could have achieved the object for which they were despatched.   Though Cecil and Willoughby were undoubtedly ignorant of sea affairs, and the morale of the seamen, through their scandalous treatment, was not up to the level of those of Elizabeth's reign, the real cause of the failure is to be found in the bad construction and equipment of the ships, as revealed in the report of Mainwaring and his colleagues, rather than in the seamen themselves.[1]   A letter-writer of the time believed that ‘ Burrell, one of the late commissioners, and the chief carpenter over these works, a man friendless and yet full of money, must pay for all.   Whether by his neck or purse, or both, I know not,' he wrote.[2] Burrell, however, never suffered bodily or financially for his misdeeds, and continued in Government employ for some time afterwards.[3]

At a meeting of the Special Commissioners on the 3rd of February, 1626–7, the question of a dock at Portsmouth was again raised by Mainwaring, and the ‘ seventeen reasons in writing ' which he produced for the edification of his

---

[1] In the nine royal ships that comprised Cecil's fleet, five of the above were included, and in Willoughby's expedition three out of the six were built by Burrell.   The *Reformation* took part in Mansell's expedition to Algiers, and the *Bonaventure, St. George*, and *St. Andrew* in Rutland's voyage to Spain.

[2] *Court and Times of Charles I*, i. 185.   Letter from London, January 19, 1626–7.

[3] Burrell died in 1630, and was succeeded as chief shipwright by Phineas Pett.

colleagues, 'were publicly read and approved of.' As a result 'it was ordered that the old dock should be repaired and new digged, or a new one made there.'

Finally, the question of the seamen's pay was discussed, and six days later a warrant was given to Mainwaring, Sir John Watts, Sir Sackville Crow, and Captain John Pennington, to repair aboard his Majesty's ships that were in the Thames, or in dock at Woolwich or Deptford, for the purpose of examining the pursers' books, and reporting any arrears of pay that were due to the Captains, Masters, and mariners.[1] A new scale of wages had been formulated in 1626, and those of the ordinary seamen, who had received 10s. a month during the reign of James I, were raised to 15s., while boys received 7s. 6d. a month in all rates of ships. For officers and others the monthly wages were fixed at [2]: Captains, 14l. to 4l. 6s. 8d. in a 6th rate; lieutenants, 3l. 10s. to 2l. 16s. in a 3rd rate; masters, 4l. 13s. 9d. to 2l. 5s. 8d. in a 6th rate; pilots and boatswains, 2l. 5s. to 1l. 3s. 4d. in a 6th rate; yeomen of halliards, sheets, tacks, and jears, 1l. 5s. to 1l. 1s. in a 5th rate; master carpenters, 1l. 17s. 6d. to 1l. 1s. in a 6th rate; pursers and master gunners, 2l. to 1l. 3s. 4d. in a 6th rate; steward and cook, 1l. 5s. to 17s. 6d. in a 6th rate; surgeons, 1l. 10s. all rates; coxswains, 1l. 5s. to 1l. in a 6th rate; quarter gunners, 1l. to 17s. 6d. in a 6th rate.

---

[1] Sir William Russell, the Treasurer of the Navy, had reported that up to the end of October, 1626, a sum of £27,303 16s. 11d. was due (S.P. Dom., xl. 52).

[2] Charnock, ii. 277. The wages of seamen and gunners were subject to a deduction of 6d. for the Chatham Chest, which had been founded in 1590 for the relief of injured and disabled sailors (Oppenheim, p. 245).

On the 18th of the month the Special Commissioners met at Whitehall in the presence of the King, and a report of their proceedings was submitted to Charles. On this occasion Buckingham acted as spokesman for his fellow commissioners, and after having summed up ' the marrow and quintessence of their consultations,' he endeavoured to persuade Charles ' to employ his whole revenue of the subsidies of tonnage and poundage towards the present defence of the seas.' His reason was ' because it was given by the Parliament to his Majesty's predecessors for that end. For this year,' Buckingham informed Charles, ' all the whole revenue must be expended in that way, but in the year to come,' he added, ' he hoped it would require the disbursement of but half.'[1] The ' pains and diligence' of his colleagues was highly praised by Buckingham, and certainly their efforts merited some recognition. For not only did they decide on repairing the then existing ships, but in view of the serious menace to our maritime supremacy that the rebuilding of the French navy presented, they suggested that eighteen new ships and two pinnaces should be forthwith commenced for the constant guard of the Narrow Seas. Of these, five were to be of 600 tons ; five of 400 tons ; four of 300 tons ; and four of 200 tons. The two pinnaces were to be from twelve to fifteen tons, with a deck, and ' to go with oars and sails.' They were to be armed with two guns each, and to have ' 12 banks on a side.'[2]

This desire of the Special Commissioners ' to speedily perfect the good work they had

[1] *Court and Times of Charles I*, i. 196.

[2] See Volume II., where this interesting document is printed in full.

begun,' was shared in no less a degree by the King, who made a determined effort to carry out their suggestions. Among the propositions for a supply which he tendered to Parliament when it met in 1628 was the following :—The furnishing of 30 ships with men and victuals to guard the Narrow Seas and along the coasts. The building of 20 ships yearly for the increase of the Navy. The supply of stores for the Navy, and the payment of arrears to the Treasurer of the Navy.[1] Unfortunately Charles, who was always at loggerheads with his Parliaments, failed to convince them of the urgency of the need, and in consequence the sparse supplies that were forthcoming would not admit of his ship-building programme being carried into effect.[2] Following on the Special Commissioners' report,[3] the only ships added to the Navy in 1627 were ten small vessels, each of 185 tons gross tonnage, known as the Lion's Whelps.[4]

At the end of February, 1628, the King appointed a committee, consisting of the Lord High Admiral, the Lord Treasurer, and others to consider the best means for raising money,[5]

[1] *Parliamentary Hist.*, vol. ii. p. 246.

[2] In 1625, £140,000 was voted (about half the cost of the fleet for that year); in 1626, nothing; and in 1628, £350,000, whereas £1,300,000 was asked for, for the needs of the army and navy.

[3] The last meeting of the Special Commission was held in the Star Chamber on May 17, 1627, at which Mainwaring, who had taken a prominent part in their proceedings from the first, was present.

[4] 'These were the only vessels constructed for the Navy prior to 1632. They were ' the first representatives, in intention, although not in form, of the regular sloop and gunboat class' (Oppenheim, p. 256).

[5] *S.P. Dom.*, Charles I, xciii. 80.

and an interesting suggestion that was propounded by Sir John Coke for obtaining money for fitting out a fleet is worth recording.   His idea was to found a Loyal Association, the members of which were to be pledged to serve the King ' with their persons, goods, and might.' The fees payable on admission to this association were to be graduated in proportion to the rank of the person admitted.   In return they were to be privileged to wear in their hats a riband or badge of the King's colour, and were to be entitled to precedence at all public meetings.[1]

[1] *S.P. Dom.*, Charles I, lxxxviii. 78.   Nothing further is heard of this suggestion, though, in view of the monetary difficulty of the country, it was certainly worthy of serious consideration.

CHAPTER VII

1627–28

THE EXPEDITIONS TO RHÉ AND ROCHELLE

WHILE the Special Commissioners were making every effort to reform and perfect the Navy and the naval service generally, the relations between England and France were daily becoming more strained. For some time both countries had been carrying on semi-privateering operations, and in December, 1626, the English people were reported to be 'frantic' over the detention of 200 ships at Bordeaux that were engaged in the wine trade.[1] The depredations committed on our merchant shipping, coupled with the success that was attending Richelieu's efforts to make France a prominent naval power, considerably widened the breach.[2]

Spain, with whom we were still in a state of war, was also fitting out a great armada, and the secret negotiations which she had been conducting

[1] *S.P. Venice*, 1626–28, No. 87.

[2] In February, 1627, Richelieu had persuaded the Assembly of Notables to keep a fleet of 45 ships in the Atlantic, and by the end of May the French arsenals were turning out a particularly powerful gun for the fleet, weighing 1,000 lbs., and firing a shot of 150 lbs. With this gun Richelieu boasted he would not only reduce Rochelle, but would enter the English ports and sink the fleet (*Ibid.*, Nos. 137, 291).

with France for some time were finally brought to a head by a treaty between the two nations in March, 1627.

The growing ascendency of the French marine under the régime of Richelieu, and the avowed determination of the latter to crush the French Protestants, or Huguenots, at La Rochelle, to whom Charles had promised protection, proved the final act that brought about a war between England and France. In consequence, though most of the English fleet were in need of repairs, Charles determined to despatch an expedition to the Isle of Rhé, which was to be used as a base of operations for the relief of the beleaguered Protestants.[1] The probability of war had been foreseen by Buckingham in January, when he had called for twenty ships to be prepared for sea by the Special Commissioners. It was impossible, however, to get such a number ready in so short a time, and in March it was decided to employ the Triumph, Rainbow, Repulse, Victory, Lion, Warspite, Nonsuch, Vanguard, and the Esperance of the King's ships, while the rest of the fleet was to be comprised of armed merchantmen. To superintend the manning and equipping of such a fleet required a person of high technical knowledge and experience, and Buckingham's choice of Mainwaring for that post bears out Sir John Oglander's statement, that Mainwaring acted as Surveyor to the Navy Commissioners.[2] About the middle of April Buckingham came to Chatham to inspect the ships, and to confer with Mainwaring regarding

[1] Rhé is about eighteen miles in length, and is divided from the mainland by a strait about two miles wide.

[2] See also *S.P. Dom.*, Charles I, lx. 54, where Mainwaring, writing to Nicholas on April 18, asked that he might have the same place in the Commission that ' the other had.'

the impressment of seamen for the expedition.[1] Bearing in mind the trouble with the workmen in the dockyard earlier in the year, the Duke addressed the shipwrights ' in courteous terms,' and urged them to use the utmost diligence in fitting out the fleet.[2]

On the 17th Mainwaring reported to Buckingham, from Rochester, that the Rainbow, Vanguard, and Repulse had been brought from their moorings and anchored safely at Queenborough. The lack of men and the leaky state of some of the ships gave cause for much concern, and the Victory, Mainwaring stated, was in such a bad condition that he feared she would be unserviceable. The following day the Commissioners of the Navy reported that the victualling of the fleet was at a standstill for want of money, and that they required £8,000 ; while Mainwaring signified that the stores of cordage for the ships were too large, and at his suggestion they were accordingly lessened. On the 19th of April Mainwaring sent word that four more of the ships were ready to sail for Queenborough, but were greatly in need of victuals and men. The Nonsuch, he informed Buckingham, could not be made ready for three weeks.[3]

The following day, accompanied by Mainwaring and others, the King paid a surprise visit to the Isle of Wight, in order to inspect Sir Alexander Brett's regiment of 1,000 men, who were billeted there.[4]

On Mainwaring's return the victualling and

[1] *Hist. MSS. Com.*, 12 i, 302.

[2] *S.P. Venice*, 1626–28, No. 242.

[3] *S.P. Dom.*, Charles I, lx. 67.

[4] *Oglander*, p. 31. The Island was a favourite place for billeting troops, owing to the difficulties it placed in the way of desertion.

fitting out of the fleet kept him fully occupied. Buckingham having inquired of the Commissioners at what rate soldiers might be victualled per day, allowing in every week three days beef, pork, and bacon, and four days butter, fish, and cheese, the same quantities as were allowed the seamen in the King's ships, they stated that it was well worth 6*d.* a man per day, without any allowance of beer. The old charge, they informed the Duke, was the same for butter, fish, and cheese, the whole week throughout, with an allowance of a ' pottle ' of beer to each man per day.[1]

On the 24th of April Mainwaring wrote to Buckingham, informing him what means he had employed to get the King's ships out of Chatham, and the merchantmen which had been hired as transports down the river. Their disinclination to take part in the expedition was apparent from the first, and Mainwaring experienced considerable difficulty in persuading them to set sail. Nor were the King's ships in a more ready state, and he was forced ' to bring the men from one ship to another ' in order to man them sufficiently. In one case, that of the Victory, there were only twenty-six seamen on board, whereas her full complement should have been about 250. To remedy the want of men, Mainwaring suggested that Buckingham should get the Masters of Watermen's Hall ' to warn all men belonging to the river ' to appear on the morrow, so that a selection could be made for the ships, which in some cases were so hopelessly under-manned that they were unable to take in their provisions.[2]

[1] *S.P. Dom.*, Charles I, lxi. 15.   April 23, 1627.
[2] *Ibid.*, lxi. 22.

MAY IT PLEASE YOUR GRACE, — Captain Marsh [1] can give your Grace an account of the executing of your command for the merchants riding below the Bridge, how unprovided I found them, not a mast aboard, nor scarce a man in some of them, and at last how unwilling to set sail. The wind indeed scanted and became more southerly than it was when I sent unto your Grace, yet with diligence some came to Limehouse, some to Blackwall, and some to Woolwich, [2] where they might have been all as well as some, and from thence the next tide at Tilbury, if they had plied it; but I believe they would have been yet at anchor had I not come and pressed them beyond their inclinations. Though the ships at Chatham ought the same day to have been all at St. Mary Creek, if not at Queenboro', yet I found them as I had left them, and there [they] would have been till now if I, or somebody else more understanding and active than myself, had not come down. With very much ado, being forced to bring the men from one ship to another (so as to man some sufficiently), we got the Rainbow and Vanguard over the chain within two warps of St. Mary Creek, whence, if the wind wester a little, they shall (God willing) go this tide to Queenboro', but the wind is here to the eastwards of the south, so they cannot stir from thence. But this tide I hope to bring the Repulse thither also, where they are ready to take any westerly wind to fall away. Also I intend to carry the Warspite [3] thither if possibly I can get men, and the next tide after, the Victory, where there are not above twenty-six seafaring men, as I am informed by the boatswain and others.

'Tis true, as your Grace is informed, that divers of the seamen are absented from thence, whether run away altogether or no I know not. I went over yesterday the Rainbow and Vanguard, when I think all the men that were known to be thereabouts or belonging to them were aboard. I found 107 men aboard the Rainbow and 89

[1] Gabriel Marsh, Buckingham's Marshal of the Admiralty.
[2] MS. Wollidge.
[3] MS. Wastspight.

men aboard the Vanguard, and a poor crew God knows as ever I saw in any ship. This I think fit to acquaint your Grace, that you may think of some course for men, for otherwise these ships thus manned are not fit to be trusted in the sea. If there be not some speedy course taken, the voyage will be overthrown for lack of men; and those two ships which lack their provisions, the Warspite and Victory, and are appointed to come to Tilbury for their provisions, cannot come thither for lack of men. I will not take upon me the boldness to advise your Grace to do things suddenly and resolutely for the getting of men, but I durst hazard the loss of those.

In the hope of your Grace's favour (without which I value my life no more), by to-morrow noon I would land at Gravesend betwixt 100 and 200 men to come that day to Chatham, with this course. Your Grace may this instant afternoon give a straight command (expressing extraordinarily the King's urgent occasions to press men), to the Masters of Watermen's Hall to warn all men belonging to the river (that are near thereabouts) to appear to-morrow by five of the clock in the morning at their Hall, and to signify that if any man bring not forth his servant that him shall be pressed, imprisoned, or the like. And then to have some two or three understanding men near to make choice of the best, and especially those who have been at sea already (whereof there are enough), and so take the Gravesend Barge [1] or others to attend them, and instantly from the Hall, without suffering them to go home, to ship them away with commanders, giving order to their masters and friends to send their clothes after them; I think Capt.

---

[1] The Gravesend Barge was of very ancient standing, dating back to the 13th century. It claimed precedence over all other craft, and no tiltboat, lighthorseman, or wherry was allowed to take passengers until the Barge was furnished and gone. In 1595 it was rowed with four men in fair weather and five in foul. It had a steersman, and was furnished with masts and sails, also an ' anchor to serve in time of distress' (Cruden, *Gravesend*, pp. 205–6).

Kettleby [1] and Capt. Porter [2] two very fit men, for they are best known there. The tide will serve very well at that time to bring them away. I have here enclosed your Grace a note of some men pressed by the gunner of the Warspite, four weeks past, and not any of them have so much as appeared, which I did (most especially), that you might apprehend them to make example of them by sending them down hither like prisoners to receive punishment here, or by disgracing them there amongst their friends with the stocks, or otherwise as shall seem best to your Grace to give example and terror to others, for I assure your Grace that if men receive no punishment for their offences, the King's service will be destroyed, and all authority and power to command men will grow neglected.

I believe much in the goodness of your Grace's disposition, which will favourably interpret my intentions in being thus bold to deliver my opinions. As also to grant me your gracious pardon if, in the pursuing of the general scope of your commands, I sometimes do those things I have not precise warrant for, whereby the service may be advanced. And this I rather hope for in regard I think your Grace hath not many that have followed or gone so far, and not many that have served their commission for the good of their employment.

Thus assuring your Grace that my diligence shall supply my disabilities to do your Grace that sufficient and acceptable service which in duty I am bound to do, and in my affection I desire to do, most humbly kissing your Grace's hand, in all duty rest

Your Grace's most humble and faithful servant,

H. MAINWARING.

Rochester,
This 24th of April, 1627.

---

[1] Capt. Thomas Kettleby, captain of the *Victory* in this expedition, and the *Charles* in the ship-money fleet of 1636.

[2] Probably Capt. Thomas Porter, brother of Endymion Porter. Served in the Algiers expedition, 1620, Cadiz, 1625, and was Captain of the *Warspite* in the Rhé expedition.

The great source from which money was forthcoming to equip the expedition was the sale of French prize goods, and on the 18th of May Mainwaring was appointed by the Judge of the Admiralty Court one of the Commissioners for that service.[1]

By the beginning of June the fleet and troops had assembled at Portsmouth, and on the 11th of the month the King came to inspect them. 'Being brought round about the bulwarks,' writes a correspondent, 'he saw what was amiss, and promised, to the great content of the inhabitants, to repair the ruinous fortifications of his only garrison town in England.' Charles next started on a tour of inspection of the fleet, and went 'aboard the Victory in the haven. From thence he went to Stokes Bay, where he boarded the Rainbow, and from her he went aboard the Triumph between 10 and 11 o'clock, where he dined and stayed till 2 o'clock.' Charles showed extraordinary interest in the fleet, and his pleasure in being amongst his ships was unbounded. 'At dinner his whole discourse was about them, and in particular about the Triumph,' inquiring of Sir John Watts, her captain, in true nautical language, 'whether she cund yar or no?'[2] A health was drunk by him to Monsieur Soubise[3] and the others for the good success of the voyage, at which five guns were discharged. 'Dinner passed away,' we are informed, 'with as much mirth as Sir Robert Deall, the fool Archie, and the Duke's musicians could make.' After dinner Charles visited the Warspite, Repulse, and Vanguard. These formalities over, he was rowed

---

[1] *S.P. Dom.*, Charles I, lxiii. 90.
[2] *I.e.*, answered the helm readily.
[3] Benjamin de Rohan, Duc de Soubise.

ashore in his barge, and carried to Broom Down in his coach to review the troops.[1]

The difficulty of finding sufficient men and victuals for the fleet seems to have been partly overcome, but the armament of the ships themselves does not appear to have met with Buckingham's satisfaction. In some of the ships he was particularly anxious to have ' whole culverins of brass ' mounted, a suggestion which caused Burrell considerable uneasiness. In order that he ' might be free from blame ' if such a procedure did not turn out a success, he asked that Watts, Mainwaring, Captains Best and Weddell, with Joliffe the master gunner, might be appointed to ' consider what is fit to be done for the supporting of them.'[2] Whether Buckingham's suggestion was found practical is not known, but, in spite of all these drawbacks, the fleet eventually left Stokes Bay on the 27th of June. It consisted of 90 sail divided into four squadrons, and with it went 6710 soldiers, besides 3848 seamen. The royal ships and their commanders were[3] :

Triumph	. Duke of Buckingham, Admiral. Sir John Watts, Captain.
Rainbow	. Earl of Lindsey, Vice-Admiral. John Weddell, Captain.
Repulse	. William, Lord Hervey, Rear-Admiral. Thomas Best, Captain.
Victory	. Earl of Denbigh, commanding the fourth squadron. Thomas Kettleby, Captain.

[1] Letter of Robert Mason to Nicholas, June 11, in *S.P. Dom.*, Charles I, lxvi. 67.

[2] *S.P. Dom.*, Charles I, lxvii. 103.

[3] *Ibid.*, lxx. 26. This list differs slightly from that given in Clowes' *Royal Navy*, ii. 65, where Lindsey is stated to have been in the *Repulse*, and Hervey in the *Victory*. No mention is made of Denbigh.

Lion   . John Pennington, Captain.[1]
Warspite   . Thomas Porter, Captain.
Nonsuch   . Sir Allen Apsley, Captain.
Vanguard . Sir John Burgh, commanding the
              troops.
Esperance, prize. Captain Skipworth.
Charles, pinnace. Captain Liddiard.

The first few days at sea were spent in chasing
Dunkirkers, whose superior sailing qualities, however, enabled them to elude the less nimble King's
ships. As a result of this exploit the fleet were
carried far to the leeward of the French coast,
where they were separated by a severe storm which
damaged the Nonsuch and other vessels. In the
meantime a Dutch vessel that left Portsmouth at
the same time as the English fleet was enabled to
reach Rhé before them, and so give information
to the French. Finally, on the 10th of July, the
advanced squadron of twenty ships anchored off the
east end of the island, where they were joined by
the rest of the fleet on the two following days.[2]
Under a protecting fire from the guns of the fleet
a landing was successfully effected, but not
without some opposition from the French. On
the 14th the troops commenced their march
inland, and the small fort of St. Marie and the
town of La Flotte surrendered to them. Three

---

[1] Pennington commanded a fifth squadron which had
sailed a few days earlier, with instructions to prey upon the
French shipping in the ' river of Bordeaux ' (*S.P. Dom.*,
lxvii. 55). On the 25th of July Buckingham wrote to him from
St. Martin's to the effect that such a design would be approved
of if he could also seize the Isle of Oleron, and for this purpose
he desired Pennington to come and consult with him (*S.P.
Dom.*, Charles I, lxxi. 81).

[2] Monson's *Naval Tracts* (ed. Oppenheim), iii. 179–181 ;
Granville's *Works*, iii. 250 ; *S.P. Dom.*, Charles I, lxxi. 23.

days later the French evacuated the town of St. Martin's, and withdrew their troops into the citadel on the east side of it, which Buckingham bombarded on the 18th.[1]   The hopes of reducing it in a short time were rudely dispelled by the fact that it was well garrisoned and vigorously defended.[2]   Within ten days Buckingham had come to the decision that the shortest way of effecting its capitulation would be to starve it into surrender. The siege will probably be a long one, he wrote to Conway, unless they had speedy supplies from England; but, he added, 'it shall be maintained with courage,' in the confidence that the King would not let them want.[3]   At the beginning of August the troops began to intrench themselves, and five hundred seamen were landed from the ships and placed under the command of Captain Weddell, in order to assist the land forces.[4]   Not only was the fort blocked up by land, but the ships of the fleet were disposed in the form of a half moon, the horns of which encompassed the citadel.[5]   It was common knowledge in the English camp that the resources of the fort were limited, but the possibility of forcing the occupants to surrender depended solely on the prompt despatch of reinforcements of every kind from England, which Buckingham had already called for.[6]   Energetic measures were therefore taken to supply the demands of the occasion, and 2000 Irishmen, under the command of Sir Ralph Bingley and Sir Pierce Crosby, arrived on the

[1] *S.P. Dom.*, Charles I, lxxi. 38.
[2] Gardiner, vi. 175.
[3] *S.P. Dom.*, Charles I, lxxii. 10, 31.
[4] Granville, iii. 254.
[5] *S.P. Dom.*, Charles I, lxxiii. 98.
[6] Gardiner, vi. 175.

2nd of September, while the Earl of Holland was to follow with further supplies of men and provisions.

Buckingham was seriously handicapped by the shortage of both men and provisions, and on the 18th of the month the King instructed Mainwaring to assume charge of the ships at Plymouth that were to transport the necessary supplies to St. Martin's. Such was the trust reposed in him that the King authorised him to press and take up any other mariners and ships that were needed, and to do ' any other act or thing ' that he thought fit for the expedition of the service.[1]

' Whereas we have caused certain ships and vessels to be pressed and taken up at Plymouth, and the parts thereabouts for transport of 1000 land soldiers unto our fleet and army at St. Martin's. And that there is likewise sufficient shipping for transport of 1000 more soldiers prepared here to go for that part.

These are to require and authorise you presently to repair to Plymouth and there to see all the said ships sufficiently prepared and fitted for that service. And if there be occasion for advancement of our said service, you are by yourself, or such as you shall appoint, to press any Pilots, Gunners, Mariners, Seamen or others, for the full manning of the said transporters.

If there be not sufficient shipping prepared there for this our service, or that you shall find any of the ships taken up defective, you are to press and take up such others to supply the said service as you shall think fit.

You are to take care that all the ships prepared for this service be made sweet and wholesome by shifting their ballast and making their decks tight, or otherwise fitting them for the best conveniency and preservation of the health of the soldiers.

[1] *S.P. Dom.*, Charles I, lxxviii. No. 50.   A rough draft by Nicholas.

You are to plan and dispose of all the officers and soldiers aboard the said ships, according to the bigness and roominess of each ship, and to cause victuals to be proportionably laid aboard for their transportation, and are to see that there be deal boards and other things necessary for accommodation and lodging of the soldiers provided and furnished.

And if there shall be occasion to employ more victuals for the expedition of this our service, than was at first proposed and taken order for in the estimate, then we will that you take up the same and give bills for it to be paid by the Treasurer of our Navy, who is to put the same in surcharge upon the next estimate.

You are to do any other act or thing that you in your discretion and judgment shall think to be most for the advantage and expedition of this our service.

And from time to time to give notice of your proceedings and in what forwardness the said ships are, unto one of our Secretaries of State.

18th Sept., 1627.

Towards the end of the month, Mainwaring reported that the two ships prepared by Sir James Bagg were ready to transport the 1000 soldiers, but were scarcely of sufficient force. He recommended that the Hector, lately employed by the Earl of Warwick, should be sent, taking 300 mariners 'that will be acceptable to the Lord Duke to supply the want at St. Martin's.' [1]

On the 29th, Mainwaring wrote to the effect that the ships would be ready by Monday night, but he was still waiting for the merchant ships from London. The Jonathan would not be ready in time, so the Hector was appointed to sail in her place. Nothing was wanting, he added, but the London ships and the Earl of Holland.

[1] Coke MSS. (*Hist. MSS. Com.*, 12 i, p. 325).

His letter is directed ' To my Worthy Friend Mr. Edward Nicholas, Secretary to the Duke of Buckingham these.' [1]

My Worthy and most Honourable Friend,—I was loth to trouble you till I had brought things to some perfection, for I found the ships as you imagined. The ships (before you can read this letter half out) will all be ready, that is by Monday night. We have no news from London of those ships. The Jonathan cannot be ready to go with this fleet, but the Hector, wherein Sir [F.] Steward was, which was with my Lord of Warwick, may go in her room, if the Earl be dealt withal, or the State please to command. I have wrote to Secretary Coke of it. Sir James Bagg tells me he wrote you an answer concerning that packet of Sir [H.] Palmer's. He hath all his provisions here in readiness, and is most dexterous in all his undertakings, and now we want nothing but the London ships and my Lord of Holland. News we have none, neither domestic nor foreign, worth the writing. Nor I hope you will not take it for news that I acknowledge myself so much bound unto you for your loving favours, that so far as I can extend either my life or fortune to do you service, I will most faithfully express myself to be as I am,

Your most affectionate friend and servant,

H. Mainwaring.

Plymouth,
This 29th of September, 1627.

Buckingham, meanwhile, began to despair of success. ' Our officers now give themselves for men neglected, and forgotten in England,' he wrote to Conway.[2] The timely arrival, however, of Sir Henry Palmer at the end of September, with the long looked-for provisions, renewed his

[1] *S.P. Dom.*, Charles I, lxxix. 62.
[2] *Ibid.*, lxxviii. 65.

hopes so much, that when the fort asked for a parley, he refused to consider anything except its surrender.[1]

At the beginning of October the London ships had not been heard of, and Mainwaring reported the Fellowship rendered unserviceable through her pilot running her on the rocks while on her way to Catwater.

'All the ships are here in readiness,' he wrote to Nicholas from Plymouth,[2] 'but there is no news of the London ships. The ship of the best force called the Fellowship, with 12 pieces of ordnance, coming to Catwater, by the indiscretion of the pilot bilged herself upon the rocks, so she is unserviceable for the voyage. . . . On Sunday last, being the last of September, there landed at Falmouth[3] one out of a small barque who said he was near St. Martin's on the Thursday before when he heard such an infinite number of ordnance go off, that he was afraid to go in. . . . I pray God send us good news of my Lord Duke. I wish from my soul this supply was there.' This last piece of intelligence probably referred to a flotilla of small craft, which had run the gauntlet of the blockade, and successfully landed provisions, sufficient for two months, to the starving citadel. On the 9th of October Buckingham shipped his sick men, and one final effort to reduce the fort was decided upon. The exertions of Mainwaring to prevent any delay in the fleet seems to have been highly commended on all sides, and on the 21st of October Viscount Wilmot, in command of the reinforcements which

---

[1] Clowes, *Royal Navy*, ii. pp. 68–9.
[2] *S.P. Dom.*, Charles I, lxxx. 28.
[3] MS. Folmouth.

were to be shipped on board Holland's fleet, wrote to Lord Conway as follows [1]:

Sir Henry Mainwaring having been employed by special instructions from his Majesty for the oversight and ordering of the ships for the transportation of these 2000 soldiers at Plymouth that is to go to his Grace to the Isle of Rhé, hath judicially and carefully answered his Majesty's trust reposed in him. In doing him but right, I could not but let your Lordship know, that his knowledge and skill hath greatly advanced the expedition of our present journey, that this day being Saturday, by the Grace of God, we purpose to set sail, though the fleet from the Thames came to us but upon Thursday in the afternoon, and yet our soldiers some companies of them being lodged twelve miles from us. The sufficiency of this noble gentleman is so well known to his Majesty and your Lordship, that my pen can add little to his worth. But in this particular your Lordship shall do very nobly to make his Majesty know his diligence in his service, which we could have very ill spared here till this day we set sail, which recommendation to his Highness, I shall humbly leave to your Lordship's noble care of him to do him right.

The ships from the Thames under the command of Sir John Chudleigh, which were to transport the soldiers to Rhé, had arrived at Plymouth Sound on the 18th of October,[2] and on the following day the Earl of Holland, who was at Portsmouth with four warships, endeavoured to join them. The 'extremity of the weather,' however, prevented their sailing, and Holland posted to Plymouth to meet Wilmot, leaving Sir Henry

[1] *S.P. Dom.*, Charles I, lxxxii. 41.
[2] *Ibid.*, lxxxii. 13.   Mervin commanded the *St. George*, Captain George Bond the *Convertive*, Captain John Harvey the *Entrance*, and Captain Francis Sydenham the *Mary Rose* (*ibid.*, 25, 30).

Mervin to follow with the ships at the earliest opportunity. On the 20th Mervin 'weighed and put to sea about St. Helens,' but contrary winds forced him back on the 23rd to Yarmouth Roads.[1] The Convertive, forming one of his squadron, was found to be so leaky, that in one hour 'she pumped 600 and odd stroke,' and Mervin strongly complained of the conduct of Burrell in permitting her to go to sea for a third time 'after having failed in two voyages.'[2]

The victualling of the relief ships proved to be one of its most serious drawbacks, and on the 24th John Ashburnham[3] wrote to Nicholas from aboard the Bonaventure, that they had been sent with such a neglect of order, that Mainwaring was forced to go from ship to ship in order to ascertain what they had.[4]

I am first [he wrote] to give you thanks for the care you have of enabling me to give an account of all proceedings to my master. You have here sent me a collection of the state of victuals of the fleet and army, wherein you nominate the provisions of victuals that are to be sent with my Lord of Holland. You only set down the quantity in general, but we are so troubled here, for the particulars of what is in this fleet, that the neglect of order in that kind cannot be forgiven ; for there is not any ship that hath either bill of lading, or any man in them that was appointed to receive the victuals and to account for them, so that Sir Henry Mainwaring is forced to go from ship to ship to search what they have ; and we reckon upon what he finds, which will amount to the maintenance of the whole army about some twenty days.

---

[1] *I.e.* Yarmouth, Isle of Wight. *S.P. Dom.*, Charles I, lxxxii. 68.   [2] *S.P. Dom.*, Charles I, lxxxii. 89.

[3] Groom of the bedchamber to Charles I, and a relative of the Duke of Buckingham.

[4] *S.P. Dom.*, Charles I, lxxxii. 80. October 24, 1627.

This allegation of mismanagement and neglect on the part of the victualler proved only too true, and as a result of Mainwaring's investigation it was found that there were only enough provisions to last the army seventeen days—a scandalous condition of things, which was aggravated by the fact that 2000 troops were living upon them in the meantime. By the time the fleet reached Rhé, it was estimated that only eleven days' provisions would be left, and the non-arrival of the four ships under Mervin considerably weakened the fleet.[1]   Mervin, however, was still weather bound at Yarmouth, and owing to the urgency of the supply, and the entreaties of the King, Holland decided to sail without him. On the 29th, therefore, .the Earl, contrary to the opinion of his seamen, ' forced the whole fleet out of Catwater ' with disastrous results. That night it was caught in a violent storm, which lasted for twenty hours, and in consequence was finally driven back into Plymouth with severe damage to the ships.[2] ' Although all diligence will be used to repair the ships,' wrote Wilmot, ' it will, for a time, hinder them putting to sea.' [3]

In the meantime Buckingham had given up all hope of the provisions and reinforcements reaching him in time. For weeks some of his

[1] *S.P. Dom.*, Charles I, lxxxii. 87.
[2] *Ibid.*, lxxxiii. 32.
[3] *Ibid.*, lxxxii. 38. October 31. On the 6th of November Holland informed the King that they were again under sail with a fair northerly wind, and he hoped for a speedy voyage and a happy one for the relief of the army at Rhé (lxxxiv. 26). Unfortunately his effort came too late, Buckingham having left the island on the 8th. No less unfortunate was Mervin, who wrote on the 5th that he was still detained in Yarmouth Roads by ' contrary winds and extreme foul weather ' (*ibid.*, lxxxiv. 23).

gallant soldiers had been posted on the house-
tops, eagerly scanning the horizon with their
telescopes for some sign of Holland's fleet, until
' they looked themselves and their perspectives
blind.' [1] In sheer desperation Buckingham, with
scarce 4000 men, attempted to storm the fort
on the 27th of October, but the result was so
disastrous that a tenth of his force perished
in the operation, without inflicting any material
damage on the enemy.[2] Two days later the
English army was in full retreat, and Buckingham and his remaining men embarked from
Rhé on the 8th of November. It was estimated
that 4000 men had perished in the expedition.[3]
Such was the dissatisfaction among the seamen on their return, that the crew of the
Assurance deserted in a body. The common
necessaries of life were not forthcoming, and
the sailors were forced to steal the soldiers' arms
at Plymouth and sell them in order to obtain
bread. The wages bill was running up to £5000
a month, because of the lack of money to pay
the crews off. Disease was rampant, and in less
than a month 500 of the seamen who had survived
the horrors of Rhé found a grave at Plymouth.[4]
Sir Henry Mervin informed the King that he
' would soon have more ships than men,' but
the remark fell on deaf ears, for Charles was

---

[1] *S.P. Dom.*, Charles I, lxxxi. 61.

[2] Granville, iii. 259. It was subsequently proved that the
French had only enough provisions to last them till the 5th of
November, and, as Dr. Gardiner remarks, ' it was lamentable
for Buckingham to be so near success and yet to miss it '
(*Hist. of England*, iv. 196).

[3] Gardiner, vi. 198. The embarkation was effected from
the small island of Loix, adjoining Rhé, west of St. Martin's.

[4] Oppenheim, *Naval Administrations*, p. 231.

bent on relieving Rochelle, where the Huguenots
were making their last stand. Another fleet
was therefore ordered to be ready for sea in
the spring, and Mainwaring, as before, was
actively engaged in its preparation. To enable
the Rochellese to hold out till then, it was imperative that provisions should be sent them from
England, and on the 13th of November Mainwaring sent a certificate to Sir John Coke, informing him of the condition in which he found
several of the merchant ships that were to convoy
them. On account of the shortage of men, the
masters of the various ships were commanded
to meet Mainwaring and Burrell at the Trinity
House by eight o'clock in the morning, to consider the best means of impressing the necessary
men. The following day Mainwaring reported
the result of the conference to Coke. With the
help of Sir John Wolstenholme, Sir William
Russell, and Denis Fleming, Commissioners of
the Navy, and the assistance of Trinity House,
' I think we have put the business in an orderly
way,' he wrote, ' so that I hope nothing but
wind and weather shall hinder their speedy
proceedings. It was the opinion of the Commissioners to have them stay at Tilbury for one
another, but (under favour) my opinion is they
should better serve the King's intention, to meet
the fleet with the victuals, to let the first stand
on their course, lest staying in this variable
and tempestuous season for some, all might come
too late.'[1] The anxiety of Mainwaring to get
the ships out of the Thames was shared also by

[1] *Hist. MSS. Com.*, 12 i, 330-1. From a private letter of
December 19th we know that 400 soldiers and 5000 quarters of
corn were prepared to be sent to Rochelle with all possible
speed (*Court and Times of Charles I*, i. 306).

the Earl of Holland, who wrote to Buckingham on the 5th of December that ' the sooner the ships are sent about the better, or, what with the sick, and the runaways, they will not be sufficiently manned.' The fleet at Portsmouth required considerable repairs, and Holland feared that few of them would be fit to put to sea. ' Most of them have leaks or other defects not to be repaired there,' he stated, ' because there is no dock, which is a great omission in some of our great officers.' [1]

On the 15th of February, 1628, a Council of War was appointed, on which Mainwaring served.[2] Its proceedings seem to have been on a similar basis to the Naval Commission of 1626, and at the first meeting, held at Whitehall on the 21st of the month, a return was called for as to the state of the King's ships, and measures were taken to put a stop to the practice, prevalent at Ipswich and elsewhere, of building ships with low decks, so that they might not be fit for war, but only for trade.[3] As the Crown

---

[1] *S.P. Dom.*, Charles I, lxxxvi. 15. Burrell, according to his contemporaries, was a good deal to blame for this. Captain Giffard informed Buckingham in the previous June that Burrell strove to hinder the building of the dock. He had caused the old one to be filled up, and would have pulled down the great storehouse, in order that he might have all the business to himself at Chatham. ' How the King has been served by him,' wrote Giffard, in reference to the finding of the Special Commission, ' has been seen, and yet he remains firm in his place ' (*Ibid.*, lxvi. 55).

[2] *Ibid.*, xciii. 37. This Council of War appears to have been appointed to carry out the duties of the Navy Commissioners who were discharged by Royal warrant on 20th of February. ' We are resolved,' runs the warrant, ' to have all these services performed by our Admiral of England, and other the ordinary officers of our Navy' (*Hist. MSS.*, 12 i, 339).

[3] *S.P. Dom.*, Charles I, xciv. i.

drew largely on the mercantile marine of the
country when fitting out an expedition, the
question was of national importance. Among
the ' advices of the Council of War,' signed by
Mainwaring, Chudleigh, Best, and Captain
Heydon, which were communicated to Buckingham two days later, mention is made of a present
fleet to guard the coasts of England and Ireland,
consisting of eight King's ships and eighteen
merchantmen, to be at sea by the end of March.[1]
The military and naval needs of the country
required an urgent supply of money, and at
the King's request the Council of War drew up
an estimate, which they presented to Charles
on the 22nd of March, showing that nearly
£600,000 would be required for the two services
during the coming year, besides an immediate
demand of nearly £700,000 for repairs and
munitions of war.[2] It was originally intended
that the fleet under the command of the Earl
of Denbigh should sail for Rochelle on the 1st
of March, but the incompetence of the Government to deal with the difficulties that its preparation presented, considerably delayed its
departure.[3]

In consequence, Mainwaring found his time
fully occupied. Besides his attendance at the
Council of War, there were his duties at Plymouth, where many of the ships had to be careened
and fitted with new masts before they could proceed to sea. Writing from there on the 16th of
March he informed Buckingham of the result
of his labours, and highly praised the help he

---

[1] *Hist. MSS. Com.*, 12 i, 339.
[2] Gardiner, vi. 239 ; *S.P. Dom.*, Charles I, xcviii. i.
[3] Dalton's *Life of Cecil*, ii. 283.

had received from Sir James Bagg (whom he
described as ' sine quo non '), the Earl of Denbigh,
and Captain Weddell. He strongly impressed
on Buckingham the need of more money, and
stated that if 600 seamen, at the least, were not
forthcoming, the expedition would be unable
to proceed. As to appointing Frenchmen[1] in
command of the fire-ships, he strongly questioned
the propriety of such a proceeding, pointing out
the miscarriage ' in a matter of so great importance, by ruining our fleet might make the
greatest delinquents meritorious in the eyes of
their sovereign.'[2]

MAY IT PLEASE YOUR GRACE,—Though I assure myself
your Excellency will receive notice from better hands than
mine, in what condition the fleet stands here, yet because
I know your Grace's earnest desire to be satisfied in
the particulars, whereof I presume no man (the Earl
of Denbigh excepted) can give you better knowledge
than myself, I think it my duty to acquaint your Grace
that all the ships in the first list appointed for this
voyage will be ready to set sail on Wednesday, the 19th
of this month, if wind and weather serve. The foremast
of the Rainbow is put into the Nonsuch for a main-
mast, which though it be short and somewhat unsightly,
yet will serve her well for the voyage, and work the ship
in all conditions ; and she will go little the worse, yet
if the shortness of time would have permitted, either to
have lengthened that, or made a newer, she should not
have gone so. On Tuesday, the 18th, the St. George and
the Nonsuch will be laid upon the careen, the Nonsuch
(because she hath but one side to trim) will be finished
that day ; the St. George, the next after. The St.
George's mast will be finished on Thursday following ;
in the meanwhile she shall take in her ballast, and
ordnance, and after her victuals ; so that (all casualties

---

[1] *I.e.* Rochellese.   [2] *S.P. Dom.,* Charles I, xcvi. ii.

excepted) she and the Nonsuch will be ready to set sail
with the rest of the fleet the 26th of this month ; this
for a certainty your Grace may build upon in point of
readiness of the ships. The Victualler will have beer
(as he undertakes) by the 22nd of this month to serve
the whole fleet, so that for the provisions of the fleet.
The wine which I acquainted your Grace came in a
Frenchman's prize, need not be appointed for the supply
of drink in the fleet ; yet Sir James Bagg[1] (whose zeal
to your Grace's service is such, that he believes in no
man's work but his own) hath made stay of it.   Your
Grace's most honoured brother (whose care and industry
I cannot sufficiently express) the Earl of Denbigh, hath
taken such course that by the assistance of Sir James
Bagg (*sine quo non*), I assure myself the fleet will be
sufficiently if not extraordinarily well fitted.   The high
and mighty difficulty which we fear is the want of men,
who rather decrease than augment.   What supplies the
press your Grace gave orders for will bring in, I know
not, but I am sure if there come not 600 seamen at the
least, the whole fleet cannot proceed.   Therefore your
Grace may be pleased to resolve what to do in that case.
The land soldiers which by your Grace's appointment
were to come in lieu of 500 seamen will not amount fully
to 400 men ; beside here is no power left with my
Lord Denbigh to take them aboard nor order which way
to dispose of the officers.   Your Grace may be pleased

---

[1] Bagg, through some family connection with Edward
Nicholas, the Secretary of the Admiralty, became an active
servant of Buckingham. He came into the West with a
commission for victualling the ships at Plymouth to the
amount of £10,000.   He rapidly rose in favour, and was made
Vice-Admiral of Devon and Cornwall, representing East Loo
in the Parliament of 1625.   Knighted by the King at Sal-
combe, on the 19th of September 1625.   He was accused of
bribery, and brought before the Star Chamber in 1635, but
Charles refused to punish him, and left him in possession of the
fort at Plymouth.   His name frequently appears in the State
Papers of the period (Forster, *Life of Sir J. Eliot*, vol. i.
pp. 201–8 ; Gardiner, viii. pp. 89–91).

to deliver your intentions on that point by my Lord Denbigh's son (the chief motive being the want of men to fit other ships). I have put French captains and French men aboard the ships appointed for fire works to rig and fit them ; but move it to your Grace (as a thing which my Lord Denbigh takes into a serious consideration) whether it be fit to entrust those ships wholly in the hands of French ; being a matter of so great importance, the miscarriage whereof, by ruining our fleet, might make the greatest delinquents meritorious in the eyes of their Sovereign. This also your Grace may be pleased to resolve. His Lordship I know to be full of industry, integrity, and resolution to perform the service faithfully which his Majesty and your Grace have employed him in. More at this time I will not trouble your Grace with, unless it be the remembrance of more money; yet if you think that, Sir James Bagg's person, his wife, children, friends, his house in Plymouth, the reversion of the Fort, his manor of Saltrum, with what else he hath can furnish us (for all these we command for your Grace's sake), your Grace may forbear any further thoughts of supplying us, if not your Grace is too wise and well experienced in these affairs to need my poor advice. For your Grace's comfort and assurance of the expediting this fleet, I must truly tell you, that nothing but your own presence can despatch it faster than my Lord Denbigh's care and pains will do, whose diligence is such that did I not fear the brand of flattery (because I so much honour and love him, and his worth) I should extraordinarily commend him for it. His example makes us all industrious, amongst whom I must ever remember to your Grace's good regards the pains and abilities of my consort Captain Weddell.[1] For my self, I shall only crave your Grace's pardon for my disabilities to serve you, and your

---

[1] John Weddell, captain in the East India Company's service, born 1583. He offered his services to the King about this period, and in 1627 and 1628 commanded the *Rainbow*. He is described as ' a gentleman of valour and resolution,' and died in the year 1642 in India (*D.N.B.*).

occasions. But when I shall either negligently or wilfully leave your Grace's commands unaccomplished, let me suffer the torture of being no longer assured that I am,

Most truly,

Your Grace's most humbly devoted servant,

H. MAINWARING.

On the 21st Captain Sydenham proceeded to impress the necessary men, but the growing spirit of dissatisfaction made it a most difficult task. At Plymouth he succeeded in impressing between eighty and a hundred, much against their will, and conveyed them to the Guildhall prior to sending them to the various ships. Seething with discontent on their arrival, they seized the opportunity to arm themselves with pikes that were laying there, and stoutly refused to obey orders. Though Mervin and Sydenham endeavoured to pacify them, their ringleader, Robert Kerby invited them one and all to die together, sooner than serve in the King's ships. The arrest of Kerby checked the mutiny for a time, but when the men heard that he was condemned to death, the smouldering flame broke out afresh. On the 22nd, the day fixed for his execution, the seamen marched in a body to the Hoe, tore down the gallows, and cast them into the sea. After leaving the Hoe their intention was to force the prison, but Bagg, who had foreseen trouble, was equal to the occasion, and had the troops in readiness to disperse them, being ably seconded by Mainwaring in his endeavours to quell the mutiny.[1] Nevertheless, it was thought prudent to guard the town, and Bagg wisely suggested to Buckingham that it would be safer to postpone

[1] *S.P. Dom.*, Charles I, xcviii. 26. Bagg to Buckingham, March 23, 1628.

the execution of Kerby till after the fleet had sailed.[1]

The cause of these frequent mutinies; the difficulty of impressing efficient seamen; and the reluctance of men generally to enter the service, is not difficult to ascertain. It was not that the spirit of patriotism was wanting, but the conditions prevailing in the Stuart Navy were so inhuman, that men, rather than be forced to serve, would have sooner gone to the scaffold; death at the hands of the public hangman was more merciful than the evils of semi-starvation, sickness, want of clothing, and lack of wages, that they would endure in the King's ships. A prominent official, in 1628, informed Buckingham of what he believed to be the ' heartburning and cause of the grief of the sailors.' ' They say,' he wrote, ' they are used like dogs, not suffered to come ashore. They have no means to put clothes on their backs, much less to relieve their wives and children. When sick, they have no allowance of fresh victuals. The sick when put ashore are suffered to perish for want of being looked to. Some of their provisions are neither fit nor wholesome. They had as lief be hanged as dealt with as they are.' [2]

At the end of March the Council instructed Bagg and Mainwaring, among others, to remove the soldiers that were being billeted in the counties of Dorset and Somerset, having given the Earl of Denbigh instructions to receive them. A new levy of 600 men was also made, the most able of whom were shipped as seamen. Those soldiers

[1] Kerby was finally pardoned, and discharged on the 18th of the following July (*S.P. Dom.*, Charles I, cx. 22).

[2] *Ibid.*, xcviii. 29. Sir F. Gorges to Buckingham, March 23, 1628.

who had been billeted in the two counties named were found to be in urgent need of clothes, and it was ordered that sufficient should be provided.[1] Nor were the Council's instructions issued a moment too soon. Loud complaints were being made by the people against the billeting of the troops upon them, and it was imperative to Charles that Denbigh's fleet should sail without further delay, if it was to succour the beleaguered garrison at Rochelle, whose privations had now reached an acute state. 'In the name of God,' wrote the Mayor of Rochelle, in a letter which reached England about the 20th April, 'come with speed and bring good store of fireworks to overthrow their practices.'[2] Within a week after the receipt of this piteous appeal, in spite of the difficulty in finding sufficient seamen to man his fleet, Denbigh left Plymouth Sound with sixty vessels. His fleet was divided into three squadrons, and comprised the following King's ships, besides armed merchantmen.[3]

1st *Squadron.*

St. Andrew	Earl of Denbigh, Admiral.
	Thomas Kettleby, Captain.
Nonsuch	Sir Francis Carew.
Antelope	Anthony Rice.
George, prize	Anthony Marbery
Squirrell, pinnace	James Butfield.

2nd *Squadron.*

Garland	Sir Henry Palmer,
	Vice-Admiral.
Vanguard	Nicholas Parker.
Mary Rose	Francis Sydenham.

[1] *S.P. Dom.*, Charles I, xcviii. 90.   [2] *Ibid.*, ci. 47.
[3] *Ibid.*, xcvi. 56 ; cii. 35.

3rd Squadron.

St. George .... John Weddell,
Rear-Admiral.
Happy Entrance .... Edward Harvey.
St. Claude, prize .... Sir David Boswell.
Esperance, prize .... Richard Skipworth.

On the 1st of May the English fleet arrived before Rochelle, and on their approach the French ships left the harbour and retreated up the river under fire of their guns. The elaborate system of defence which had been constructed at the entrance to the harbour, consisting of palisades and moles, had been further strengthened with 'two floats of ships, within and without, moored and fastened together.' This formidable obstruction, coupled with the ordnance which the French had planted on both sides of the harbour, had virtually rendered Rochelle impregnable from the sea. In fact, the town was so completely blocked up by land and sea, that the garrison were unable to communicate with the English commander.[1] The only chance of success Denbigh saw, was to make an attack with his fireships, and on the first fair evening Captains Allen and Williams approached the works with six 'floaters.' In this dangerous operation the former unfortunately lost his life, being blown up with seven of his crew through one of his 'engines' taking fire.[2] On the 8th the English fleet were face to face with an unlooked-for difficulty. The wind was blowing off the land, and lying as they were in shallow water, there was a probability of the French retaliating with their own fireships. A council of war was

[1] *S.P. Dom.*, Charles I, ciii. 50, 57 ; cv. 30.
[2] *Ibid.*, cv. 86.

therefore held, and as a precautionary measure it was decided to retire a little out of range. This retrograde movement, however, proved fatal to the discipline of the English sailors, and despondency spread from ship to ship.[1]   On the 17th an urgent message was sent from the King to the Earl of Denbigh, telling him to hold on to Rochelle as long as possible, and await reinforcements, which were being sent. That same day Coke, Mainwaring, Bagg, Pennington, and Nicholas were ordered down to Portsmouth to expedite the relief ships.[2] On the following day Denbigh's son, Lord Fielding, and Mainwaring were instructed by the Council to press, take up, and send away as great a proportion of victuals (particularly biscuits and beer), seamen, ships, and any other necessaries that they could make ready for the fleet at Rochelle.[3]   Nevertheless, in spite of all these efforts to reinforce the English fleet, Charles on the 19th received intelligence that Denbigh was on his way home. Three of his vessels laden with corn were captured by Dunkirk privateers within sight of the English coast, and on the 27th he arrived off the Isle of Wight. In the meantime the soldiers who had been poured into the various towns proved a source of trouble to the authorities. The Mayor of Southampton informed Coke that the place was overcharged with soldiers, their being some 400 of them, besides two Irish companies billeted in the town, which caused many of the inhabitants to leave.[4]

---

[1] Gardiner, vi. 292.   [2] *Hist. MSS. Com.*, 12 i, 343.

[3] *S.P. Dom.*, Charles I, civ. 16. On the 20th, Fielding informed Buckingham that Mainwaring had not yet arrived. If he did not come they would ' have land hearts, but not sea heads,' he wrote (*ibid.*, 34).

[4] *Hist. MSS. Com.*, 12 i, 344.

On Denbigh's arrival off the Isle of Wight, Coke reported that the fleet only required fresh victuals and water. On the following day, however, Mainwaring ' insisted on going aboard the ships again, but brought no news of any imperfection.' Acting on the instructions of Coke, he persuaded Denbigh to anchor his ships nearer to Cowes, ' otherwise the bringing of fresh water will breed excuse for their stay. They send their staves in pieces,' he wrote, ' instead of their water casks, and all the coopers are not sufficient to make these casks fit.' [1] The difficulty of re-victualling the ships ' without money' presented a serious obstacle to both Coke and Mainwaring. Though they had ' all impediments, and no help from the fleet, except in the Earl and some very few others,' they informed Buckingham that they did all they could, and were ' discouraged by nothing.' [2] On the 1st of June Mainwaring left his colleague at Portsmouth, and came up to London to consult Buckingham regarding the fleet, and to inform him of the difficulties that had been raised against its return. A rumour had been circulated stating the impossibility of success at Rochelle, which so disheartened the seamen, that Coke and Mainwaring toiled almost in vain to reorganise the expedition. The crew of the Nonsuch mutinied, and Coke was forced to appeal to Denbigh for his help in appeasing them. Mainwaring expressed an opinion that the commanders themselves, and not the seamen, were the prime movers in the discontent.[3]

[1] *S.P. Dom.*, Charles I, cv. 84, 85.   [2] *Ibid.*

[3] *Ibid.*, cvi. 10. Coke was of the opinion that the strength of the fleet when at Rochelle was sufficient to encounter all the force that Richelieu could prepare (*ibid.*, cv. 58).

I.

Coke himself certainly had his suspicions in that direction, and on the day that Mainwaring started for London, he wrote Denbigh the following letter [1] :

I heard an evil report raised in the fleet, and from thence spread abroad, of his Majesty's resolution to send back this fleet to an impossible work . . . For my part I believe not that such worthy gentlemen can have so ignoble thoughts. . . . I do confidently publish what is told me from some of them . . . who are so far from declining any service his Majesty commandeth, for fear of difficulties and dangers, that they think it a special honour to be trusted in such attempts. . . . Now, whether it concerneth both your Lordship and all these worthy gentlemen in like manner to disavow and cry down the unworthy bruits and slanders cast upon your actions, and the designs of the State, your wisdoms may consider. . . . Now there is no way to redeem or make good your honour with his Majesty and the world but by advancing the action, encouraging the mariners, and making way through all fears by your wisdom and courage, for in greatest dangers greatest captains get praise, and where there no danger is every man can command.

Such noble words from one of the most patriotic Englishmen of the day, it is to be hoped duly impressed the officers, though Denbigh himself avowed they had been ' much wronged by ill-information.'

As a result of Mainwaring's audience with Buckingham more fireships were ordered to be prepared, and £4000 worth of corn was provided to go with the fleet for the relief of Rochelle. Denbigh's ships were to be victualled by petty warrant so long as they remained in harbour, in order that their sea victuals might be spared and lengthened. Eventually it was decided that

1 *Hist. MSS. Com.*, 12 i, 346.

the ships should remain in England until the whole maritime force of the country could be fitted out to sail under the command of Buckingham. To this end the King expressed a resolve to come to Portsmouth as soon as money had been raised upon the credit of the subsidies,[1] and in the meantime Buckingham charged Coke ' to continue the diligence and care ' he had hitherto shown.[2] Unfortunately the expedition had been delayed so long that by the end of June the plight of the Rochellese was pitiful in the extreme. Famine ravaged the beleaguered town, and grass, roots, shell fish, and boiled leather formed the only food for the women and children.[3] The sands were fast running out, and if relief did not come soon, the garrison would be forced to capitulate. To none was this more apparent than to Coke and Mainwaring, and their endeavours to get the fleet away were worthy of the highest praise. On the 25th of June Coke put the case before Buckingham in plain words : ' Every day the fleet stayeth in this harbour,' he wrote, ' it will be less ready and worse provided to put to sea. The victuals and provisions daily waste, and supplies cannot be made so fast ; and if it linger till towards the autumn, when the winds will blow high, they will require more supplies of anchors, cables, and all things else than I fear all the stores of the Navy can supply ; and what is most important, the men, part by sickness, part by running away, do every day go fewer.' [4]

[1] Five subsidies had been voted by the Commons in April, amounting to £350,000, but the formalities necessary for making the vote a bill were not completed.

[2] *Hist. MSS. Com.*, 12 i, 346–7, 357 ; Gardiner, vi. 293.

[3] Gardiner, vi. 342.   [4] *Ibid.*, vi. 345.

Finally an effort was made to bring order out of chaos, and at the beginning of August the King went down to Portsmouth to superintend the fitting out of the fleet, while Buckingham remained in London to hasten on the much needed supplies. Unfortunately, the success of the Duke's undertaking was marred by the hostility of his own officers, who, as Dr. Gardiner writes, ' opposed the force of inertia to his reiterated commands.' [1] Added to this, there was the bitter hatred of the seamen towards him, a combination of circumstances which filled his wife and family with grim forebodings of evil.

For the expedition men had been pressed into the service, who had hitherto earned their livelihood ashore ; and who, forced to serve against their will, were face to face with the prospects of semi-starvation and no pay.[2] Underhand methods were resorted to by the pressmasters, and Buckingham gave instructions that the crews of certain vessels should not be paid off until some of his own ships were ready, and then Peter White was to be present to press them immediately for further service.[3] Such intolerable conditions could not last for ever, and Buckingham's career was rapidly drawing to a close. During the second week in August he arrived at Portsmouth, and while driving in his coach to visit the King, his progress was interrupted by 300 sailors who demanded their pay. One of their number, more daring than

---

[1] Gardiner, vi. 345.

[2] On the 8th of August Buckingham wrote to Coke that ' if the mariners make difficulty to go until they are paid some of their arrears, I pray cause the Treasurer of the Navy to pay what shall be needful ' (*Hist. MSS. Com.*, 12 i, 362).

[3] Oppenheim, *Naval Administrations*, p. 234.

the rest, made an attempt to pull the Duke from his coach, but Buckingham, seeing what was about to happen, caught the offender up and conveyed him to Captain Mason's house a prisoner.[1] On the 22nd the mutineer was condemned to be hung, at which news the sailors armed themselves with cudgels and stones, and a fight ensued. The captains of the various ships made an endeavour to pacify the men, but were themselves drawn into the fight. The news meanwhile had reached the Duke, and when he appeared with ' a great company on horseback,' 200 swords were drawn, and many were killed and wounded, before the seamen returned to their ships. Their ringleader was hung on a gibbet between Portsmouth and Southsea Castle, the office of hangman being performed by a sailor who had received his pardon for that special purpose.[2]

That same day John Felton, who had held a Lieutenancy in the Rhé expedition, was nearing Portsmouth. The promotion which he had expected was not forthcoming, and after purchasing a knife on Tower Hill for tenpence, he tramped in search of his victim to Portsmouth. The night of the 22nd he slept some three miles from the town. The next morning he awoke early and made his way to Buckingham's lodging, where, on account of being known to many of the guard, he had no difficulty in gaining admittance into the hall. That morning Buckingham was in high spirits, for intelligence (which proved false) had reached him that Rochelle had been relieved. After breakfast he made haste to carry the glad tidings to the King, and coming out

[1] Oglander, *Memoirs*, p. 45.
[2] Account of an eye-witness (in *Rous's Diary*, Camden Soc., pp. 27–8).

of his parlour he met one of his officers, Colonel Sir Thomas Fryer. Fryer was of short stature, and while Buckingham was returning his salute, Felton seized the opportunity, and drove his knife over Fryer's shoulder into Buckingham's left breast, mortally wounding him. Thus ended the career of George Villiers, a favourite of two monarchs, and a man who had virtually wielded the destinies of the nation.

With the death of Buckingham, Mainwaring lost one of his staunchest supporters, for the Duke, as we have seen, was always willing to listen to any project or suggestion that he cared to put forward concerning the Navy and sea service. Though history has not passed a favourable verdict on the actions of Buckingham generally, in fairness to his memory it must be stated that under his régime as Lord High Admiral the Navy had been considerably augmented and improved. ' He possessed,' writes Charnock, ' that mixture of character to which, though it was not possible to afford unqualified applause, it was not by any means fair to condemn in that extent some historians have thought proper, who have only regarded his political conduct.' [1] Briefly, the result of Buckingham's naval administration may be thus summarised :—The tonnage of the Navy had been raised from 26 ships and 11,070 tons to 53 ships and 22,122 tons. Various improvements had been carried out in the dockyards at Chatham, Deptford, and Portsmouth, as far as the finances of the country would allow.

---

[1] Charnock, *Marine Architecture*, ii. 278. In the only expedition that he took part in, that of Rhé, his personal gallantry was highly extolled by his contemporaries.

Encouragement had been given to private ship-builders to build ships of above 100 tons burden, so that, in the event of war, they could be taken up by the Crown. The manufacture of great cables had been introduced, and Buckingham had provided for the home manufacture of cordage generally by persuading Dutchmen to teach Englishmen their art. The wages of seamen had been considerably augmented, and lighthouses were erected at various points round the coast. Buckingham's zeal was evidenced at the meetings of the Council, where his suggestions for maintaining a fleet for the constant guard of the coast were propounded. The re-introduction of Lieutenants and corporals on board ship was due to the Duke, as was also the systematic gunnery and naval instruction in the service.[1] His purchase of the Lord Wardenship of the Cinque Ports was a desirable amalgamation of the two offices of Lord Warden and Lord High Admiral, and the papers printed by Dr. Gardiner[2] tend to show that the Duke's action was prompted solely by patriotic motives. In short, the period of Buckingham's administration over the naval affairs of the country was marked by incessant activity and zeal, which was maintained up to almost the last hour of his life.

A fortnight after Buckingham's death the fleet, with the Earl of Lindsey as Admiral, set sail for Rochelle. It comprised the following

---

[1] Notes made by Nicholas, five years after Buckingham's death, in *S.P. Dom.*, Charles I, cxli. 85. See also the report of the Officers of the Navy in 1629, in *S.P. Dom.*, Charles I, cxxxviii. 73, and Mr. Oppenheim's *Naval Administrations*, p. 280.

[2] Documents relating to impeachment of Buckingham (Camden Soc.).

King's ships and merchantmen, besides corn
and munition ships, and fireships.   With it went
1613 seamen and 4000 landsmen.[1]

The Admiral's Squadron.

St. George ...... Earl of Lindsey, Admiral.
            John Weddell, Captain.
Garland .... Sir John Chudleigh.
Dreadnought .... Captain Plumleigh.
St. Claude, prize.. Sir David Boswell.
1st Whelp ...... Capt. Taylor.
4th Whelp .... Capt. Pardoe.
7th Whelp ...... Capt. Browne.
10th Whelp .... Capt. Powell.
        Besides 4 pinnaces and 9 merchantmen.

Vice-Admiral's Squadron.

Swiftsure ...... Earl of Morton, Vice-Admiral.
            John Burley, Captain.
Nonsuch .... Capt. Butler.
Antelope .... Capt. Povey.
St. James, prize.. Capt. Richard Fogge.
2nd Whelp .... Capt. William Jewell.
5th Whelp ...... Capt. William Button.
8th Whelp .... Capt. Bamford.
        Besides 3 pinnaces and 7 merchantmen.

Rear-Admiral's Squadron.

St. Andrew .... Earl of Newport, Rear-Admiral.
            Thomas Kettleby, Captain.
Happy Entrance . Captain Harvey.
Mary Rose ...... Captain Sydenham.
Black George .... Captain Marbery.
3rd Whelp .... Captain Batten.
6th Whelp .... Captain John Pett.
9th Whelp .... Captain Bulger.
        Besides 3 pinnaces and 8 merchantmen.

[1] *S.P. Dom.*, Charles I, cxvi. 84.

On the 18th of September the three squadrons arrived in the roadstead of St. Martin's, the scene of Buckingham's failure in the previous year. For some days the fleet was kept in a state of inactivity, owing to adverse weather conditions. On the 23rd the weather became more favourable, and an attack on the enemy's ships lying at anchor under Charlebois Point was decided upon. Owing to the shallowness of the water, it was impossible for the larger King's ships to come to close quarters, and, in consequence, the attack devolved mainly on the merchant ships and whelps. Neither the commanders nor their men, however, entered into it with any zeal, and they were content to spend their shot at ' too remote a distance.' On seeing this, Lindsey sent them peremptory commands, threatening them with execution if they did not go within caliver-shot and see the fireships grapple with the enemy ; but it was all to no purpose.[1]

No sooner had the King learnt of the failure of the first attack than he sent Lindsey a personal letter, charging him to take care of his own honour and the honour of the nation. The passage could not be opened without hazard to some of his ships and loss of his subjects, he wrote, and therefore Lindsey was to make ' a vigorous trial for beating the ships ' and forcing the passage for the relief of Rochelle. ' We do rely,' Charles informed Lindsey, ' upon the courage of our own subjects, which we hope will never deceive us, and particularly upon this occasion.'[2] It was one thing for Charles to issue

---

[1] Lindsey to the King. *S.P. Dom.*, Charles I, cxviii. 8.

[2] *S.P. Dom.*, Charles I, cxviii. 66.

commands, and another thing for the English admiral to have them carried into effect. The crews of his ships, as we have seen, were most of them pressed men, and this system, which had helped to ruin the Cadiz expedition in 1625 and Denbigh's efforts in the previous spring, was still undermining the effectiveness of the English fleet. The courage and enthusiasm necessary for the success of an enterprise such as Lindsey's could not be had to order, and this was the cardinal lesson that the King and Government had yet to learn.[1] On the 24th of September Lindsey essayed another attack with his fireships, but it was delivered in the same half-hearted fashion, and his commands were not obeyed. Instead of directing the course of the fireships they were allowed to drift in, a precedure which enabled the French to tow them aside and place them out of harm's way.[2] Under these circumstances the only course open to the English commander was to wait for the spring tides, which would enable him to bring his large ships nearer the mole.[3] The discontent among the crews of the various ships was aggravated by the lack of unity among the officers. 'The councils held,' wrote Captain Plumleigh of the Dreadnought, 'were rather tumults. Every man spake, and nothing was put to votes, but what Weddell and Chudleigh

---

[1] Gardiner, vi. 364.

[2] *S.P. Dom.*, Charles I, cxviii. 8. Several captains, including Sir David Boswell, Marbery, and Fogge of the King's ships were subsequently brought before the Council and charged with cowardice, and seven of their number were committed to the Marshalsea (*Court and Times of Charles I*, i. 448 ; ii. 3).

[3] Gardiner, vi. 365.

thought fit.'[1] These dissensions, and the excellent gunnery of the Frenchmen which cowed the English sailors,[2] made Lindsey's task certainly an unenviable one.

From the beginning of October till the 14th of that month, negotiations were in progress between Charles and Richelieu regarding Rochelle, but the Cardinal stoutly refused to withdraw either his ships or his army. The English agent was politely conducted over the moles, and was convinced by Richelieu that the works were impregnable by any force at Lindsey's disposal.[3] Nevertheless, Lindsey, who had already commanded one ill-fated expedition, refused to abandon the task as hopeless without a further effort, and an officer on board his flagship furnishes us with an account of the subsequent proceedings of the fleet.[4]

The 15th of this October [he wrote] my Lord General gave order to shoot off a piece of ordnance, and to put out a pennant in the fore-topmast's head to give sign for the leading ships to weigh anchor, and to fall on the enemy the third time. Yet were we forced to lead the way in the St. George, having but $4\frac{1}{2}$ fathom water, we went so near. But when we tacked about at the flood, to linger for the leading ships, which at three foot flood came on, but did then as they did the second time, shooting off many pieces to small purpose, and the tide being at the lowest, after two hour's fight, came off again, and nothing done. The 17th there was called a council of war, and a new way propounded for attempting the enemy, which was to go side by side by the enemy with the men-of-war, and to send in a mine ship to the pallisado. But God, who disposeth of all things, had otherwise determined of the event.

---

[1] *S.P. Dom.*, Charles I, cxx. 72.   [2] *Ibid.*
[3] Gardiner, vi. 365.
[4] Ellis, *Original Letters*, ser. 1, vol. iii. 273.

The Rochellese, discovering the futility of the English efforts, had surrendered to Richelieu's forces on the 18th. It was reported that 16,000 persons had died of starvation during the siege, the rest of the garrison having existed on hides, leather and old gloves.[1]

Certainly no part of the blame for the failure of the three efforts to relieve the town can be laid on the shoulders of either Coke or Mainwaring. The evidence that has been produced shows that they left no stone unturned to make the expeditions a success, and the late Commissioners of the Navy wrote of Mainwaring to the following effect[2] :

We understand that by his extraordinary pains there [*i.e.* at Plymouth], that the fleet under the command of the Rt. Hon. the Earl of Holland was suddenly hastened out of the harbour and dispersed to sea, and therefore in recompense of his great pains and his extraordinary charges and expenses in travelling post, and for boat hire from ship to ship, and for the diet of himself and servant for 45 days, we hold him worthy of 26s. 8d. per day. For the employment which after that he received at His Majesty's commands, namely the hastening of the ships out of the river that did transport victuals to Portsmouth at the return of the fleet from the Isle of Rhé, we think it fitting that for his pains, his horse hire, boat hire, diet, and other expenses, he be also allowed 26s. 8d. a day.

---

[1] Ellis, 274.

[2] *S.P. Dom.*, Charles I, cix. 22. Signed by Sir J. Wolstenholme, J. Osborne, and William Burrell. On the 1st of February 1628 Mainwaring had written to Nicholas asking for an allowance, as he was nearly £100 out of pocket by his services (*ibid.*, xcii. 8).

CHAPTER VIII

1629–34

MARITIME REVIVAL

By the 12th of November the whole fleet, with the exception of two ships, reached Portsmouth, but the expenses of the expeditions to Rhé and Rochelle had so drained the resources of the country, that it was only with the greatest difficulty that sufficient money could be found to pay off the crews of the various ships, for which a sum of £29,000 was required. Not only was the Government embarrassed by the monetary question, but the naval stores had been so depleted that, on the return of the fleet, the Comptroller of the Navy reported that he was unable to have the ships repaired on account of the stores at Portsmouth being exhausted.[1]

Parliament, which had been prorogued since the 26th of June, assembled again on the 20th of January 1629, when any hopes that Charles may have had of obtaining supplies were rudely dispelled. Concessions were demanded from the King, to which he refused to submit, and after a short but stormy session he finally dissolved the Parliament on the 10th of March. The dissolution wrought dismal effects at home, and the

---

[1] Sir G. Slingsby to Lords of the Admiralty. *S.P. Dom.*, Charles I, cxx. 45, 60.

merchants generally refused to set out ships, ' so
as all men began to tremble at the consideration,
what the issue might prove, for by the discon-
tinuance of trade, both the strength and riches
of the kingdom must of necessity in time decay.'
Thus wrote Sir Simond D'Ewes, a shrewd observer
of the day.[1] Such was the want of money that
further offensive operations against France and
Spain became impossible, and only ' a few ships,
not worthy to be called a fleet, could be kept afloat
for the guard of the Narrow Seas.'[2] Even these
were not sufficiently provided, and it was suggested
to the Lords of the Admiralty that it would be
more profit to the King, and as much for his honour,
not to have ships abroad, unless a more certain
course could be taken to supply them. Mervin,
who was in command, beseeched them for the
honour of the State, not to let the naval service
become a scandal, for ' foul winter weather, naked
backs, and empty bellies ' made the ordinary
seamen view service in the King's ships worse than
being galley slaves. ' Without better order,' he
wrote, ' his Majesty will lose the honour of his
seas, the love and loyalty of his sailors, and his
Royal Navy will droop.'[3] Under such distressing
circumstances the idea of peace naturally presented itself, and from the time when such a course
became inevitable, the interests of the King and
his subjects became more fully concerned with
affairs at home.[4] With the death of Buckingham the warlike ambitions of the country came
to an end, and in consequence the demand on

---

[1] *Diary*, i. 407.

[2] Mr. Bruce's preface to *Cal. S. Papers*, 1629-31, p. 1.

[3] *S.P. Dom.*, Charles I, cxlix. 90, 92.

[4] Peace was signed with France in April 1629, and with
Spain in December 1630.

the services of the maritime population became less.

In spite of this, the next two years of Mainwaring's life were in some respects the most romantic of his eventful career, and matrimonial ventures, colonial ambitions, and naval affairs, kept him fully occupied. He was now in the prime of life, and sought to find a bride from among the more wealthy citizens of the metropolis. Therefore, early in 1629, like many other impecunious cavaliers, he became a suitor for the hand of Elizabeth Bennett,[1] the widow of Richard Bennett, a rich mercer and alderman of the City of London. The widow, who was ' near about thirty years of age,' resided with her only son in the parish of St. Olave, Old Jewry. She was reported to be handsome, and to have inherited under the will of her husband an estate of twenty thousand pounds. In the words of a contemporary, she was ' for person and parts, fit for a gentleman of worth.' Her comfortable position in the world drew round her a host of admirers, and the Navy was well represented in the persons of Sir Sackville Crowe, its Treasurer, Sir John Eliot, a former Vice-Admiral of Devon, and Mainwaring. Prior to Mainwaring's début the three foremost in the field were Sir Heneage Finch, Speaker of the House of Commons and Recorder of London, Sir Sackville Crowe, and Dr. Raven, a physician of note. This trio, needless to remark, provided amusing gossip, and led to much bantering by the wits of the city, in songs and ballads on the Finch, Crow, and the Raven. The most ardent lover of the three was Dr. Raven,

[1] Daughter of William Craddock, Esq., of Staffordshire. Her husband's father, Sir Thomas Bennett, was Lord Mayor of London in 1603.

and on the 19th of November in that year he created
a scene by bribing the servants to admit him into
the lady's bedchamber, which escapade caused
him to be entrusted to the care of the custodians
of the peace.   The next day he was brought before
the Recorder, Finch, who, seeing a favourable
opportunity to be rid of a serious rival, committed
Raven to gaol till the following sessions.

Sir Edward Dering of Kent now joined forces
with Finch, and, like his predecessor, commenced
to buy over the widow's servants.   His exploits
are humorously recorded in his diary thus :

Nov. 21. I inveigled G. Newman with 20s.
Nov. 24. I did re-engage him 20s. I did also oil
the cash-keeper 20s.
Nov. 26. I gave Edmund Aspull (the cash-keeper)
another 20s.
Nov. 27. The cash-keeper supped with me.

Numerous letters were also despatched to the
lady, but all to no effect.   Suitors came and went,
and ladies drove to Old Jewry to champion the
claims of their various knights.   Lady Skinner
pleaded the cause of a Mr. Butler, whose suit was
abruptly ended by the widow describing him as
a 'black blunt-nosed gentleman.'   Sir Peter
Temple assured the lady of his superiority in
birth and estate over Sir Edward Dering.
Following Temple, came Sir Henry Mainwaring,
who was introduced by no less a personage than
the Countess of Bridgewater,[1] and certainly his
prospects seemed brighter than some of his rivals,
as the widow had openly stated her desire ' to
match where there was no children.'   Sir Edward

[1] Frances Stanley, daughter and co-heiress of Ferdinando,
Earl of Derby, married John Egerton, 1st Earl of Bridgewater, who was M.P. for Shropshire in 1601.

Dering had been married twice previously, and Sir Heneage Finch was a widower. An interview of an hour, however, terminated our hero's suit. Lord Bruce and Viscount Lumley were others that sought the widow's hand, the latter proving Dering's most serious rival. Sir Edward Dering was ably seconded by his old friend, Izaak Walton, and Lumley by the widow's brother-in-law, Mr. Loe. Lumley's suit appears to have triumphed over Dering's, and he succeeded in persuading the widow to accept a ring, under circumstances which almost amounted to a marriage contract. His hopes, however, were soon shattered, for on the 14th of February his suit was dismissed and the ring returned.

Hearing of Lumley's fate, Sir Edward's friends renewed their exertions more vigorously on his behalf, only to be met with a sad rebuff, for on the 16th of April 1629 Mrs. Bennett was married to Sir Heneage Finch, at St. Dunstan in the West, much to the dismay of Mainwaring and others.[1]

The wealthy widow having failed Mainwaring, an uninhabited island off the coast of Brazil, named Fernando do Noronha, next engaged his attention. With his brother, Sir Arthur, and Captain William King,[2] a man of experience in colonial adventure, he accordingly petitioned Charles for a grant of it, owing to the possibility of its being taken possession of by ' the subjects of some other Prince, if not speedily

---

[1] Dering : *Proceedings in Kent*, ed. L. Larking (Camden Soc.), pp. xiv.-xxxiii., where this story is fully chronicled.

[2] King was one of the original adventurers to whom James I granted the second charter of incorporation for the Virginia Co. (Brown, *Genesis of the U.S.*, i. 219).

I.   P

prevented.' Their petition is couched in the
following terms[1]:

To the King's most Excellent Majesty.

The humble petition of Sir Arthur Mainwaring, Sir
Henry Mainwaring, and Captain William King.

Shewing that whereas there is a small island commonly
known by the name of Fernando do Noronha,[2] being
situated between four and six degrees south latitude, and
distant from the main land of America, betwixt 80 and 120
leagues or thereabout, and is not inhabited by the subjects
of any Christian Prince in league with your Majesty,
nor as yet granted to any by your Majesty. And the
same very likely suddenly to be possessed by the subjects
of some other Prince if it be not speedily prevented, by
taking into your Majesty's royal protection.

May it therefore please your Majesty at the humble
request of your petitioners to grant the said Island to
them and their heirs, with all such privileges and
immunities as in like cases your Majesty hath graciously
been pleased to grant to others, and to that end to give
order to your Majesty's Attorney General for preparing
a book, containing a grant thereof accordingly to your
petitioners for your Majesty's royal signature.

And as in duty bound your petitioners will daily
pray for your Majesty's long and happy reign.

This request was granted, and the above
document is endorsed by Sir Thomas Aylesbury[3]
as follows :

At the Court at Whitehall, 3 Feb. 1629.[4]

His Majesty is graciously pleased to grant the request
of these petitioners for the above-mentioned island, so
as the same be not already granted to any by his

---

[1] *S.P. Colonial Papers*, vol. 5, No. 52.

[2] MS. Fernando Lorinha:

[3] Aylesbury was secretary to the Earl of Nottingham,
when Lord High Admiral, and also to his successor Buckingham. He was Surveyor of the Navy from 1628 to 1632.

[4] Old Style, really 1630.

Majesty, or be not inhabited by any Christian Prince or his subjects in league and amity with his Majesty. And that Mr. Attorney General prepare a bill thereof accordingly with such clauses and articles, and in such form and manner as his Majesty hath heretofore granted to others in cases of the like nature, fit for his Majesty's royal signature.

THOMAS AYLESBURY.

This island, which is in S. latitude 3° 50', and W. longitude 32° 25', has a curious history, and is worthy of a brief notice. It is situated about 194 miles north-east of Cape San Roque, the most eastern point of the Brazils, and lies off the beaten track of shipping, being one of the most seldom visited islands in the South Atlantic. It was probably discovered by Gaspar de Lemoz as early as 1500, and rediscovered by Fernando do Noronha, a Portuguese navigator, in 1502.[1] The following is extracted from Americo Vespucci's account of his stay at the island, which was previously unknown to him, in August, 1503.

When we had sailed for 300 leagues, being 3° to the south of the Equinoctial line, a land was sighted at a distance of 22 leagues, at which we were astonished. We found that it was an island in the midst of the sea, very high and wonderful in its formation, for it was not more than two leagues long and one broad, and uninhabited. . . . We found the island supplied with abundance of fresh water, quantities of trees, and full of marine and land birds without number. They were so tame that they allowed us to take them with our hands. We caught so many that we loaded a boat with these animals. We saw nothing but very large rats, lizards with two tails, and some serpents.[2]

---

[1] *Biographie Universelle*, article 'Noronha.'

[2] *Vespucci's Letters*, ed. Sir C. Markham (Hakluyt Soc., 1894), pp. 53-5.

In 1504 the King of Portugal rewarded Fernando do Noronha, giving to him and his descendants the gift of this isle—hence its name.[1]

The island is about four miles long, and, on an average, about one mile in breadth. It now serves as a Brazilian convict settlement, and is chiefly an ' undulating plateau from 100 to 300 feet above the sea level, sloping steeply towards sandy beaches or bays, or ending in bold bluffs or cliffs, but rising occasionally into what the inhabitants jocularly term " mountains," of which there are four or five, from 500 to 700 feet high.'

At the eastern end of Fernando do Noronha are several small islands, chiefly rocky and uninhabited. Dr. Rattray, writing in 1872, stated that Brazilian men-of-war, and on an average ten or twelve whalers, visit the place during the year. The scenery is described ' as by no means unpicturesque, the climate fine and healthy. . . . The whole island is well worth a visit, and would especially repay the naturalist.'[2]

Though a charter was granted by the Crown for a settlement in Fernando do Noronha, it was not destined to become part of the British Empire. For some reason—probably a failure to find financial support—the grant to Mainwaring and

[1] Capt. John Davis, the famous navigator, during his voyage to the East Indies, touched here in 1598 ; also again in 1605, when he found ' nothing but a wild country, inhabited only by six negroes, which live like slaves.' They were left there by the Portuguese, whose carracks used to water at the island (Davis, *Voyages*, Hakluyt Soc., 1880, pp. 133, 159).

[2] ' A visit to Fernando Noronha ' (*Royal Geog. Soc. Journal*, xlii. pp. 431–8). It has also been visited by the following explorers and scientists : Ulloa, Capt. Cook, Foster, Darwin, and by the Rev. T. S. Lea in 1887, whose paper is printed in the *Royal Geog. Soc. Proceedings*, x. 1888, pp. 424–35.

his partners seems never to have proceeded further. No trace, at any rate, is to be found of any attempt to operate the concession, and Mainwaring's colonial ambitions came to an end.

It is to this year, 1630, that we may assign the marriage of Mainwaring to a daughter of Sir Thomas Gardiner of Basing's Manor, Peckham. We are unable to glean many particulars of the lady or her marriage. The only information that is forthcoming is that she was the fourth and youngest daughter of Sir Thomas, by his wife Frances, daughter of Ralph Skipworth, of Parkbury, Herts. She was baptised on the 4th of October 1607 at St. Giles', Camberwell, and received the christian name of Fortune.[1]

The Gardiners, a Bermondsey family, had been resident at Peckham since the latter part of the 16th century, and the manor of Basing was purchased by them during the reign of Elizabeth. Sir Thomas Gardiner was a Justice of the Peace for the county of Surrey, and there are several curious letters from him to persons of high rank, preserved in the Public Record Office.[2]

No record is extant of Mainwaring's courtship, but it is possible that he first saw his future wife during one of the King's visits to Basing's Manor, when he probably formed one of the royal suite. Unlike his wooing of the previous year, it was a case of love and not riches. No exact date can be assigned to the marriage, but the manner in which it was celebrated suggests that it was a runaway match, and the lady must have been of a peculiarly romantic temperament, which found

[1] *Coll. Topog. et Geneal.*, iii. p. 15.
[2] Sir T. Gardiner died 10th August 1632, and was buried at St. Giles', Camberwell. His wife was also interred there 4th September 1638.

an ideal hero in a man of Mainwaring's character
and antecedents.

The only account handed down is contained
in a letter of Sir Thomas Gardiner to the King,
preserved among the State Papers. Sir Thomas,
who had been summoned to appear before
the Star Chamber, on a warrant brought against
him by Endymion Porter, petitioned the King,
on account of illness, to be excused. Part
of his letter is here reproduced [1] : ' I humbly
pray that my coming may be spared because of
mine infirmities, if the matter be not great that
is made against me.' Then follows some curious
details relating to his children, in which he says :

And when the time came that I should bestow my
daughters in marriage, and conceiving that all hopes
was frustate for money by my son, then I was driven
for to lessen my estate, and to sell lands for my daughters'
portions, and I gave unto three of them two thousand
and three hundred pounds, besides the charges and their
raiment in marriage. But my youngest daughter,
which is the fourth (who your Majesty did once vouchsafe
to see at my house, and King James often) she, without my consent or knowledge, mounted up to top of
Paul's, the nearer to heaven, for to shew God there, how
wise she was in her actions, and there she was married
unto Sir Henry Mainwaring ; and yet she was not there
taken up into heaven, but came down again upon earth,
here further to trouble me before I die, although the
great care and charge I had in breeding her up did not
deserve such disobedience.

Sir Thomas finishes his quaint epistle by stating

[1] *S.P. Dom.*, Charles I, clxxv. 128 (undated, but probably
November 1630). Endorsed ' a true copy of the original
presented unto the King.' It occupies seven closely written
folios, and commences, ' Your Royal Gracious Majesty.
Humbly showeth ; that I sitting ill in my Chamber,' etc.

that his only son, who served in the Low Countries and Denmark, has returned home, and lies at his (Sir Thomas's) house to no little charge, ' for soldiers will not be pleased nor contented without money and gilt.'

The writer is, of course, speaking of St. Paul's Cathedral,[1] and the incident has been thought sufficiently interesting to be mentioned by a modern authority on the cathedral.[2]

In the year of his marriage, Mainwaring was elected to the important post of Master of the Corporation of Trinity House, his connection with which has been fully traced in a subsequent chapter. Though the office must have occupied most of his time, he nevertheless found sufficient leisure to interest himself in our right of fishery in the Narrow Seas. The importance of this can be fully understood when it is stated that during

[1] It is worthy of note that Dr. Donne was Dean of St. Paul's at this period. He had, in 1601, married a cousin of Mainwaring, Ann, a younger daughter of Sir George More of Loseley. Donne's eldest daughter, Constance, married at St. Giles', Camberwell, 3 December 1623, Edward Alleyn, the famous actor-manager and founder of Dulwich College. Donne's third daughter, Bridget, married Mainwaring's brother-in-law, Thomas Gardiner, youngest son of Sir T. Gardiner, at Camberwell, about 1633.

[2] Dr. S. Simpson, *St. Paul's and Old City Life*, 262–4. Dr. Simpson believed that the ' top of Paul's ' might have been the ' High Altar at the upper end of the choir,' but the context, he states, will not bear that interpretation. In *The Gull's Hornbook*, written by Dekker in 1609, ' the gallant is advised to pay tribute to the top of Paul's steeple with a single penny ; and before you came down again, I would desire you to draw your knife, and grave your name (or for want of a name, the mark which you clap on your sheep) in great characters upon the leads . . . and indeed the top [*i.e.* the leads] of Paul's contains more names than *Stowe's Chronicle*.' For other instances of this, see Rye's *England as seen by Foreigners*, p. 202.

the first half of the 17th century, the main issue
in determining the English claim to the sovereignty
of the seas was based upon her right of fishery in
those quarters. In 1630, therefore, Mainwaring
presented to Sir John Coke, one of the Navy
Commissioners, a discourse on the inconveniences
and abuses that resulted from allowing the French
to fish at the Sowe, a fishing-ground[1] situated
between Rye and Dieppe, the ' outwardmost ' part
of which extended about a third over the Channel.
This fishery came within the jurisdiction of the
Lord Warden of the Cinque Ports, and the French
kings, ' time out of mind,' had been accustomed
to obtain licences for a limited number of their
boats to fish there, for the ostensible purpose of
supplying the court of France with fresh fish.

The fishing-ground was stated to be the 'choice
nursery for turbots, halibuts, pearls, sole,
weavers, gurnets, etc.' During the reign of
Queen Elizabeth the licences were very restricted,
and the French could only obtain four. James I,
however, ' who did not much love fish,' was more
liberal, and during his régime their number was
increased to 14. These boats and their masters
were chosen by the Governor of Dieppe, who
sent them over to Dover Castle to be approved
of. If on examination their nets were found to
be of lawful scale, five inches, they were granted
a licence for one year on payment of four crowns.
At what period this custom originated is uncertain,
but it was evidently of considerable antiquity, and
may have even come down from Norman and
Angevin times.[2]

---

[1] Three leagues long and three broad ; depth 26 and 28
fathoms. The discourse (*S.P. Dom.*, Charles I, clxxx. 96) is
printed, for the first time, in vol. ii.

[2] Fulton, *Sovereignty of the Sea*, p. 65.

The granting of these licences proved to be very unsatisfactory, and brought many complaints from the fisher folk of Rye, whose fishery was principally carried on at the Sowe. Nor were their complaints unreasonable. Whereas the French had leave to fish in season and out of season, the 'Reyers' were restricted to certain times of the year, and were not allowed to fish in the night, a privilege which was granted the French. For every French boat that took a licence another one was in readiness to attend her, 'that as one goes in, the other stays out and takes the licence.' Besides this fraudulent dealing, 40 or 50 other boats from places adjacent to Dieppe took the liberty to fish without licence, an abuse which was added to by their using unlawful nets.

The evils resulting from allowing the French to fish at the Sowe had been apparent to Mainwaring for some time, and during his Lieutenancy of Dover Castle several cases of illegal fishing had come under his jurisdiction.

To the town of Rye, the licences and their attendant abuses proved disastrous. From a very early period Rye had been celebrated for her own fishery, and the 'ripiers'[1] of Rye had the privilege of supplying the royal table and London with fresh fish. Though Rye had hitherto been in a flourishing position, by 1630 Mainwaring reported that the town had fallen to such great decay that the houses were being pulled down for want of tenants. The navigation of the port was 'almost laid down,' and there were only six or seven fisherboats. Whereas there were formerly '500 seamen of the train band, there is now few more than 100,' he wrote. To remedy the abuses com-

---

[1] Those who carried the fish to London in panniers on horses' backs.

mitted by the French he suggested that Charles should appoint boats of his own subjects to attend the French king's service, and that only sufficient to supply the immediate needs of the French court should be granted the privilege to fish.   If the King of France, he informed Coke,

desires to enrich his subjects, to increase and strengthen his navigation by impoverishing and weakening ours, I think the law of nature, and reason of state, will oblige our King to prefer and perform his own strength to prevent such intentions, especially now the French begin to talk of Mare Liberum. The affairs, privileges, and prerogative of the Narrow Seas so highly concern his Majesty, that beware whosoever shall aim to make himself Pompey, our King must still be *Cæsar aut Nullus.*

In conclusion, Mainwaring enumerated the various benefits that would be bestowed on the kingdom if this reformation were carried out, first and foremost among them being that ' the Port and Town of Rye will again flourish and be re-populated ; ' while seamen, shipping, and divers crafts belonging to the same would be increased and maintained.

That Mainwaring's advice was acted upon may be inferred from the fact that in May 1631 the Lords of the Admiralty instructed Pennington to cause some of the ships under his command to range the Sowe near Rye, and in the event of finding any Frenchmen fishing without licence from the Lord Warden, their nets were to be seized, and the masters and their boats sent into one of his Majesty's ports.   Similar instructions were also issued to the fleet in the spring of the following year.[1]

The year in which Mainwaring was advocating our claims in the Narrow Seas marks, by a strange

---

[1] *S.P. Dom.*, Charles I, cxcii. 7 ; ccxv. 15.

coincidence, the beginning of a period when a further revival in England's maritime interests is noticeable.[1] There is evidence that the suggestions propounded by the Special Commissioners in 1626–27 were at last being seriously considered, and one result of the welcome peace with both France and Spain was to stimulate Charles and the officers of the Navy to strengthen England's first arm of defence. In October 1630 an account of the present state of the Navy was called for by the King. A list of ships that had been at sea during the year was drawn up, and the captains themselves were ordered to prepare a statement of their various employments. The reason for this was that information had reached the King of much negligence in the Narrow Seas. 'The King's end is princely,' wrote Coke, ' and if they (the captains) can give him satisfaction for the present, they will for the future put things into a due form of account both for the better government and his Majesty's better contentment.' [2]

Early in the following year the King started on a tour of inspection of the various dockyards, accompanied by Mainwaring and other prominent officials. In April, Charles and his party were at Woolwich, where they were shown over the yard and entertained by Phineas Pett. On the 15th and 16th of June they were at Rochester and Chatham, and in a gossipy letter which Nicholas sent to Pennington, we get a vivid account of the King's personal interest in the Navy.[3] 'Charles

[1] Following on Mainwaring's discourse, Sir John Borough's work on the *Sovereignty of the British Seas* was written in 1633, and Selden's monumental work appeared in 1635.

[2] *S.P. Dom.*, Charles I, clxxiv. 21. In the Coke MSS. there is an ' Account for Sea Services,' being Coke's report of an inquiry into the Navy in this year (*Hist. MSS. Comm.*, 12 i, 415–16).

[3] *S.P. Dom.*, Charles I, cxcv. 6.

went aboard every ship, and almost into every
room in every ship. There was no office in any
ship that his Majesty went not into himself, and
into the holds of most of them. He afterwards
beheld and counted the ordnance belonging to
every vessel, which lay ashore marked and sorted
for his Majesty's view. He then went to the dock
at Chatham, and visited all the rooms and store-
houses there, and saw the making and tarring of
the cordage.'

The result of the visit was highly satisfactory
both to the King and the Lords of the Admiralty,
who, according to Nicholas, ' got great honour
by this survey,' so much so, that there was ' not a
thought of a Lord Admiral,' the office of which
had been in commission since Buckingham's death.
The favourable impression which the King's visit
created was also shown during his stay at Portsmouth, where he arrived on the 2nd of August, to
inspect the Triumph, Swiftsure, St. George, St.
Andrew, Warspite, 3rd Whelp, 8th Whelp, Maria,
and Esperance, which were in harbour there.[1]

As a result of the King's tour the officers of
the Navy were informed by the Lords of the
Admiralty that

his Majesty hath thought fit for your better strengthening in the government of his Navy, to join with you his
servant Sir Kenelm Digby, a gentleman of worth, and
well acquainted with the sea. We do admonish, and
entreat you, that with united councils and endeavours
you will reform all such abuses and disorders as have
crept into any part of the service.[2]

Digby was a personal friend of Mainwaring, and
had only recently returned from a successful
privateering expedition in the Mediterranean.

---

[1] *Oglander*, p. 58 ; *S.P. Dom.*, Charles I, cxcviii. 7.
[2] *Hist. MSS. Comm.*, 12 i, 413.   October 13, 1631.

The principal reason for this renewed activity
on the part of Charles is to be found in the fact
that up to 1631 the French had built no less
than thirty-nine war ships within the space
of five years,[1] while the Dutch had practically set
the English claim to the sovereignty of the
seas at nought.   This rapid building on the part
of our continental rivals could not be ignored,
and it became imperative that England should
wake from her lethargy if she was to preserve
her position as the foremost naval power.   The
race for maritime supremacy had at last begun
in earnest, and following on the visit of the King,
the English dockyards responded slowly but
surely to the call made on them.   During the
next three years they were kept fully active, and
at the end of that time they had turned out six
new vessels for the Navy.   In furtherance of
the King's policy the Lords of the Admiralty
on the 21st of April 1632 issued instructions
for Sir Robert Mansell, Sir Henry Mervin, Sir
Kenelm Digby, Sir Henry Mainwaring, and Sir
Sackville Trevor ; with Captains Best, Rainborowe, and Kyme, to attend a meeting of
the Board, for the purpose of determining the
number of men necessary for manning each of
the King's ships, and to give their opinion as to
the ordnance required for the same.   Unfortunately there appears to have been some difference
of opinion among these gentlemen, and a month
later we are informed that Mansell and his party
were busy measuring the ships, and that Mainwaring, Digby, and the Trinity House had
subscribed what they thought were the number
of men necessary, but kept the information to
themselves.   On the 4th of July a meeting was

---

[1] Fulton, *Sovereignty of the Sea*, p. 246.

arranged with Mansell, but after a long discussion they failed to agree, and it was decided to deliver their opinions separately to the King.

The Trinity House men [wrote Digby to Coke] forebore presenting their opinions to his Majesty, to give way to Sir Robert Mansell for measuring the ships, which being done, and Sir Robert not making use of it for this service (but for some sinister end), they beg the King to assign a time when they shall attend him.

The controversy seems to have lasted the whole year, and was not finally settled till the end of March 1633, when the King finally approved of the numbers propounded by the Trinity House. The original list, which gives the names of the ships, their measurements, burthens, and the number of men appointed for each, both on the coast and for foreign service, is here reproduced.[1]

'A list of his Majesty's ships with their several measures and burthens, and the numbers of men appointed for each, entered by his Majesty's express command. The numbers of men propounded by the Trinity House for service on this coast, and for foreign service, are approved and established by his Majesty, whereof the Lords Commissioners for the Admiralty are prayed and required to take notice, and to give order accordingly.' (See p. 223.)

During March and April[2] of this year, a

---

[1] *S.P. Dom.*, Charles I, ccxx. 16 ; ccxxxiv. 52.

[2] In the April of 1633 Mainwaring suffered a sad bereavement by the death of his wife. The love match which ended under such romantic circumstances at the ' Top of Paul's' was destined to be shortlived, and it is to be regretted that among the many letters written by Mainwaring, not one has been preserved that enables us to get a passing glimpse of him in his domestic life. Lady Mainwaring was buried at St. Giles', Camberwell, on the 26th of April (*Coll. Topog. et Genealog.*, iii. p. 15).

Ships.	Length of the keel. Ft.	breadth within the plank. Ft. In.	the breadth to the upper edge of the keel. Ft. In.	in tons and tonnage. Tons.	Number of ordnance.	Men in harbour.	Number of men at sea.	of men for our own coast.	men for foreign service.
								Propounded by the Trinity House.	
Prince Royal	115	43 0	18 0	1187	55	21	500	500	500
Merhonour	112	38 7	16 5	946	40	20	400	350	350
Anne Royal	107	37 4	15 4	828	44	13	400	300	350
Triumph	110	36 6	14 6	776	44	20	300	300	350
St. George	110	36 5	14 10	792	44	14	250	260	300
St. Andrew	108	36 5	14 8	783	42	14	250	260	300
Repulse	108	37 0	14 4	764	40	9	250	260	300
Defiance	104	36 7	17 3	875	38	9	250	250	280
Vanguard	112	36 4	13 10	751	40	9	250	250	280
Swiftsure	106	36 0	14 8	746	44	14	250	260	300
Rainbow	112	36 0	13 6	731	40	9	250	240	270
Reformation	106	36 3	15 0	742	40	9	250	250	280
Victory	106	35 0	14 7	721	40	9	250	250	300
Warspite	97	35 0	15 0	702	36	14	250	220	250
Charles	105	36 2	16 3	810	44	9	250	250	280
Henrietta Maria	106	35 7	15 8	793	42	9	250	250	280
Red Lion	103	35 9	14 5	698	40	9	250	220	250
Nonsuch	88	35 3	15 0	619	38	9	250	220	250
Assurance	104	35 2	13 0	601	34	7	250	200	225
Convertive	96	33 4	15 0	621	34	7	200	200	225
Garland	96	32 4	13 10	567	34	7	200	170	190
Bonaventure	96	32 0	13 6	557	32	7	200	170	190
Dreadnought	92	32 5	14 6	552	30	7	200	140	150
Happy Entrance	96	31 0	13 1	539	30	7	200	160	180
St. Denis	104	32 2	11 9	528	38	7	200	160	180
Antelope	92	32 5	10 10	512	38	7	160	160	180
Mary Rose	83	31 9	9 5	321	26	6	100	100	110
Adventure	88	26 0	9 0	287	24	6	100	100	110
1st Whelp	62	25 0	9 0	186	14	3	60	60	60
2nd Whelp	62	25 0	8 2	186	14	3	60	60	60
3rd Whelp	62	25 0	9 0	169	14	3	60	60	60
4th Whelp	62	25 0	9 0	186	14	3	60	60	60
5th Whelp	62	25 0	7 10	186	14	3	60	60	60
8th Whelp	62	25 0	9 0	162	14	3	60	60	60
9th Whelp	62	25 0	9 0	186	14	3	60	60	60
10th Whelp	62	25 0	6 6	186	14	3	60	60	60
Henrietta	52	15 0	6 6	68	6	1	25	25	25
Maria									

thorough survey of the Navy and naval stores took place at Chatham, Portsmouth, and Deptford, under the superintendence of Sir William Russell, Kenrick Edisbury, and Denis Fleming, the three principal officers of the Navy.[1] As a result, a praiseworthy effort was made to get some of the fleet ready for sea, and by the beginning of June, Pennington, who had been appointed Admiral for the guard of the Narrow Seas, was patrolling the Channel with six warships under his command. His principal charge was 'to preserve his Majesty's honour, coasts, and jurisdiction within the extent of his employment, so that no nation should intrude therein.' In the event of meeting with ' ships of any foreign prince,' he was instructed ' to expect the Admiral and chief of them to perform their duty and homage in passing by, and if they refuse he is to enforce it.' [2] From these instructions it is clear that the idea of enforcing the English claim to the sovereignty of the seas was gradually maturing in the mind of the King and his Council, and Pennington's cruise in 1633 was but the germ of a much larger naval demonstration, the famous ship-money fleets which were inaugurated two years later. Before giving an account of them, it is interesting to examine the naval force that Charles had at his disposal in 1634. The

---

[1] *S.P. Dom.*, Charles I, ccxxxiii. 79, 84, 91 ; ccxxxiv. 62, 70, 75 ; ccxxxvi. 85. The report of the Survey occupies in all 165 quartos.

[2] *Ibid.*, ccxxxvii. 1. Though Pennington's cruise two years earlier was ' for the protection of trade, and securing the Narrow Seas from pirates,' he had nevertheless received ' private instructions ' that in the event of meeting any fleet ' belonging to any foreign prince,' he was to compel the Admiral, ' in acknowledgement of his Majesty's sovereignty, to strike his topsail in passing by ' (*ibid.*, cxc. 52 ; cxcii. 3).

two last vessels which had been added to the Navy were the Leopard and Swallow, and their inception was due to Mervin, Mainwaring, Pennington, and Button, to whose dimensions they were built in 1634.[1] The total number of the King's ships was now 42, comprising 4 first rates ; 16 second rates ; 10 third rates ; 2 fourth rates ; 8 of the 10 original Whelps, classed as fifth rates ; besides 2 sixth rates, the Henrietta and Maria.[2] In addition to the King's ships, it is necessary to consider the strength of the mercantile marine, which formed an integral part of the Navy. All the fleets set forth by Charles I contained a large proportion of armed merchant ships, and when it is remembered that no fewer than ninety-five of over 100 tons each had been built between the years 1630–34,[3] we begin to realise what a powerful naval force Charles had at his disposal when the first ship-money writs were sent out in 1634.

[1] *S.P. Dom.*, Charles I. cclix. 91.

	Keel.	Beam.	Depth.	Gross tonnage.
Leopard	95 ft.	33 ft.	12·4 ft.	515
Swallow	96 ft.	32·2 ft.	11·7 ft.	478

[2] Mayo, *Trinity House*, p. 20. A navy list of 1633, printed in Derrick, *Royal Navy*, pp. 59–61, gives 50 ships—obviously erroneous.

[3] Oppenheim, p. 271.

I.   Q

CHAPTER IX

1635-36

THE SHIP-MONEY FLEETS

' Who is so wilfully ignorant or so grossly blinded as not to see, and seeing, not to acknowledge, the being of a navy in this kingdom to be one of the greatest and [most] deserving undertakings of the State, worthy the care of the greatest peer, and the prayer of the greatest prelate? '

' If either the honour of a nation, commerce or trade with all nations, peace at home, grounded upon our ememies' fear or love of us abroad, and attended with plenty of all things necessary either for the preservation of the public weal or thy private welfare, be things worthy thy esteem . . . then next to God and the King give thy thanks for the same to the Navy.'[1]

MAINWARING'S career as a naval officer now brings us into contact with an important development in our naval policy, the true significance of which, affecting as it did the status of England as a great sea power, has been overshadowed by the constitutional crisis to which it ultimately led.

The lines quoted above, though written as long ago as 1638, were just as true then as they are in the twentieth century, but unfortunately the writer's views did not find the same whole-hearted support as they would at the present

[1] John Hollond, *Discourse of the Navy* (Navy Rec. Soc.), pp. 4-5.

day. It is true that the majority of his countrymen were willing to acknowledge that a powerful
fleet was desirable both for the credit and safety
of the nation, yet the inception of a permanent
naval force was looked upon as a very unequal
recompense for the national liberties, which were
to be sacrificed to establish it.[1] The position of
foreign affairs in 1634 had certainly reached an
acute point, and besides the Dutch, the French,
to quote a contemporary, were now challenging
a dominion in those seas ' where anciently they
durst not fish for gurnets without licence.'[2]
Therefore the necessity of placing the English
fleet on a sounder basis became apparent, and
towards the end of January 1634 the Lords of
the Admiralty, ' having taken into consideration
the depredations committed in the Narrow Seas,
and even within his Majesty's ports and chambers,
by men-of-war to the dishonour of his Majesty's
sovereignty in those seas, the discrediting of his
harbours, and the disturbance of trade,' instructed
Sir Henry Marten, the judge of the Admiralty
Court, and the Attorney-General, Noy, ' to compose a reglement whereby his Majesty's ancient
right in the Narrow Seas, and in his chambers and
ports,' might be preserved.[3] Though Charles
was without a Parliament, he resolved to meet
the monetary difficulty that such a step would
involve by reviving a tax that had been
imposed once or twice previously,[4] and for this

[1] Ewald, *Stories from the State Papers*, ii. 165.
[2] *S.P. Dom.*, Charles I, cclxxviii. 3.
[3] *Ibid.*, cclix. 7.
[4] Under the Plantagenets it had been the custom to call
upon the port towns to furnish ships for the defence of the
kingdom. In 1626 a fleet had been created in this manner,
during the war with Spain (Ewald, ii. 163).

purpose the first issue of ship-money writs was sent out towards the end of 1634.

After due deliberation by the committee to whom the King referred this ' business of guarding the sea,' [1] it was thought safest, or more in accordance with the former precedent, to limit the writs to the port towns; but finally all maritime places were joined with them.   Each was called upon to maintain a proportion of the shipping for the defence of the Narrow Seas [2]—that is, the two seas between England and France, and England and the Netherlands.[3]   Whatever may be thought of the financial measures which were adopted to give the new idea material shape, there can be no doubt that the policy itself struck the keynote of the development of British power, and it is this side of the question that we are able to see more clearly through the aid of Mainwaring, for it was in the fleets that resulted that he held important commands.   The objects of the fleet are so fully set forth in the instructions issued by Coke, that we cannot do better than reproduce them in full.   It will be observed that the importance which Mainwaring attached to our right of fishery in the Sowe is duly recognised.[4]

Our intention is not to offend or incommodate our neighbours or allies, or in any sort to break that peace which, by God's great blessing, we enjoy with all Princes and States.   Our seas, commonly called the four English seas, are much infested by men-of-war and others, tending to the denial or impeachment of that sovereignty,

---

[1] *Hist. MSS. Com.*, 12 ii. 59.

[2] *I.e.*, to provide the King with ships, or pay an equivalent sum of money (*Cal. S.P.*, 1634, pref. xxvi.).

[3] Edmundson, *Anglo-Dutch Rivalry*, p. 161.

[4] ' Instructions for the Fleet.'   Draft by Sir J. Coke in *Hist. MSS. Com.*, 12 ii. 104.

peculiar interest, and property, which we and our progenitors, time out of mind, have had and enjoyed in
the said seas. We have therefore now put our navy
in order for the maintenance of this right. And because
this sovereignty is exercised especially in guarding
of our seas, we command you not to suffer our power
and right to be therein usurped upon. But if any Prince
or State shall, by their fleets or men-of-war, take upon
them to keep a guard on our seas, you shall first prohibit
them and require them peaceably to retreat. And in
case they shall resist or refuse you shall force them to
quit the seas. And that in the due execution of all
these our sovereignty may be acknowledged and maintained, we require you to let none pass by you of what
quality soever without veiling bonnet and performing
the due homage of the sea. That which, in the next
place, we require you to look unto as a branch of our
sovereignty is to free and secure trade in every part
of our seas. And whereas the inveterate war between
the subjects of Spain and the United Provinces hath
introduced an innovation prohibiting free commerce,
contrary to our undoubted right and the practice of
former times, and law of nations, by seizing and con-
fiscating the persons, ships, and goods of our subjects
trading on either side, as forcing all their neighbours
to submit to their interests, we, following the example
and resolution of our progenitors, require you to oppose
and vindicate this wrongful restraint of trade by whom-
soever it shall be made. And in case you cannot rescue
and recover what shall be taken, you shall cause due
restitution by way of reprisal. As trade must be opened
and protected, so with equal care you must in the fishing
restore and preserve our ancient rights. The fishing
betwixt the English and French coasts hath ever been
acknowledged to be proper to this Crown, and the
French kings themselves have fished there only by our
licence. For the herring and other fishings, though we
permit our neighbours to partake with us in God's
blessings upon our coasts, yet therein you must take care,
first, that our own fishermen have precedence and

advantage for their better encouragement in this hopeful trade ; secondly, that all strangers yield to us such duty and acknowledgment as heretofore hath been allowed. By these instructions you are sufficiently directed in general in the things concerning the interest of our State. We forbear to descend to particulars, relying therein upon your own discretion, who, with the advice of a well-chosen council of war of experienced commanders, will be best able to resolve upon emergent occasions what is fittest to be done. Other instructions concerning the government of your fleet in what belongeth to every man's proper office we leave to the direction of the Commissioners of our Admiralty in the usual form.

These instructions were issued to the Earl of Lindsey, on whom was conferred the command of the first ship-money fleet, and with him, as his Vice and Rear Admirals respectively, were Sir William Monson, the old Elizabethan sailor, and Sir John Pennington, who had recently been knighted. Though Mainwaring's name figures third on a list of captains drawn up for presentation to the King on March 1635, for some reason he was not actively employed.[1] This is the more curious as Mainwaring sailed with all the subsequent fleets, but possibly ill-health may have been the cause. It was originally intended that the fleet should assemble at Portsmouth, but owing to an outbreak of small-pox the Downs was substituted, and by the beginning of June the whole fleet, consisting of 19 king's ships and 6 merchantmen, assembled in this famous roadstead.[2]   The ships and their commanders were[3] :

[1] *S.P. Dom.*, Charles I, cclxxxiv. 84, 85.
[2] Clowes (ii. p. 73) says 26 merchant ships, but both Monson and Lediard state 6.
[3] Lediard, ii. 524 ; Monson's *Naval Tracts* (ed. Oppenheim), ii. 223-4.

Merhonour .	.	Earl of Lindsey, Admiral.
James .	.	Sir William Monson, Vice-Admiral.
Swiftsure .	.	Sir John Pennington, Rear-Admiral.
St. George .	.	James Montague, Captain.
St. Andrew	.	Walter Stewart, Captain.
Henrietta Maria	.	Thomas Porter, Captain.
Vanguard .	.	Sir Francis Sydenham, Captain.
Rainbow .	.	John Povey, Captain.
Lion . . .	.	John Mennes, Captain.
Reformation	.	Lord Poulett, Captain.
Leopard .	.	Lewis Kirke, Captain.
Mary Rose .	.	George Carteret, Captain.
Adventure .	.	Richard Parramour, Captain.
Swallow .	.	Henry Stradling, Captain.
Antelope .	.	Richard Fogge, Captain.
1st Whelp .	.	Anthony Penruddock, Captain.
3rd Whelp .	.	Peter Lindsey, Captain.
8th Whelp .	.	Thomas Price, Captain.
10th Whelp.	.	William Smith, Captain.

and the following merchantmen :—Sampson, Royal Exchange, Freeman, Pleiades, William and Thomas, Minnikin, ketch.

On the 6th of the month the whole fleet sailed westward from the Downs, but contrary winds detained it at St. Helens for some time, and it was not until the 20th that Lindsey reached Dartmouth. A large French fleet which had been driven into Portland Roads by stress of weather considerably alarmed the inhabitants of Weymouth, who appealed to Lindsey for protection. The French admiral, de Manty, however, assured the mayor that he had no hostile intentions, and in order to pacify the inhabitants he offered to show his instructions, which bound him ' to honour and respect ' everything belonging to the King of Great Britain.[1] As soon as the weather permitted

[1] *Cal. S.P.*, 1635, pref. xiv ; *S.P. Dom.*, Charles I, ccxci. 23.

the French fleet sailed westward, with Lindsey
on its heels. The English admiral was 'once so
near them, as with the same wind that he came
into Portland Road they (the French) put to sea.' [1]
On the 21st the English fleet reached Plymouth,
and from thence proceeded to the 'furthermost
part of Scilly,' during which time they met with
a few Hollanders, who performed 'their due
obeisance.' [2] On returning along the coast
Lindsey was informed that the French fleet had
been joined by a Dutch squadron, and had proceeded either to the French coast or the Bay of
Biscay. Accordingly, the English fleet plied
towards the coast of France, and Lindsey in a
despatch from Plymouth on the 21st of July
stated that he had caused 'a boat to be taken up
at Plymouth, and sent to Ushant, Conquet, and
other parts of France to bring him intelligence
what ships were thereabout.' The only information that was forthcoming, however, was to
the effect that the combined French and Dutch
fleets were 'supposed to be on the coast of Biscay.'
This was actually the case, and in order to prevent
hostilities, Richelieu had instructed the French
admiral to cruise in the Bay in concert with the
Dutch. Nevertheless, a rumour was current that
17 French men-of-war were off the Lizard, and,
the wind being favourable, Lindsey made all haste
to intercept them. On arrival no trace was to be
found of the French fleet, and the English admiral
went on to the Lands End, but with the same result.
If the French 'did appear,' wrote Lindsey, 'they
were late come, and soon gone.' [3] In fact, neither
pirate nor enemy of any kind was to be found,
and on the 4th of August the fleet returned to the

---

[1] *S.P. Dom.*, Charles I, ccxci. 82.
[2] *Ibid.*, ccxi. 82.   [3] *Ibid.*, ccxiv. 20.

Downs to revictual. Early in September it was again ready for sea, and the English admiral sailed west, with the intention of ranging along the coast as before, but unfavourable weather detained him off the Isle of Wight until the end of the month. It being late in the year, Lindsey decided to return to the Downs, arriving there on the 5th of October, the cruise of the first ship-money fleet ending three days later. Though Lindsey's fleet had not met with any resistance, its presence in the Channel no doubt raised the general opinion of England as a maritime power. The moral effect of the fleet was certainly great, and Sir Kenelm Digby, one of the Navy Commissioners, writing to Coke from Paris on the 29th of September, stated that if the King kept ' a fleet at sea, and his navy in that reputation it now is—for I assure your honour that is very great—and although my Lord of Lindsey do no more than sail up and down, yet the very setting of our best fleet out to sea is the greatest service that I believe hath been done the King these many years.' [1]

As a display of naval force it was certainly an event of which Charles was justly proud, and when the second writs were issued, he was determined that the resulting fleet should be on a much grander scale. For this purpose the writs were extended from the maritime places to the whole of the kingdom, a procedure, Laud wrote, ' I pray God bless . . . for if it go well, the King will be a great master at sea, and in these active times we, by God's blessing, may be more safe by land.' [2] In some of the country places people were found who ' assumed the character of

[1] *Hist. MSS. Com.*, 12 ii, 95.
[2] Strafford, *Letters*, i. 438.

patriots,' and refused to pay their contribution towards the tax, but the majority of the writs were executed with great facility.[1]

The command of the second ship-money fleet was bestowed on the Earl of Northumberland, and Mainwaring was commissioned to the Unicorn, a second rate of 34 guns, built in 1633. Though the number of ships under Northumberland's command only exceeded that of the previous year by two, it comprised no less than 24 king's ships as against the 19 that sailed with Lindsey. The following list gives the names of the ships, with their commanders, guns, and crews.[2]

Ships.	Commanders.	Tons.	Ord-nance.	Men.
Admiral's Squadron.				
Triumph . .	Earl of Northumberland, Admiral	776	44	300
Unicorn . .	Sir Henry Mainwaring	621	34	250
Convertive .	John Mennes	621	34	200
Victory . .	Walter Stewart	721	40	260
Swallow . .	Thomas Kirke	478	34	150
Jonas[3] . .	Richard Fielding	×	×	220
Neptune[3] .	Ben. Johnson	×	×	220
4th Whelp .	Sir Elias Hickes	186	14	60
Greyhound Pinnace	Robert Turner	×	×	50

[1] *Cal. S.P. Dom.*, 1636–37, pref. x.

[2] This list differs slightly from that given in Clowes, ii. pp. 73–5, and in Mr. Oppenheim's edition of Monson's *Naval Tracts*, iii. 252, both as regards ships and commanders. It is taken from Northumberland's own Journal (*S.P. Dom.*, Charles I, cccxliii. 72). × Blank in the original.

[3] Merchant ships fitted out by the City of London.

Ships.	Commanders.	Tons.	Ord-nance.	Men.
	Vice-Admiral's Squadron.			
St. Andrew [1] .	Sir John Pennington	783	42	260
Henrietta Maria	Thomas Porter	793	42	250
Nonsuch . .	John Povey	619	38	220
Repulse . .	Lewis Kirke	764	40	260
HappyEntrance	George Carteret	539	30	160
Bonaventure .	Henry Stradling	557	32	170
Adventure .	Thomas Price	287	24	100
10th Whelp .	Francis Smith	186	14	60
Roebuck . .	Robert Slingsby	×	×	50
	Rear-Admiral's Squadron.			
James . .	Sir Henry Mervin	875	48	260
Charles . .	Thomas Kettleby	810	44	250
Garland . .	Richard Fogge	567	34	170
Defiance . .	David Murray	875	38	250
Assurance .	Jeremy Brett	610	34	200
Mary Rose .	John Fletcher	321	26	100
5th Whelp .	John Burley	186	14	60
2nd Whelp .	Phillip Hill	186	14	60
True Love [2] .	Peter Lindsey	×	×	100

The instructions given to the Earl of Northumberland were almost identical to those issued to Lindsey in the previous year, but in addition 'Brief instructions for a sea-fight' were also given, whereas in the 'Instructions' of 1630, only one article (No. 18) dealt with tactics, the rest being constituted of 'articles of war, sailing instructions, and general directions for the conduct

[1] Substituted for the *Anne Royal*, which was wrecked on her way to join the fleet.
[2] Merchant ship fitted out by the City of London.

of a fleet at sea.' [1]   An eminent naval authority
has written that ' the inaccessibility of the official
Fighting Instructions from time to time issued to
the fleet has long been a recognised stumbling-
block to students of naval history,' [2] and therefore it may be permissible to print those issued
by Northumberland in 1636, which, though brief,
have hitherto not been published, as far as we are
aware.   They are entitled :

Brief directions for a sea-fight in case of encounter. [3]
Our rendezvous whilst we are to the north-west is
Flamboro' Head, and so to the northward some ten
leagues off the shore.

If we meet with an enemy that will oppose us, we are
to use all diligence to get the wind of them if possible
we can, and then to fetch them up.   The Admiral to
join fight with their Admiral, the Vice-Admiral
with their Vice-Admiral, and the Rear-Admiral with
their Rear-Admiral, if it may be done without losing
any good advantage ; and so for the Admiral, Vice,
and Rear Admiral of the squadron.

Directions for the Admiral's squadron.

1. If the Admiral be engaged the Victory is to
second him, and the Neptune the Victory.

2. If my Vice-Admiral be engaged, the Jonah is to
second him, and the 4th Whelp to second him.

3. And if my Rear-Admiral be engaged, the Swallow
is to second him, and the Swan to second him.

4. Every ship is to keep such a distance that they
hinder not one another, and that they be sure not to
hurt any of our fleet with their ordnance, nor come foul
one of another.

---

[1] Corbett, *Fighting Instructions*, 1530–1816, p. 76 (Navy
Records Soc.).

[2] Sir Julian Corbett, *ibid.*, pref. i.   The instructions
issued in 1635 are printed in Monson's *Naval Tracts*, ed.
Oppenheim, vol. iv. (Navy Record Soc.).

[3] *S.P. Dom.*, Charles I, cccxliii. 72.

5. If the Admiral be laid aboard by a ship of war, or by a fire ship, and that the enemy with a ship, or ships, lie close by, plying him with small shot, and hinder him from putting out the fire, or clearing himself, then his second is to thrust in between the enemy's ship and the Admiral, to give him time to clear himself and put out the fire; if he be not near, then the next of his squadron is to do it, and so for all the fleet.

6. If it happen that any of our fleet be engaged, so that he is like to be lost unless he be relieved, then in that case the ship that is next him, although he have the vantage of an enemy's ship, yet he is to leave the pursuit of that ship, and presently to succour that ship of our fleet that is engaged.

7. If any man that is side by side with an enemy's ship receive a shot under water, or have a mast, or yard shot by the board, or have plied their ordnance so long till they be hot, and cannot well come off, then his second to thrust in between him and the enemy's ship, till he can free himself and come into his place again, and so of any second, or any of the squadrons if they have none side by side with them; in the meantime they are to ply their chase and luff pieces to rake the enemy's ship, or ships, fore and aft.

8. If we do assail an enemy's fleet, then the Vice-Admiral of the fleet to go ahead with his squadron, and to begin the fight, and so his second as before, unless it be thought fit to lie side by side till he have spoiled, or disabled his enemy, in that case his second to rake the enemy fore and aft.

9. If any ship being in fight with an enemy's ship which shall bear room, or forsake the fight by way of flight, you shall not chase the said ship out of the fleet, but engage yourself where you shall see the most resistance to be made by the enemy, to weaken the force of those that shall most strongly oppose us.

10. The uncertainty of a sea fight is such that no certain instructions can be given, by reason till we come to it we know not how the enemy will work, and then (as often befals) one ship will becalm another, and some not possible to luff or board up as they would

because of ships that are near them, and many other accidents, which must be left to every captain to govern by his own discretion and valour.

On paper the fleet presented a formidable appearance,[1] but its strength was seriously undermined by the twin evils of the Stuart régime— bad victuals and inefficient seamen. In many cases the food served out to the men proved so unwholesome that it was thrown overboard. During the voyage from Chatham to the Hope, there was scarce a seafaring man on board Mainwaring's ship, with the exception of the officers ! Pennington's flagship, the Anne Royal, was wrecked in the river through the indiscretion of her master, Peter White, who, contrary to orders, had left the ship unmoored. When informed by the steward that the hold was full of water, he hoisted the top-sails, and so overset the ship ' which had fallen flat if the main-yard, being stricken, had not held her up.'[2] This was Nottingham's Ark Royal of 1588, rebuilt and renamed, which he lovingly stated ' was the odd ship of the world for all conditions.' That she was held in scant veneration by Northumberland's seamen is revealed by the fact, that when wrecked, the carpenter and others cut holes in her side to enable them to get their clothes out ![3] The St. Andrew was afterwards commissioned to take the place of the Ann Royal, and on the 20th of May part of the fleet weighed and sailed west from the Downs. The French were known to have a large fleet at Rochelle, and Northumberland's

---

[1] It was stated to have been the most powerful fleet fitted out from England up to that date.

[2] *S.P. Dom.*, Charles I, cccxix. 4, 13.

[3] Oppenheim, 221. *S.P. Dom.*, Charles I, cccxix. 15.

instructions were to watch it. While his ships were waiting in the Downs, two Dunkirk frigates, with four French vessels which they had taken at sea, came into the harbour under Pendennis Castle, Falmouth. After a brief stay of two or three days they set sail, and were encountered by a Hollander, the Black Bull of Amsterdam, commanded by Captain Van Galen,[1] who chased one of the frigates back into the harbour. Thereupon the fort opened fire on the Black Bull, which promptly tacked about and chased the other frigate into Helford, following her about a mile into the river, until they both touched ground. Not content with that, Van Galen landed thirty musketeers on the south bank of the river, and succeeded in capturing the frigate. This was 'an insolency not to be endured,' and Northumberland was instructed to give order for some of his fleet to scour the seas for the Hollander, and apprehend him, so as to secure those seas 'from pickeroons, and sea rovers, who violate his Majesty's roads and ports.' It stands to the credit of Northumberland's men that they effected the capture of the Black Bull soon after receiving these instructions, and on the 23rd of May the Hollander was brought into Portsmouth Harbour. In order that she should not escape, her rudder was unhanged and her sails taken ashore.[2]

Three days later the fleet 'had beaten up' to Portland Road, where it was detained by

---

[1] Van Galen was a typical Dutch sailor. As Admiral Van Galen he is remembered by his courageous bearing, when mortally wounded, during an action with the English fleet off Leghorn in 1653.

[2] Northumberland's Journal, *S.P. Dom.*, Charles I, cccxxv. 20.

contrary winds. While off Portland eight Dutch
men-of-war were encountered, to which Northumberland gave chase, but owing to the superior
sailing qualities of the Hollanders, the English
were unable to come up with them.[1]

In the meantime both Pennington and Mainwaring were detained in the Downs by not having
sufficient men to man their ships. In this respect
Mainwaring was not so unfortunate as his
colleague, and on the 1st of June he was able
to join Northumberland off the Lizard. Out of
the 250 men turned over from the Anne Royal
to Pennington's flag-ship, the St. Andrew, 220
deserted, and though 20 new gunners were pressed
for service, not one put in an appearance. To
such an extent was Pennington handicapped,
that it was not until the 12th of June that he was
able to set sail to the westward to join his
Admiral. 'Never,' he wrote, had he been 'so
troubled to get men since he went to sea.'[2] On
the 5th of June Northumberland records that
'we saw 13 sail that held in their course towards
us for a while, and then stood off again, but
they being to windward of us none of our ships
could reach them.' The following day, however,
the English fleet 'fetched them in,' when they
proved to be Hamburgers and Flemings bound
from St. Lucar to Dover. It afterwards trans-
pired that at first they believed the English ships
to be French men-of-war on account of the 'blue
and white flags of our squadrons,' and had

---

[1] Except where otherwise stated, the whole of the operations of the 1636 fleet is taken from Northumberland's own
Journal in the *Domestic State Papers*, Charles I, cccxliii. 72.

[2] *S.P. Dom.*, Charles I, cccxxvi. 10. Several other ships,
including the *Repulse*, *Swallow*, *Assurance*, and *Mary Rose*,
were also detained for the same reason.

resolved to run their ships aground sooner than fall into French hands. By the 9th the English ships were 'half seas over betwixt Lands End and Scilly,' when intelligence was received that the French fleet were at Belle Isle. Northumberland immediately shaped his course to meet it, but that same evening the wind began to blow hard from the north-west, and the English fleet were forced to ride it out all night. As a result they were driven 'easterly off Yarmouth,' and during the storm the Defiance spent her foretop-mast. The following day the weather showed no signs of improvement, and owing to many of the fleet being in need of fresh water and ballast, it was resolved to make for Plymouth Sound. Here they anchored on the 11th, but it continued so tempestuous that the ship's boats could not stir to fetch either water or ballast till the 16th of the month.[1] Northumberland continued to receive rumours concerning the French fleet; and while at Plymouth he was informed that it had cruised towards Dunkirk. Putting on all sail he hurried up Channel in the hope of meeting it, but on arriving in the Downs on the 24th, he found that the report was false. Meanwhile the season for fishing in the King's seas and on the north coasts had begun, and the English fleet remained in the Downs till the

---

[1] The humorous side of the cruise is depicted by Viscount Conway in the *Triumph*, who, writing about this time, states that owing to the continual bad weather they could 'neither sleep nor eat quietly.' He goes on to state that one night while at supper 'a tumble of the ship flung all the dishes on the ground. Dowse let go the hold of a post to take up a shoulder of mutton, but his unsteady footing made him sit down on the sauce of one dish, with his feet in the buttered meat of another' (*Hist. MSS. Com.*, 14 ii, 35).

I.   R

19th of July, 'expecting directions for our
northern voyage, and in providing pilots and
other necessaries for the same.' The Lords of
the Admiralty had prepared 100 licences signed
by the King, with blanks for such busses and
other fishing-boats ' as will take the same.' For
the privilege of fishing in these seas, the foreigner
in future was to obtain a licence, and Northumberland was instructed to repair to the Holland
fishing-fleet, and exact such duties as had been
fixed (12*d*. a ton from each vessel that carried
a licence), in acknowledgment of the King's
'sovereignty and hereditary dominion in his
seas.' In the event of a buss fishing without a
licence, Northumberland was empowered to bring
the vessel and fish into one of his Majesty's ports.[1]
Having received his instructions and 'other
necessaries,' the Earl 'loosed' from the Downs,
shaping his course northward. By the 24th of
July the fleet had reached 'about the height
of Tynemouth,' when Northumberland resolved
to call all the captains together in order that
there should be no misunderstanding concerning
the instructions that had been given to every
one of them. Four days later the fleet arrived

---

[1] Northumberland MSS. (*Hist. MSS. Com.*, iii. 72–3).
The northern herring fishing was almost entirely monopolised
by the Dutch. They kept 3000 busses at sea, and their
catch of herrings on the English coast was reputed to amount
to £1,000,000 a year (Clowes, ii. 72). During the first half
of the 17th century their operations were carried on between
the Shetlands and the Kentish coast. Their fleets sailed
to the fishing-grounds in June and the autumn. From June
24 to July 25 the fishery was carried on in the north; from
July 25 to September 14, south of Buchan Ness; September 25
to November 25, off the coast of Yarmouth; November 25 to
January 31, off the mouth of the Thames and the Kentish
coast (Edmundson, *Anglo-Dutch Rivalry*, p. 160).

at the fishing-grounds, where they found sixteen sail of busses guarded by one of their own men-of-war. As soon as the Dutch discerned the English ships, they made from them 'with all the sail they could pack on,' and owing to their superior sailing qualities, Northumberland found it impossible to fetch them up, with the exception of the man-of-war, which, from the first, was far astern. On the following day, the 29th, it was decided to divide the fleet into three squadrons, in the hope that the busses would not find it so easy to elude their vigilance. Accordingly the Vice-Admiral's squadron was despatched to the north as high as Buchan Ness, while Mervin, the Rear-Admiral, was sent to the south as low as Flamborough Head. Before departure it was impressed upon all the captains the necessity of using their best endeavours to make the Hollanders accept the licences. In the meantime Northumberland had arranged to ply to and fro between Buchan Ness and Flamborough Head for the same purpose. By the 5th of August his ships were off Aberdeen, and up to then they had only succeeded in distributing a few licences. Nevertheless, he continued to beat off and on the coast till the 8th, and in the afternoon of the following day he was joined by his Vice-Admiral, Pennington, who was even less fortunate, having persuaded only three busses to accept the licences. On the 10th the two squadrons passed to the south of the Firth of Forth, and on the following day they found themselves among a great fleet of about 200 fishing-boats, zealously guarded by five Dutch men-of-war. To Mervin, the Rear-Admiral, belonged the honour of discovering this fleet, and prior to Northumberland's arrival he had persuaded about thirty of them to accept the licences, and now the combined squadrons effected the distribution of 100 more. What ultimate success would have attended their efforts it is impossible to say, for on the morning of the 13th a sudden storm dispersed the English fleet, and the Triumph, Northumberland's flagship, was forced to make for Scarborough, where it was eventually joined by the rest of the fleet. The Earl now sailed for the Downs, and on the morning of the 20th, a fleet of twenty sail was descried on the horizon. On coming up with them they proved to be Dutch men-of-war, and as soon as the English ' stood with them,' the Hollanders ' took in all their flags, struck their topsails, and every ship one after another saluted us with their guns, which we answered.' These formalities over, the Dutch Admiral, Van Dorp, came aboard the Triumph to explain the purpose of his presence, which was to prevent the licences being forced upon his countrymen. His dismay when he learned that the English fleet had already effected their mission, can better be imagined than described, and it was unfortunate for Van Dorp that he had received his instructions too late to render assistance. Two days later Northumberland arrived in the Downs, and remained there for some time while his ships were revictualled. At the end of August he despatched three or four of the fleet to the west, to ply along the coast between Lands End and Scilly, and pursue all ' Turks ' and other pirates infesting those parts, the King desiring that his subjects in the western counties might ' take knowledge of his care of them, and find the benefit of his fleet at sea.' The satisfactory result of Northumberland's cruise among the Dutch fishing-fleet stimulated the King to further action, and he therefore resolved to send the Earl to the east coast on a similar mission. Accordingly, on the 16th of September, having taken in most of their provisions, the fleet 'loosed from the Downs' with a fair wind, and anchored in Yarmouth Roads on the 18th. Here it remained till the 22nd, getting pilots and other necessaries, when information was received that some Hollanders were cruising outside the roadstead. The fleet thereupon weighed, and 'stood off to sea,' but failed to find any trace of them. Their vigilance, however, was soon rewarded, for on the 28th a fleet of fifty sail of busses and two or three men-of-war were descried to windward. The Earl immediately set sail, and while following the Hollanders, which 'would not come near them,' they ran into a larger fleet of sixty sail, guarded by three men-of-war. Northumberland records that 'when we came amongst them, we let fall our anchors, and made their men-of-war do so too.' Following on this 'all the busses came about us'; but it was found that most of them had formerly taken licences, and such as were unprovided agreed to accept them. The distribution of these occupied Northumberland till the 5th of October, by which time he had begun to despair of giving out any more, so the fleet made for Yarmouth, where it arrived on the following day. From Yarmouth the ships were dispersed to their various bases, and on the 25th of October Mainwaring brought the Unicorn into Portsmouth, having received orders to revictual his ship for the winter guard of the sea.[1]

[1] *S.P. Dom.*, Charles I, cccxxxiv. 30 ; dxxxvi. ; November 1636.

Though the second ship-money fleet accomplished little more than its predecessor, its presence had the salutary effect of keeping the French out of the Channel. This in itself was enough to justify the existence of a regular fleet, and Charles was now determined that, ' sooner than surrender his dominion of the sea, he would give up England itself.' [1] In furtherance of this policy the third ship-money writ was issued on the 9th of October.

There were many defects both in the *personnel* and the *matériel* of the second ship-money fleet, and it stands to the credit of Northumberland [2] that he used his best endeavours to remedy them for the succeeding fleets. He was young and full of zeal for the King's service, and had carefully noted the abuses and defects that flourished in the fleet of 1636. Soon after coming ashore he drew up a statement, and embodied the same in thirteen articles for presentation to the King. The points to which he drew the King's attention were [3] :

1. Divers of your Majesty's ships are so old and decayed that the repair of them is a great and continual charge, and the ships are able to do little service.

2. The girdling of some of your Majesty's ships and taking away their galleries will add much to their force.

3. The leakiness of so many of his Majesty's ships and illness of their masts must proceed from some negligence.

4. That all his Majesty's ships are furnished with much ill cordage.

[1] Gardiner, viii. 158.

[2] Algernon Percy, 10th Earl of Northumberland, born 1602, Lord High Admiral 1638, died 1668.

[3] Hollond's *Discourse* (Navy Rec. Soc.), ed. by Dr. J. R. Tanner, pp. 376–87.

5. The making mean men press-masters doth occasion many abuses.

6. Laying in six months' victual is very incommodious.

7. Much of the victuals naught and short in the proportions.

8. The want of a treasurer very inconvenient to all the fleet.

9. The paymaster refuseth to pay men turned over from other ships, if they bring not tickets from the ships where they have first served.

10. The paymaster will pay no tickets but to the parties themselves unto whom the money is due.

11. If the paymaster have it in his power to refuse whom he will, he may draw men to what composition he pleaseth.

12. Great sums are owing to the Chest.[1]

13. That 2s. in the pound is usually abated upon all such moneys as are lent to supply the poor men's wants upon any occasion.

The truth of these articles was fully testified to by the various officers serving under Northumberland, and a court of inquiry was held, which examined Pennington, Mervin, and Mainwaring among others. It was generally agreed that several of the King's ships were very much decayed, unfit to be repaired, and of little use. The most serviceable were the Assurance, Adventure, Black George, Defiance, and Repulse. The St. Denis, Dreadnought, and divers others, the witnesses stated, were not worth the charge bestowed on them. Two of the fleet, the Repulse and Defiance, being so old, were not able to bear out their lower tier of ordnance in any weather.[2]

Mainwaring's evidence is still preserved, and is headed: 'Concerning those articles sent down

---

[1] *I.e.*, the Chatham Chest: founded by Sir John Hawkins and Drake for disabled seamen.

[2] Hollond's *Discourse*, pp. 362–6.

by the Lord-General, my opinion and knowledge is as followeth'[1]:

To the first my opinion hath been long, and is still, which is likewise the opinion of the ablest seamen we have, that it were better husbandry for his Majesty to build new ships in the room of the old that are decayed, rather than to patch them up, which, as we had experience this voyage, proved dangerous and unserviceable.

To the second, concerning girdling, I think I know it fit to be applied to all his Majesty's ships that are tender sided, to some more, to some less, as the quality of their defect will require, the experience whereof I had this voyage in the Unicorn, which being a ship condemned as unserviceable for not bearing, being girdled only with 3, 4, and 5 inch plank, 7 strakes, is now as stiff a ship to bear sail as I think any is in the kingdom. As for galleries, I am utterly against such as are exorbitant, as the Triumph's now are, and the George and St. Andrew were, but being as they are now reformed, I hold them a great ornament to the ship without board, a great conveniency within board, and no prejudice to the quality or sailing of the ship, nor any danger in fighting, being galleries by reason they are not pitched, but seared and painted, are not so apt to fire as the chain wales, or other parts of the ship that are pitched.

To the third for the leaking, we had very good experience to his Majesty's great disservice this voyage; that divers ships were sent in by reason of their leakiness, and so all the charge the King was at in setting them out was lost, and the fleet so much the weaker by their absence, the fault must needs be in the negligence of the caulkers, or carpenters, who were to oversee them.

To the fifth, I never saw a ship so meanly manned as the Unicorn was when she came from Chatham to the Hope, scarce a seafaring man except the officers; men of poor and wretched person, without clothes,

---

[1] Brit. Museum, *Add. MS.*, 9294, ff. 489-91, and *S.P. Dom.*, Charles I, cccxxxviii. 39. One account supplements the other.

or ability of body, tradesmen, some that were never at sea—a thatcher, glover, or the like,[1] who these men did affirm, that in the same place there were store of sufficient seamen, which the press-masters refused or dispensed with, so that I can impute the ill manning of our ships to the ill choice of men in that service; the inconveniency to his Majesty's service is more apparent in losing conduct money, in loss of the service of his ships whilst they stay to be re-mended in the river.

To the sixth, that four months' victual for the service of the Narrow Seas laid in at the first, whereof at the most there should be but one month dry salted, the rest in repacked pickle, and the other two months meat new killed and packed would be very wholesome for the company, and good of the service.

To the seventh, concerning the victuals, I have had many complaints this voyage, and much ado with my company. There was in the Unicorn much bad victuals, as appears by the certificate of the officers of that ship, who are to give account of the victuals on behalf of the company, who testify that of the first six months' victuals all the dry salted beef proved very bad, which was for four months, and that it was without reason so to victual, for it was white and blue mouldy, not fitting to be spent but on necessity. The pickled beef was very faulty, because it was not repickled from the bloody pickle, except ten hogsheads, which being repickled proved well. Two or three hogsheads of pease were faulty. One hogshead of pork stank. Both the ling and haberdine [2] was very bad, so that there was little or

---

[1] Captain Carteret stated that in his ship, the *Entrance*, out of a crew of 150, not more than twelve besides the officers could take the helm. In Raleigh's day the same difficulty was experienced, and owing to the bribery prevalent among the press-masters, it became a proverb among seafaring men, ' that the muster-masters do carry the best and ablest men in their pockets' (*Works*, viii. 346).

[2] Mervin in the *James* reported that about 300 lings were so corrupt that they tainted the hold and were thrown overboard (Hollond, pp. 382–3). Haberdine was sun-dried cod.

none of it dressed all the voyage, except the two first months, for when it was boiled the men would not eat it, but threw it overboard. The bread was some of it old, some new, mingled together. The second victualling for one month, which was taken in at the Downs, proved well.[1]

To the eighth, I conceive it a very necessary thing for the service of his Majesty, in preserving the company in health, to have one or more treasurers in a fleet who may issue out money to the sick, who for want of money, and their own, which they have served for, we must either keep aboard, or turn ashore in great danger of starving, or not to be received into any house, so that I have seen some die upon the strand for lack of relief. Also, that men who have served long, and their clothes worn out, may have some part of their money to furnish them, the want thereof this last voyage some of the best men daily fell sick, or are not able to stand to their labour upon the decks, or to keep their watches in the winter. That by paying discharged men the King saves conduct money. And it is requisite to have money to pay for ballast and other petty charges, the want whereof is a great discommodity.

To the rest I cannot answer anything, for they are out of my knowledge, being I have not lately been employed in his Majesty's service, and so was not at my pay, nor know the manner of their proceedings in that way.

H. MAINWARING.

That the Lords of the Admiralty were greatly incensed by Northumberland's action is shown in a letter of the latter to Strafford, in which he writes : ' The Lords Commissioners are not well pleased at my proceedings, because I did not first

---

[1] The surgeon of the *Unicorn*, William Thorp, certified that the musty bread sent aboard ' caused a soreness of the mouths and throats of the crew,' sixteen or seventeen of them being affected at the same time.

acquaint them with these things ; I suppose that they think, that these things passing for some years unquestioned may be imputed to a negligence in them.' [1]

Even in those days the country suffered from the effects of officialdom, for on the 7th of February 1637 Northumberland again wrote to Strafford : ' The slackness in punishing the offenders hath made them so insolent that they now justify those facts, which hitherto they have tacitly committed. This hath brought me to a resolution not to trouble myself any more with endeavouring a reformation, unless I be commanded to it.' [2]

However, on the 16th of March the King, with the Lords of the Admiralty, considered the evidence in council, at which Northumberland was present. Although measures were recommended for remedying the abuses, the only point on which the council appear to have agreed was with regard to the paymaster ; this official they decided should not in future ' abate or take to himself two shillings of the pound of the seamen's wages for collecting any money for the creditors.' [3]

[1] Strafford, _Letters_, ii. p. 40.   [2] _Ibid._, ii. p. 49.
[3] Hollond, pp. 403-4.

CHAPTER X

1637–42

THE SHIP-MONEY FLEETS

WHILE Charles was discussing with his Council and the Lords of the Admiralty the serious charges raised by Northumberland, preparations for the third ship-money fleet were in active progress. Earlier in the year it had been estimated that the total sum due under the writs would amount to £210,600, and that the resulting ships would number 45. Of these, it was proposed that 28 should be fitted out for the guard of the coast, and 6 for an expedition against the pirates of Sallee. The remainder of the money was to be expended thus : (1) Repairs to ships, £24,000 ; (2) for the continuance of ships at sea beyond eight months, £6,000 ; (3) for reimbursing the overplus paid out of the Exchequer in 1636, £30,000 ; (4) repairs of forts, castles, etc., £5,000 ; (5) towards preparations for 1638, £13,459.[1]

For three successive years the tax had now been levied, and in February 1637 Charles sent to have the opinion of the judges on the legality of the impost.[2] Their answer, delivered a few days later, was entirely favourable to the King's ambitions.

[1] *S.P. Dom.*, Charles I, cccxliii. 15, January 5, 1637.
[2] *Ibid.*, cccxlvi. 11.

We are of opinion [they informed Charles] that when the good and safety of the kingdom in general is concerned, and the whole kingdom in danger, your Majesty may by writ under the great Seal of England command all the subjects of this kingdom at their charge to provide and furnish such number of ships, with men, victual, and munition, and for such time as your Majesty shall think fit for the defence and safeguard of the kingdom.[1]

Though it may be argued that we were not actually engaged in hostile operations at the time, and that therefore the safety of the kingdom was not imperilled by the dangers of invasion, there is no knowing what the powerful French and Dutch fleets, which were afloat, would have done had they found us unprepared on sea. Having satisfied himself as to the legality of ship-money, Charles therefore persisted in his policy that a powerful navy was both desirable and necessary for preserving the safety of the kingdom and protecting its commerce, besides being a valuable diplomatic asset. To this end a fleet comprising 19 ships of the Royal Navy and 9 armed merchantmen was ordered to assemble in the Downs, and was placed under the command of the Earl of Northumberland as before. The ships and their captains are set forth in the list on pp. 254-5.

From this list it will be seen that Mainwaring was again commissioned to the Unicorn of 46 guns ; but on proceeding to join her at Chatham at the end of March, he found that the officers of the ordnance had a ' design to take six principal pieces of ordnance from her.' The reason for their action is not quite clear, and may

---

[1] *S.P. Dom.*, Charles I, cccxlvi. 14, February 7, 1636-7.

'A List of his Majesty's Fleet set forth for guard of the coast for eight months from the 20th of April, 1637, to the 20th of December following.' [1]

Ships.	Tons.	Men.	Captains.
Triumph . .	776	300	Earl of Northumberland, Admiral.
Swiftsure . .	746	260	Sir J. Pennington, Vice-Admiral.
Bonaventure .	557	170	Sir H. Mervin, Rear-Admiral.
Unicorn . .	767	250	Sir H. Mainwaring.
James . .	875	260	Capt. John Povey *up till September, afterwards* Captain Walter Stewart.
Henrietta Maria	793	250	Captain Thomas Kettleby and Captain David Murray *successively.*
Rainbow . .	731	240	Captain Povey.[2]
Vanguard . .	751	250	Captain John Mennes.
St. George .	792	260	Captain David Murray.
Convertive .	621	200	Captain Richard Fogge.
Dreadnought .	552	140	Captain Henry Stradling and Captain Thomas Kirke *successively.*
Mary Rose .	321	100	Captain Lewis Kirke and Captain Thomas Trenchfield *successively.*

[1] *S.P. Dom.*, Charles I, ccclxxxviii, 72, and *Pipe Office, Declared Accounts*, 2278.

[2] After September, probably in succession to Captain Stewart.

Ships.	Tons.	Men.	Captains.
1st Whelp . .	186	60	Captain Richard Donnell and Captain Robert Slingsby *successively.*
2nd Whelp .	186	60	Captain Phillip Hill.
5th Whelp . .	186	60	Captain Edward Popham.
Greyhound .	×	×	Mr. Thomas Rabnett, Master.
Roebuck . .	×	×	Mr. Ruben Broad, Master.
Swan Frigate .	×	×	Henry Dunning.
Nicodemus Frigate	×	×	Captain Richard Bullard.

Merchant ships: Unicorn, Industry, Mayflower, Richard and Mary, Pleiades, Margaret, William, Royal Prudence, Defence.

have been due to Pennington reporting her crank and tender sided, though Edward Boate, the keeper of naval stores, believed it to have been 'an act of malice,' which he requested should be put a stop to.[1] As nothing further is heard of the matter, it is to be presumed that the intention of the ordnance officers was frustrated, and that she sailed with her full armament.

On the 15th of April Northumberland received his commission as ' Admiral, Custos maris, and General of all our forces, for this present intended service ' ;[2] and by the 20th of the month nearly

× Blank in the original.
[1] *Cal. S.P. Dom.*, Charles I, March 28, 1637.
[2] *Northumberland MSS.*, p. 74.

all the fleet had 'entered into sea victuals.'
Though Pennington was again appointed Vice-
Admiral, the Lords of the Admiralty were un-
decided in their selection of a Rear-Admiral.
The choice lay between Sir Henry Mervin and
Mainwaring, and up till the last week in May
the matter was still unsettled.   On the 22nd
of that month Pennington wrote to Nicholas
that he was told 'Sir Henry Mainwaring rides
yet Rear-Admiral,' and that he would be glad
to know who should have the place.[1]   At what
date the decision was arrived at is not known,
but Mervin eventually received the command
and hoisted his flag in the Bonaventure.   In
the meantime Northumberland was detained
by not having his 'despatch from court,' so
Pennington was instructed to cruise in the
Channel with a number of ships ; while Captain
Stradling in the Dreadnought received orders to
repair to the west with a whelp and a pinnace for
the 'securing of those coasts.'   On the 2nd of
May Pennington reported the Dutch Admiral,
Van Dorp, sailing between Dunkirk and the
Downs in command of 20 stout men-of-war,
and at the beginning of June Stradling was in
action with 4 sail of Dutchmen homeward bound
from Brazil. He had ordered them to strike
to the King's ships, a request which the Admiral
and Vice-Admiral complied with. The Rear-
Admiral, however, refused to strike his flag, and
Stradling, in accordance with his instructions,
boarded him, and eventually lodged the Dutchman in Plymouth Fort, where he was detained
for a fortnight, until a satisfactory explanation
was forthcoming.[2]   On the 7th of June Northum-

---

[1] *S.P. Dom.*, Charles I, cccliv. iii ii ; ccclvii. 25.
[2] *Ibid.*, ccclxi. 41.

berland came aboard the Triumph, which was then riding in Tilbury Hope in company with six others of the fleet ; and eight days later he joined his Vice-Admiral in the Downs. There the fleet remained in a state of inactivity till the end of the month, and even then its only employment consisted of convoying the Elector Palatine over to Holland. For this purpose the whole fleet weighed from the Downs on the 29th of June, but they were hardly clear of the North Foreland when a sudden gale was encountered, which 'carried by the board' the main and mizzen top masts of the St. George. By the afternoon of the 30th they 'made the coast of Holland,' and anchored about 3 or 4 leagues off the entrance to Goree, while the Vanguard and the St. George escorted the Elector into Helvoetsluys amid salutes from the rest of the ships. This mission being accomplished, the fleet shaped its course for the Downs. At sunset on Sunday, July 2, Northumberland records, 'we had sight of a high land which we conceived to be Calais cliffs,'[1] and to avoid coming near the shore in the night, the fleet tacked about. On the following day the ships anchored in Dover Road, coming into the Downs with the next morning's tide. There they remained from the 4th of July till the 9th of August. No foe was to be found, and with the exception of employing ships for the transportation of ambassadors and others, and going with convoys to various places, Northumberland's fleet played a watching game. To the Earl these trifling employments did not appeal, and on the 15th of

---

[1] Northumberland's Journal, 1637 (in *S.P. Dom.*, Charles I, ccclxxii. 93). Except where otherwise stated, the whole of the proceedings of the 1637 fleet are taken from this Journal.

July he wrote to Strafford from aboard the
Triumph in the Downs, expressing his dissatisfaction : ' To ride in this place at anchor a whole
summer together without hope of action, to see
daily disorders in the fleet, and not have means to
remedy them, and to be in an employment where
a man can neither do service to the State, gain
honour to himself, nor do courtesies for his
friends, is a condition that I think nobody will be
ambitious of.' [1]

By this time the season for fishing in the
King's seas had commenced, and Northumberland
was instructed to send one of his ships to the
north, for the purpose of distributing licences
to the Dutch fishermen, who in return for accept-
ing them were promised protection against the
Dunkirk privateers.[2] About the middle of July,
Captain Fielding in the merchant ship Unicorn
was commissioned for this duty, and on the 18th
of the month he arrived among the busses off
Buchan Ness. The fulfilment of his mission
was impossible from the first. At the fishing-
grounds he found as many as six or seven hundred
busses, zealously guarded by twenty-three of their
own men-of-war, and an attempt to distribute
the licences was strongly opposed by the Dutch
Admiral, who refused to let any boat pass among
the fishermen. Fielding, therefore, had no alternative but to return with his mission unaccomplished. At the beginning of August, Northumberland, for want of better employment, was
ordered to sail to the westward, and on the 9th

[1] Strafford, *Letters*, ii. p. 84.
[2] ' The state of the negotiations with France, and other
causes,' prevented the King from renewing his enterprise
against the Dutch fishery on the same scale as the previous
year (Fulton, p. 319).

of the month he weighed from the Downs, cruising down Channel towards Lands End.[1] Considering the time of the year, the weather was of the worst, and on the 13th the fleet were forced to anchor in Torbay, where, Northumberland records, ' the foulness of the weather held us all that day and the next.' On the 15th the fleet passed close to Plymouth, anchoring at night off the Start. The next morning it blew a hard gale, and the weather was so thick, that some of the ships fell foul of one another, but eventually they managed to anchor in Plymouth Sound about eight o'clock in the evening. Here they were forced to remain till the 24th, when, ' with a bare wind,' the Earl states, ' we got forth to sea; but in the evening, the leeward tide being come, we stood in for Plymouth again.' The same unsettled conditions prevailed till the 28th, when the ' wind coming fair,' the fleet weighed and passed in sight of the Lizard towards the west. At night the weather again became ' thick and gusty,' and in consequence, Northumberland states, ' we handed [2] all our sails and so drove.' On the 30th, the ' wind being changed and overblowing,' the fleet bore up for Plymouth and there anchored. Here Northumberland awaited further despatches from Court, but as they were delayed, and his victuals were running short, he decided to sail for the Downs. With a very hard gale of wind the fleet succeeded in

[1] Seven ships were left in the Downs for service there. Prior to this, the *Mary Rose* and the *Roebuck* had been sent with a supply to Rainsborough before Sallee, and the *Fifth Whelp* had been wrecked, so the fleet during the westward cruise consisted of nine King's ships (*Northumberland's Journal*).

[2] Handed, *i.e.*, furled.

reaching Beachy Head on the 3rd of September, anchoring in the Downs on the following day. Here the cruise of the third ship-money fleet ended, and Northumberland was informed that 'His Majesty, taking notice that victuals in the fleet are near at an end, and considering the foulness of the weather, is pleased to give you leave to return to his presence, as soon as you have given order for the Winter Guard of the Seas.' [1]

The sailors, like Northumberland, were no doubt heartily glad to be quit of their charge, for during the western cruise it is recorded that they scarcely saw a sail, with the exception of those 'of the poor fishers that dwell upon this shore.' [2] The ships to form the Winter Guard were left to Northumberland's choice, and were to be under the command of Sir John Pennington, 'among which His Majesty' was 'well contented that Sir Henry Mainwaring's should be one.' [3] Accordingly, the Unicorn was victualled for further service, and on the 17th of October Mainwaring received orders to sail for Dieppe to bring over the French Ambassador, M. Pomponne de Bellièvre. The outward voyage was safely accomplished, but the return journey was not without incident, and owing to the tempestuous weather, Mainwaring was 'much put to it,' losing his pinnace, also an anchor and a cable, before he was able to make Dover roadstead. Severe as the buffeting was, the Unicorn, which three years previous had proved unseaworthy, managed to land the Ambassador and his suite at Dover on the night of the 25th, but the four French vessels laden with the Ambassador's belongings,

[1] *S.P. Dom.*, Charles I, ccclxvii. 38.
[2] *Ibid.*, ccclxvii. 1.
[3] *Ibid.*, ccclxvii. 38. The other ships were the *Swiftsure*, *Bonaventure*, *First Whelp*, *Second Whelp*, and *Greyhound*.

which left Dieppe at the same time, were not
so fortunate, only one of their number reaching
Dover. Of the others, one put into Hastings,
while the other two turned back. M. de Bellièvre,
naturally alarmed, feared that he had lost plate,
jewels, and money to the value of £30,000, and
Pennington ordered the Second Whelp over to
Dieppe to ascertain what had happened, but
for a whole fortnight, in spite of the endeavours
of her captain (who was repeatedly driven back),
she was weather-bound at Dover.[1]

On the 2nd of December Mainwaring brought
the Unicorn into Chatham, and his commission
ended thirteen days later.[2]

The fleets that resulted from the levy of ship-
money had up to now not met with serious
opposition, and in consequence many who were
called upon to maintain their share of the tax
were loth to forget the faults of its inception.
Nevertheless, the presence of a regular fleet in
the Channel had exerted a silent pressure on
both the Dutch and the French, and had brought
about a feeling of security to the Kingdom.
'Methinks we have a very great calm both of
the French and Dutch,' wrote that staunch
seaman Pennington,[3] and the moral effect of the
fleet on both these nations was certainly borne
out by subsequent events.

For maintaining the welfare of the State
no unprejudiced person can affirm that a powerful
fleet was not a necessity, but when the writs
were sent out for a fourth time, early in 1638,
the collection was accompanied by more general
dissatisfaction than had previously prevailed.[4]
The writs called for £70,000, but the response

---

[1] *S.P. Dom.*, Charles I, ccclxx. 64.
[2] *Ibid.*, ccclxxiii. 10.   [3] *Ibid.*, ccclxxxv. 65.
[4] Gardiner, viii. pp. 269–70 ; *Cal. S.P.*, 1637–8, pref. ix.

represented a figure far below that sum, though
the machinery for collecting the tax had attained
its perfect working order.¹ In spite of this
opposition, a fleet of 24 King's ships and 7
merchantmen was ordered to be ready by the
20th of April, and owing to the illness of the Earl
of Northumberland they were placed under the
command of Sir John Pennington. Earlier in
the year Mainwaring had been confined to his
bed through a fall from his horse, though fortunately he had sufficiently recovered by the end
of April to take his place in the fleet. The
Unicorn not being refitted in time, he was commissioned to the Charles, a ship of 44 guns, built
in 1632. As will be seen from the following list,
the fleet was considerably stronger than that of
the previous year.

'A List of his Majesty's ships that are to be
employed at Sea, Anno 1638.' ²

Ships.	Men.	Captains.
St. Andrew . .	260	Sir John Pennington, Vice-Admiral.
Victory . . .	260	Sir Henry Mervin, Rear-Admiral.
Charles . . .	250	Sir Henry Mainwaring.

¹ *Cal. S.P.*, 1637-8, pref. vii. By September 1639 the
amount received for 1638 was £41,161. The arrears for the
previous years then stood at—1635, £4,536 ; 1636, £7,181 ;
1637, £20,924 (*S.P. Dom.*, ccccxxviii. 41).

² *S.P. Dom.*, Charles I, ccclxxxvi. 99 ; ccclxxxix. 86 ;
Pipe Office, Declared Accounts, 2280. The *Sovereign of the
Seas* was inserted in the list, but she was not ready in time.
The *Convertive* was substituted for the *Antelope*. In addition
to the above there were seven merchant ships, one of which,
the *Confident*, was commanded by William Batten, the famous
admiral of the Civil War. While commissioned to this ship
he received 6s. 8d. per day (*P.O. Accounts*, 2280).

Ships.	Men.	Captains.
St. George . .	260	John Newcombe, Lieutenant.[1]
Constant Reforma-tion	250	John Povey.
Nonsuch . .	220	John Mennes.
St. Denis . .	200	Thomas Kirke.
Leopard . .	160	Henry Stradling.
Garland . .	170	David Murray.
Entrance . .	160	Richard Fogge.
Convertive . .	—	George Carteret.
Adventure . .	100	John Hall.
Expedition . .	100	Robert Slingsby.
Providence . .	100	Edmond Seaman.
1st Whelp [1] . .	60	—
6th Whelp . .	60	Richard Burley.
8th Whelp . .	60	Richard Donnell.
10th Whelp . .	60	Robert Foxe.
Greyhound . .	50	Abraham Wheeler.
Roebuck [1] . .	45	—
Swan . . .	50	Francis Simonds.
Nicodemus . .	50	Anthony Woolward.
Fortune Pink .	25	William Pett.
Mary Rose . .	—	Thomas Trenchfield.

The activities of the fleet were even more limited than in the previous years. In May, two merchant ships, the Providence and Mayflower, were employed to transport gunpowder to Dunkirk, and Pennington was ordered to stand over with the whole fleet towards that place and give them safe convoy. This may seem to have been a trivial employment for such a large fleet as Pennington's, but the salutary effect its

---

[1] I have been unable to find out who commanded the *St. George, 1st Whelp,* or *Roebuck.*

presence had on the Dutch is clearly shown by the fact, that though over 14 States men-of-war were in the roadstead, the English commander was able to report that he had passed through the blockade and seen the merchantmen safely anchored under the fort at Dunkirk. On the 8th of June the whole fleet arrived back in the Downs without meeting with any opposition, a circumstance of which Pennington was naturally proud.[1] At the beginning of August, on an alarm occasioned by the presence of ' Turkish ' pirates on the Dorset coast, the Leopard and a merchant ship were sent to those parts. So well did they do their work that by the end of the month there was no sign of the ' Turks,' and the English ships were reported to have ' at least freed the coast of them.' As a preventive against further raids, the Tenth Whelp and the Greyhound were also despatched to the west, with orders to cruise there for six weeks.[2] In the meantime the troubles in Scotland had reached an acute stage.[3] It was known that the Scots were shipping large supplies of arms and ammunition from Rotterdam and Bremen, and to intercept these the services of the fleet were requisitioned. On the 11th of August Pennington sent two of his ships to lie off the mouth of the Maas, with instructions to search all ships of Holland and the Low Countries that were bound to the northward. At the same time the Entrance

---

[1] *S.P. Dom.*, Charles I, cccxcii. 40.

[2] *Ibid.*, cccxcvii. 93.

[3] The ' National Covenant ' had been signed at Edinburgh in the early part of 1638, and in the winter following a General Assembly was held at Glasgow at which Prelacy was abolished and Presbyterianism restored (Dodd, *Covenanters*, pp. 30–33).

and the Providence were ordered to cruise off
the coast of Scotland and intercept all manner
of warlike material.[1]

These were the only employments of the
fourth ship-money fleet, and Mainwaring for his
services this year was remunerated at the rate
of 8s. a day.[2]

At the time his commission ceased a post
happened to be vacant in which his technical
knowledge and skill would have been of the
highest value to the State.   This was the Surveyorship of the Navy, rendered vacant by the death
of Kenrick Edisbury, who had held the office
since 1632 in succession to Sir Thomas Aylesbury.
It was a department in which Mainwaring had
already been employed, for it will be remembered
that during the proceedings of the Special Commission of 1626, he had undertaken the Surveyor's
duties, and the thoroughness with which he
discharged them eminently fitted him as a
successor to Edisbury.   To possess an expert
knowledge on all things that pertained to the
welfare of the Navy generally was not, however,
in those days counted as the primary qualifica-
tion for the post, and the prospect of securing it
depended solely on the length of a man's purse.
Though it was reported to be 'a troublesome
place,' and the purchase price £1500,[3] applicants
were numerous.   Mainwaring, being unable to
raise the necessary money, was one of the unsuccessful candidates, the post being eventually
granted to Captain (afterwards Sir) William
Batten, a record of whose appointment is contained in the following extract from a letter of

[1] *S.P. Dom.*, Charles I, cccxcvii. 93.
[2] *Pipe Office, Declared Accounts*, 2280.
[3] Monson's *Tracts* (Churchill's *Voyages*, iii. 339).

Northumberland's secretary, Thomas Smith, to Pennington.[1]

On Sunday last Captain Batten kissed his Majesty's hand for the Surveyor's place. His patent is drawing during pleasure only, as all patents must be hereafter. Here has been much striving for the place, Sir Henry Mainwaring, Captain Duppa, Mr. Bucke, *cum multis aliis* ; but the King, with the help of somebody else, thought him the fittest man.

Clarendon describes Batten as ' an obscure man, unknown to the Navy,' and the mysterious ' somebody else ' alluded to in the letter confirms Clarendon's other statement that Batten was ' made Surveyor for money.' [2]

During the autumn of 1638 the usual ship-money writs for the following year's fleet did not appear. In view of the serious state of affairs in Scotland it was thought wiser to decrease the amount of the writs, which were consequently not issued till January 1639. Even then the sum demanded only amounted to about a third of that levied on previous occasions, but it was estimated that this would be sufficient for the fitting out of 19 ships, which were intended for a service quite different from that of the previous fleets. The Marquis of Hamilton, High Commissioner for Scotland, who had been sent by Charles to endeavour to bring about a settle-

[1] *S.P. Dom.*, cccxcviii. 113. The post was also offered to Pennington, and Smith informed him that if he had ' a stomach to it . . . I will be cook to make ready that dish for you.'

[2] *Clarendon Rebellion*, 1826, ii. p. 340. Batten was not quite so obscure as he is represented. An hitherto unnoticed reference shows that he was sufficiently worthy to be entrusted with the command of a merchant ship in the fleet of 1638. (*See* p. 262, note.)

ment with the Covenanters, had hopelessly failed
in his mission, and in the November of 1638
he informed the King that the only way to crush
the rebellion was to blockade Scotland and cut
off its commerce by sea. Hamilton realised
what a powerful weapon the King had at his
disposal, and he believed that the situation might
be solved by the silent pressure of sea-power if
he could only persuade the King to accept his
views. He therefore ventured to unfold his plan
of campaign to Charles.

Their being is by trade [he wrote], whereof a few
ships of your Majesty's, well disposed, will easily bar
them. . . . In my opinion your ships would be best
ordered thus, eight or ten to be in the Firth. There
should be some three or four plying to and again betwixt
the Firth and Aberdeen, so long as the season of the
year will permit them to keep the seas, and when they
are no longer able, they may retire into the Firth.[1]

The ships that were in the Irish Sea, Hamilton
believed, would be sufficient to intercept all
trading vessels from the west of Scotland. Charles
eagerly seized on this suggestion, and a fleet was
immediately ordered to be prepared. At the
same time the King decided to raise an army of
30,000 horse, and lead them in person towards
Scotland. To cover the concentration of this
large army on the borders it was proposed to
hold Berwick and Carlisle.[2]

This, then, was the plan of campaign, and in
February 1639 the choice of competent commanders for the ships was under careful
consideration. The seriousness of the situation
was fully recognised by the Lords of the Admiralty,

[1] Hardwicke, *State Papers*, ii. 118.
[2] Burnet, *Dukes of Hamilton*, 113 ; Gardiner, ix. p. 1.

and, in the words of Northumberland's secretary,
they were 'troubled whom to choose for a Vice-
Admiral.[1] I desire a little of your advice herein,'
he wrote to Pennington, 'as being a business of
great consideration, for now sea-captains must
not expect to play as they have done heretofore,
but must look for such times of action as will
require commanders of skill, courage, and
fidelity.'[2]

One of his reasons in writing to Pennington
is to be found in the fact that Sir Henry Mervin,
who had sailed as Rear-Admiral in the last
three fleets, had 'given in his resolution' to
Northumberland not to accept a command in
that of 1639. At this news, we are informed,
the Earl was 'very well contented,' and Northumberland's secretary expressed the opinion that
he believed Mervin would not come into the fleet
again in haste.[3] Whatever advice Pennington
offered his chief, it must have been in the nature
of a strong recommendation of Mainwaring. He
was certainly a commander who fulfilled in a
high degree all the essentials required of a seaman,
'skill, courage, and fidelity,' and in March he
was appointed Pennington's Vice-Admiral, with
his flag in the Henrietta Maria.[4] The full list of
the fleet is here given :

[1] *S.P. Dom.*, Charles I, ccccxiii. 56.
[2] *Ibid.* It will be remembered that two years previous
there had been some talk of superseding Mervin by Mainwaring.
Mervin claimed the Admiralty of the Narrow Seas, and in
February 1639 he was suing the King for £1000, or £500 per
annum for seven years, for which sum he stated he would
relinquish his claim. Northumberland's secretary (Thomas
Smith) informed Pennington that he believed he would get
nothing (*ibid.*).
[3] *Ibid.*
[4] *Ibid.*, ccccxv. 105.

FLEET FOR THE GUARD OF THE NARROW SEAS, 1639.[1]

Rainbow . . .	Sir John Pennington, Admiral.
Henrietta Maria . .	Sir Henry Mainwaring, Vice-Admiral.
Vanguard . . .	John Povey, Rear-Admiral.
Unicorn . . .	David Murray [2]
Victory . . .	John Mennes.
Leopard . . .	George Carteret.
James . . .	Richard Fogge.
Providence . . .	Edmond Seaman.
Antelope . . .	Henry Stradling.
Mary Rose . . .	Thomas Price.
Dreadnought . .	John Hall.
Expedition . . .	Robert Slingsby.
Greyhound . . .	Abraham Wheeler.
Bonaventure. . .	Richard Fielding.
Roebuck . . .	Anthony Woolward.
2nd Whelp . . .	Richard Burley.
3rd Whelp . . .	Philip Hill.
8th Whelp . . .	Robert Foxe.
Unicorn . . .	Edward Popham.

In March, Pennington and Mainwaring with eight King's ships were ordered north. At Harwich there were 20 transports with 5000 soldiers under the command of Hamilton, and the English Admiral was instructed to call there and convoy them to the Firth of Forth. By the 29th of April the fleet and transports appeared off Berwick, which had been entered that day by strong forces under the commands of the Earls of Lindsey and Essex respectively. On the 2nd of May the English ships anchored safely in Leith Roads. The arrival of Pennington's fleet was

[1] *Pipe Office, Declared Accounts*, 2282 ; *S.P. Dom.*, Charles I, ccccxii. 20 ; Peter White's Account.

[2] Capt. Murray commanded the *Rainbow* during July and August, when Pennington transferred his flag to the *Unicorn*.

viewed with apprehension by the Scots, and the damage which it afterwards inflicted on their commerce did not tend to minimise their discomfort. The first thing to be done was to dispose of the troops, and on the 4th and 5th of the month they were landed on two islands (Inchkeith and Inchcolm), ' to exercise them in the use of their arms.' So well did the Navy do its work that by the 22nd Pennington was able to report that they had

done a very great service by making a diversion. The Scots durst not draw any men from these parts, but have been forced to keep continual guards night and day on both sides of the Firth, for fear we should land and burn their towns. Besides, we have so blocked them up by sea that they cannot stir in or out with a boat but we snap them, which does infinitely perplex and trouble them more than all the King's army.[1]

In order that the blockade should be complete, the Dreadnought, Greyhound, 9th Whelp, and some smaller vessels were sent from Dublin ' to watch Scotland on the other side,'[2] thus completing the plan of campaign as suggested by Hamilton.

That the duties which the fleet were carrying out were of a particularly arduous nature, and called for constant vigilance both on the part of the captains and the men, is shown by the fact that Pennington wrote that he was ' so tired out with a multitude of business both night and day ' that he had ' neither time to eat, drink, or sleep.'[3]

In the meanwhile the army was not inactive, and on the 31st of the month Coke wrote to

[1] *S.P. Dom.*, Charles I, ccccxxi. 128.
[2] *Ibid.*, ccccxxi. 142.   [3] *Ibid.*, ccccxxi. 128.

Mainwaring from Berwick, ordering him to proceed to Newcastle, and take aboard the Henrietta Maria various Scotchmen who had been detained as prisoners.

To my honourable friend Sir Henry Mainwaring, Knight, &c.[1]

It is his Majesty's pleasure that you take into your custody aboard your ship the persons mentioned in this paper, and dispose of them in such sort as his Majesty shall be pleased to direct.

The names of the Scottishmen to be received by you.

Lieut.-Colonel Milles.
Captain Carr.
John Hamilton.
Robert Hamilton.[2]
Mr. James Home.[3]
David Donaldson.
Alexander Penniwick.[4]
Alexander Dixon.
George Home.[4]
Hans Hofler.[5]
Captain Primrose.[5]
George Buchanan.

John Sibett, Sergeant.
David Belly.
William Admiston.
Peter Hamilton.[6]
Andrew Ramsey.
Alexander Wallace, servant to Lieut.-Colonel Milles.
John Graunt.
George Peeker.
John Rough.[5]

(Signed)   JOHN COKE.

Berwick, the last day of May 1639.

The following day the Earl of Arundel informed Windebank that the King was sending divers Scotch officers and soldiers, lately stayed by

---

[1] *S.P. Dom.*, Charles I, ccccxxii. 114.

[2] Marked 'discharged at Berwick, being never aboard.'

[3] Marked 'discharged by warrant by the Earl of Arundel, June 1.'

[4] *Ibid.*, June 4.

[5] Marked 'discharged by my Lord Marquess in the Frith, never aboard.'

[6] 'Discharged to Sir James Hamilton.'

the Marquis of Hamilton, to be embarked in the ship commanded by Sir Henry Mainwaring, who was to make for the Hope, and to ride there till he received further orders.   During the voyage to Newcastle Mainwaring met with rough weather, and in consequence the Henrietta Maria had the misfortune to lose her foremast before she anchored off that town on the 6th of June.   How this difficulty was temporarily overcome is described in the following letter to Pennington.[1]

SIR,—For all the stories of Berwick I wrote not to you because you had by word of mouth from those who know you a perfect relation. With my jury mast, which is my foretop-mast, set upon the stump of my foremast some 8 foot from the deck the ship works very well, and I have fitted to my main stay a mizzen sail, which by quartering did us good service.

I came to an anchor before the bar of Newcastle the 6th of this month, and have taken in the Scotch officers and followers about the number of 30, which I am to deliver into the hands of Secretary Windebank. The Shallop I left at Berwick with the governor, because I am commanded to return hither with all speed.

Though I have not your commands to London, I shall not fail to study wherein I may do you service, which I shall perform faithfully and affectionately.

I am,

Your affectionate friend and servant,

H. MAINWARING.

The Shields, this 7 of June.

On the 11th Mainwaring with his charges arrived at Gravesend, and during the short time they were in his company he seems to have found them a great nuisance, so much so, that he wrote to Windebank the same day, asking him to forward instructions for their removal.

[1] *S.P. Dom.*, Charles I, ccccxxiii. 51.

His letter, which is directed to ' the Right Honourable Sir Francis Windebank, Knight, his Majesty's Principal Secretary at Drury Lane,' and superinscribed ' hast these—hast—hast,' is here reproduced.[1]

RIGHT HONOURABLE,—By order from his Majesty, signified under the warrant of the Earl of Arundel, his Excellency General of his Majesty's Army, I have brought with me from Newcastle, 31 Scottish commanders and other soldiers delivered over by the Mayor of that place. And also from Berwick eleven delivered me by the Earl of Lindsey there, which I received by warrant from Mr. Secretary Coke. The copy whereof I have herewith sent your Honour with a declaration what is become of some included in that note, which are not brought by me, to show you how they were disposed of. I am commanded to address myself to your Honour for order what to do with them, which I humbly desire to receive with as much expedition as shall seem fit unto you, for I am not very fond of their company, they being a great trouble and charge to me. I have warrant to press boats or barges to bring them to you, or if it please your Honour to direct any other way, how I may be discharged of them, I shall either land them at the place you shall appoint, and in such sort, as you think fit as prisoners, with a guard or otherwise, or in any other way be ready to obey your commands for the discharge of them, as becometh one who most earnestly desireth to be esteemed

Your honour's most humble servant,

H. MAINWARING.

From on board his Majesty's Ship the Henrietta Maria, at anchor a little below Gravesend, this 11 June, 1639.

I think fit to acquaint your honour that the tide of flood will serve very well about 1 of the clock in the afternoon to-morrow, being the 12th, to bring away

---

[1] *S.P. Dom.*, Charles I, ccccxxiii. 78.

the Scotchmen for London, therefore I humbly desire
to know your honour's resolution early in the morning.

A prompt answer not being forthcoming,
Mainwaring wrote again two days later, this
time in somewhat sharper tones. In this letter,
which was composed at 3 o'clock in the morning,
he stated that while the Scotchmen were with
him he was unable to see to the refitting and
victualling of the ship.[1]

Right Honourable,—I wrote to you by packet,
dated the 11th of this month, concerning divers Scottish
officers and others, in all to the number of 42, which I
was appointed by the Lord-General the Earl of Arundel
to deliver to your Honour. I humbly desire that since
I have had them on board me this long time to my great
charge and trouble, that you will be pleased to discharge
me of them, by sending for them, or else to order that
they may be delivered on shore to the Mayor of
Gravesend, the rather for that I have a new fore-mast
to set, and a bowsprit ; to be revictualled, doctored,
and other businesses concerning the ship to despatch
with all speed, to return to his Majesty as he commanded
me, and whilst they are here we can do nothing. It
makes me doubt your Honour hath not received my
letter, that being not farther distant than 20 miles, you
have not vouchsafed an answer to
　　　　　Your honour's most humble servant,
　　　　　　　　H. Mainwaring.

*From aboard his Majesty's Ship the Henrietta Maria,
this 13 of June at 3 of the morning, 1639.*

Eventually the prisoners were sent to London,
but on the treaty of peace being signed at Berwick
on the 18th they were all liberated.[2]

[1] *S.P. Dom.*, Charles I, ccccxxiii. 94.
[2] *Ibid.*, ccccxxiv. 47, 78. The exact date on which they
were embarked is not recorded.

A week later Pennington, who was still with the fleet off Leith, was ordered to convoy the transports with the troops back to Harwich, and then to make for the Downs with all diligence.[1] The reason for his hurried recall was owing to the presence of a powerful Dutch squadron in the Channel, and on the evening of the 7th of July he arrived in the Downs, where he was joined by Mainwaring on the following day.[2] After a stay of about a fortnight in which to refit, the fleet put to sea again. During the short time Pennington had been in the Rainbow he found her very unserviceable. She was ' tender sided,' he reported, ' and her lower tier of guns were too near the water,' so he transferred his flag to the Unicorn, while Mainwaring remained in the Henrietta Maria.[3]   The King having received complaints from the merchants ' of many insolencies committed upon them in his own seas,' Pennington was instructed to cruise to the westward to prevent the like disorders, ' that trade may be kept open. It is most requisite,' wrote Northumberland, ' that some course be taken to preserve his Majesty's sovereignty at sea, which, by our own remissness, has been of late so much encroached upon by our neighbours.' [4]

No sooner had the fleet sailed than it was confronted with the serious problem of finding a Dutch squadron of 30 sail cruising off Portland.[5] The freedom of the Channel as a means of getting reinforcements and supplies to her garrisons in Flanders meant everything

[1] *S.P. Dom.*, Charles I, ccccxxiv. 60.
[2] *Ibid.*, ccccxxv. 36.   [3] *Ibid.*, ccccxxv. 88 i.
[4] *Ibid.*, Nos. 72, 76.
[5] *Ibid.*, ccccxxv. 88 ; ccccxxvi. 28.

to Spain. During the early part of the year,
English ships had been chartered to transport
men from Spain to Dunkirk ; and for the purpose
of intercepting these vessels, Tromp, the Dutch
Admiral, was lying in wait.[1] In the summer of
1639 the Spaniards had gathered together a
huge armada, consisting of 67 large ships and
galleons, with 25,000 seamen to man them,
transporting at the same time 12,000 soldiers.
Their supposed mission was to dislodge the
Dutch ships before Dunkirk ; but by some it was
believed that their destination was England.[2]
The command of this formidable fleet was given to
Don Antonio de Oquendo, and on the 26th of
August he sailed from Corunna. By the 1st
of September the Spaniards were reported off
Plymouth, and we can believe that the thoughts
of many of the inhabitants went back ' to the
day when Drake and Hawkins finished their
game of bowls on the Hoe.'[3] The following
day William Wislade, master of the Hopewell,
of Southampton, reported them off the Start.
He records that ' he came out of Dartmouth,
and about 6 o'clock at night off the Start saw
70 sail, whereof 40 or more were great ships,
and that the Admiral was a very great and
warlike ship.'[4] In the meantime Tromp's Vice-
Admiral, de With, had been despatched with
17 men-of-war to intercept the Spaniards, and
on the 6th he came up with Oquendo. Though
hopelessly outclassed in point of numbers, de
With kept up a running fight, during which one

[1] Gardiner, ix. p. 57 ; *S.P. Dom.*, ccccxxvii. 81, Tromp to
Pennington.
[2] Sir W. Penn, *Life*, 1, App. E, No. 2.
[3] Gardiner, ix. p. 59.
[4] *S.P. Dom.*, Charles I, ccccxxviii. 21 ii.

of his ships was blown up by accident. At night the wind shifted, and ' came to the S.W. fair weather.' The Spaniards in consequence were forced to ' lay all night by the lee,' and until after noon the following day, before they could fit themselves, being then driven between Beachy Head and Fairlight. Mainwaring, who had received instructions to cruise between Beachy and Dungeness with six ships, having been roused by the sound of firing, came up with Oquendo's armada on the 7th. After a hurried council aboard the Henrietta Maria, he resolved to send Captain John Hall of the Dreadnought to the Spanish admiral, to command him to strike his flag to the King's ships. Hall was courteously received by Oquendo, who related to him particulars of the previous day's fight ; but when the English captain announced the purpose of his mission, the Spanish admiral was indignant, and returned a message to the effect ' that he did expect to have as much freedom in the English seas as his master did give unto our King's ships in his harbours, which was to wear their flag,' and therefore he refused to strike. Such an argument, however, carried little weight with a seaman who was no friend to Spain, and on Hall's return Mainwaring immediately took steps to enforce the English claim. ' A fair shot at the Admiral ' had the desired effect, for both he and his Vice-Admiral struck their flags, ' and hoist them up again,' which, we are informed, ' was as much as could be required of them in the sea.' [1] The Spaniards now steered along

---

[1] From a rare tract by Peter White, one of the Masters in the English fleet, entitled, ' A memorable sea fight . . . narrative of the principal passages which were transacted in the Downes in 1639.' London, 1649.

to the eastward, the Hollanders continually running before them ' with a short sail.' [1] After the incident with Oquendo, Mainwaring shaped his course for the Downs, and despatched his lieutenant to Pennington with the following letter [2] :

Sir,—Because I suppose the notice of the Spanish fleets arrival in these parts is of importance for you to take knowledge off, with divers passages concerning the Hollanders and them, with what past betwixt them and us (whereof to relate the particulars in writing would be to hinder the expedition of this intelligence), I have (because the tide and wind did not serve for a ship), sent my pinnace with my lieutenant, who can relate to you all the passages, and the certificate of all the captains and masters, concerning their opinions of what was done under their hands, hoping you will like it well. And so for the present, having nothing else to advertise you of, and loth to lose time, I take my leave, and rest

Your affectionate friend and servant,
H. Mainwaring.

From on board the Henrietta Maria this 7 of September at 3 in the afternoon, The Ness, N.N.E. 3 leagues.

I intend to be to-morrow betwixt Folkestone [3] and Dover to expect my pinnace, and to stand off and on during the time limited.

Tromp, who was at Dunkirk, had heard the firing, and on the 8th he joined de With with 15 ships. Between one and two o'clock in the morning, the combined Dutch squadrons attacked Oquendo in the Straits of Dover. [4]

[1] Peter White's Account.
[2] *S.P. Dom.*, Charles I, ccccxxviii. 38.
[3] MS. Fowlstone.
[4] *S.P. Dom.*, Charles I, ccccxxviii. 52.

The attack was successful, and during the fight three Spanish galleons were sunk and one captured. Before nightfall the Spaniards had exhausted all their powder, and were forced to take shelter in the Downs, with Tromp following hard on their heels. Oquendo met with as cold a welcome from Pennington as he had received at the hands of Mainwaring. On entering the roadstead he was made to haul down the Spanish flag, while Tromp was informed that no hostilities would be permitted there, and that he must keep to the southern part of the anchorage, the Spaniards being assigned the northern part.[1]

On the 12th Northumberland wrote to Pennington approving of the discretion and care shown to the rival fleets, but desiring him ' still to have a watchful eye upon them,' and to give him ' advertisement from time to time of all that shall occur in this affair.' [2] The very day that this letter was penned, the Spanish admiral, having the best of the anchorage, despatched under cover of night fourteen of his smaller vessels to Dunkirk with troops. Incensed at this action, Tromp appealed to the King, and on the 16th Pennington was informed that

a complaint has been made unto the King, that before the fourteen sail of Spaniards stole away, the Holland admiral would have placed some ships towards the North Foreland, to prevent the Spaniards going away in the night, but that you refused to suffer him, engaging your word to him that none of the Spanish fleet should slip away in the night.[3]

Whatever Pennington may have promised, it is difficult to see how he could have prevented

[1] Gardiner, ix. 60.　　[2] *S.P. Dom.*, ccccxxviii. 66.
[3] *Ibid.*, ccccxxviii. 93.

any action of the Spaniards in this direction, for at the time there were only ten ships under his command, besides sundry merchantmen that happened to be in the Downs.[1] After this event there followed one of the most humiliating episodes in our naval history, Charles offering the protection of the English fleet to whichever party was the highest bidder.

On the 15th the Spaniards were informed that for the sum of £150,000 their ships would be placed in safety. The money, however, was not forthcoming, though the Spaniards purchased English gunpowder at 2s. a pound to the extent of 500 barrels. As a solatium Charles received £5000, and the Earl of Newport, Master of the Ordnance, £1000, besides the value of the powder.[2] On the 23rd Pennington issued instructions that if either of the two fleets should presume to attempt ' anything here in the King's Chamber, contrary to the laws and customs of nations,' the English vessels were to fall upon them, and to do their best ' to take, sink, or destroy them.'[3] Three days later Mainwaring was sent aboard Tromp's flagship to demand satisfaction for the behaviour of a Dutch captain, ' that did

---

[1] Peter White's Account, p. 9. The fleet consisted of *Unicorn*, Sir J. Pennington; *Henrietta Maria*, Sir H. Mainwaring; *Antelope*, Captain Stradling (Rear-Admiral); *Bonaventure*, Captain Fielding; *Dreadnought*, Captain Hall; *Providence*, Captain Slingsby; *Second Whelp*, Captain Burley; *Third Whelp*, Captain P. Hill; *Roebuck*, pinnace, Mr. Woolward; *Unicorn*, merchantman, Captain E. Popham. On the 15th ten English merchantmen were stayed in the Downs by warrant from Pennington (*ibid.*, p. 15).

[2] *S.P. Dom.*, Charles I, ccccxxviii. 113 ; Gardiner, ix. p. 61. The Spaniards pretended that the want of powder was the sole cause of their long delay, whereupon Tromp offered them 500 barrels at the usual rate, which they refused (*Sidney Papers*, ii. 612).   [3] *S.P. Dom.*, ccccxxix. 15.

presume to wear his Majesty's colours' in the roadstead, and had taken two 'catches'[1] full of Spanish soldiers. Meanwhile, Tromp had been reinforced from Holland by the welcome addition of fireships, and the fleet under his command numbered about eighty sail. The patience of the Dutch seamen was now nearly exhausted. Pennington himself saw that the spark might be kindled at any moment, and his crew would have been hard put to it if called upon to assist the Spanish fleet. He therefore resolved to ask Northumberland for more precise instructions. To this end a despatch signed by himself, Mainwaring, and six others was sent to the King and the Lord Admiral, asking how far they should 'proceed' or 'engage' themselves in the event of the rival fleets fighting in the road. The King, who happened to be at Windsor celebrating the feast of St. George, returned an answer to the effect that he would return to London in four days' time, when he would appoint a day for both fleets to leave.[2] This message Pennington was requested to convey to the Dutch admiral, the King being confident that no act of hostility would be committed in the meantime. To Tromp this was welcome news, and on being informed of the King's resolve he 'rejoiced and wished that time were come.'[3] To the English commander, however, Charles' instructions were puzzling and contradictory. At first he had instructed Pennington to enforce the neutrality of the roadstead, and now, on the 8th of October, he ordered him

to send to the Spanish admiral to inform yourself in what state they are to defend themselves, and to resist

[1] *I.e.*, Ketches. White's Account, p. 24.
[2] White's Account, pp. 39–41. [3] *Ibid.*, p. 41.

the great force of Hollanders which now threatens them. If when the Hollanders assault the others you see the Spaniards defend themselves so well, that with the help of those few ships that are with you they shall be able to make their party good, which the King upon the report of some is well inclined to believe, then you are to give them your best assistance, otherwise you must make as handsome a retreat as you can in so unlucky a business.[1]

Though it cannot be denied that the English fleet were involved in an 'unlucky business,' its commanders had no intention of carrying into effect the latter portion of these instructions. Pennington and Mainwaring were certainly not the type of men who, even in the face of overwhelming odds, would have been content to make 'a handsome retreat,' and the same splendid spirit no doubt animated the rest of the fleet. Two days after receiving these instructions, thirty ships laden with men and provisions reached Oquendo from Dunkirk, and preparations were made to take aboard the 500 barrels of gunpowder that he had purchased.[2] Tromp now saw it was time to strike a decisive blow. For this purpose he ordered his pinnace to be got ready, and sailed with it through the Spanish fleet. What he had no doubt foreseen happened ; the Spaniards, angered at the sight of the pinnace, shot a hole through her foresail, excusing themselves on the ground that they believed it to be a fireship. The next day one of the Dutch seamen was shot dead with a musket. This was enough. Tromp reminded Pennington that the King had promised his aid against whichever party fired the first shot. He pointed out that

---

[1] *S.P. Dom.*, Charles I, ccccxxx. 47.
[2] *Ibid.*, ccccxxx. 77.

the neutrality of the road had been twice infringed, and ' if,' he informed Pennington, ' you will not follow the King's order by helping us, we expect, at least, that you will let us go on against our enemy and fight with him.'[1] After this polite but emphatic request, Tromp seized a favourable opportunity while powder was being brought on board Oquendo's fleet on the evening of the 10th, and decided to attack. Ere the morning fog had lifted, his fleet were under sail, and the roar of cannon across the water announced to the English commander that the battle had commenced in earnest. Pennington immediately summoned a council aboard his flagship, and although his ships were the ' leewardmost ' of all, and in danger from the fireships of the rival fleets, he afterwards succeeded in getting the ' weather gage,' chasing and shooting at many of the Dutch ships and forcing them to take in their flags until clear of the Downs.

The result of the action was disastrous to the Spaniards, and in a few hours the majority of their galleons were either burnt, sunk, or driven ashore. An account of the battle was subsequently drawn up by Pennington, Mainwaring, and the other officers for presentation to Northumberland, and as it has never been printed verbatim before, we cannot do better than give it here[2] :

The Spaniards being berthed altogether in the best of the road, the Hollanders without them to the eastward and northward, and the King's ships to the southward. About eight in the morning, the wind being at north-west, the Hollanders were all on sudden under sail ; whereupon our Admiral called a council. We

[1] *S.P. Dom.*, Charles I, ccccxxx. 80.
[2] *Ibid.*, ccccxxx. 74.

were no sooner aboard with him but we heard some
shot betwixt the fleets, but which began we could not
certainly know by reason of the fog, but as some of our
men affirm, and by circumstances it is possible, it was the
Hollanders gave the first occasion by weighing with their
whole fleet, endeavouring to get the wind of them, and
coming so near that they might justly expect their
intentions to board them with their fireships.   Our
ships being all loose, we had not time to advise long,
being at that time the last quarter flood.   We all agreed
that we being the leewardmost ships of all, by reason of
the fog, the thickness of the ships together, and the
smoke, we could neither avoid the being entangled (to
a great disadvantage) betwixt the fleets, nor the danger
of the fireships, nor yet assist the Spaniards, unless
we stood to the northward to get the weather gage
of them, which we did.   At which time the Holland
admiral sent a captain aboard with a letter, which
being in Dutch we understood not, but the captain,
in the name of his admiral, made a protestation that
they had not broke the peace, but the Spaniards, who
begun with them.   The fog was so thick that the ships
could not see one the other, so that in an hour's time we
heard few or no shot, neither was there very many shot
in all.   The weather clearing up a little, that we could
see we had got the weather gage of them, we stood
in again with the Hollanders, and shot many guns from
all our ships, shooting many of them through, but they
did not return one shot at us.   We continued chasing
and shooting at them till they were all out of the Downs,
all beyond the South Foreland, neither did they put
out their flags till [they] were all out of the Downs and
a good way off, and then, seeing some Hollanders to the
northward and eastward, we tacked and stood into
the Downs again to prevent them that they should not
fetch off those Spanish ships which were run on shore,
being to the number of twenty-four, one of which was
the Vice-Admiral, who did all willingly run on shore,
save some of them which were forced to avoid the
fireships which burnt out by them.   In regard that
the Spanish fleet was so much disabled by the loss of

half their ships at the first onset, and the rest flying, we did not think fit to pursue them any farther, neither do we conceive that if his Majesty had at this time a force equal with the Hollanders it had been possible to prevent this action, seeing we were not to begin with them, whereby they might take their own time and best opportunity of wind and tide most for their advantage.

This is a true relation of this day's action, which we Captains and Masters of his Majesty's fleet are ready to testify upon our oaths.

As we were signing this we made stay of two Hollanders who had run on shore in the fog, between the two castles, who made many shot at them, who never returned any to them again. But considering, as is probable, that the Holland fleet will speedily come in again, and that we shall not be able to keep these by force if they require them, which we conceive will be a greater affront to his Majesty than what is past, if they should take them from us, we have therefore thought it convenient at this time to dismiss them.

(Signed) J. PENNINGTON, HEN. MAINWARING, HEN. STRADLING, RICHARD FIELDING, EDW. POPHAM, R. SLINGSBY, JOHN HALL, WILL. BROWNE, PETER WHITE, JAMES BAMFORD, WILL. NICHOLLS, JOHN SWANTON, PHILLIP JOHNSON, THO. ROCKWELL, JOHN ROCHESTER.

So complete was Tromp's victory over Oquendo's armada, which some six weeks earlier had set out for Dunkirk, that less than twenty ships reached their destination. For the crushing defeat of the Spaniards England had cause to thank the gallant Dutchmen. The supposition that the armada was intended for our shores, and not for Flanders, was not groundless. The county of Kent had exhausted its arms in supplying trained bands on the borders; and the governor of the Isle of Wight, who was supposed to be a Catholic, had shot away all his powder as a salvo at the drinking of healths, thus crippling the Island's chance of resistance against a foe.[1]

In December the fleet was paid off, and for services rendered this year, Pennington was remunerated at the rate of 40s. a day, and Mainwaring at 20s. a day.[2]

The means by which Charles contrived to fit out his fleets was yearly becoming a more difficult task. By 1640 the sheriffs in some parts of the country had almost despaired of collecting the money demanded by the ship-money writs. Against the organised resistance of the inhabitants they were powerless, and by the end of May less than a tenth of the sum required had been collected. In London the Lord Mayor, with the sheriffs and other city officers, made a house-to-house visit on a particular day, 'but not above one paid.'[3] Before both Houses of Parliament, the Lord Keeper, Finch, explained that the King 'was not wedded to this particular way' of fitting out a fleet, and if some other method could be devised for raising the necessary money, he was willing to commute the tax.[4]

In addition to the hostility which was shown to his personal government at home, the King found himself once again embroiled with a rebellion in Scotland. The treaty of Berwick was but a

[1] Gardiner, ix. p. 69. This peril was even more dangerous than that of 1588, the King of England being on the side of the invaders. Martin Harpertzoon Tromp, the heroic victor in thirty-three sea fights, was shot in his action with Monk, July 31, 1653.

[2] *S.P. Dom.*, Charles I, ccccxxxv. 76 ; 14 December 1639.

[3] *Ibid.*, cccclvii. 36 ; *Cal. S.P.*, 1640, pref. xliii–xliv.

[4] Gardiner, ix. 107. The Short Parliament met on April 13th and was dissolved three weeks later.

few months old when both parties were accusing one another of violating its terms.[1] The King was determined never to abandon the cause of episcopacy in Scotland, and the Covenanters on their part refused to sanction bishops. In consequence, early in 1640, arrangements were in progress for raising an army to invade Scotland. The fleet was also ordered to be ready by the end of March, and, in spite of the growing discontent, 21 ships were commissioned for sea, under the command of the trusty Pennington. The Admiral's ship was the James, of 875 tons, with a crew of 260 men, and carrying 48 guns, while Mainwaring was commissioned to the Charles, mounting 44 pieces of ordnance, with a crew of 250 men.[2]

Though the list (*see* p. 288) gives the name of Captain John Mennes as Vice-Admiral, his appointment must have been subsequently cancelled, for there is abundant proof that during the whole of 1640 he was attached to the King's army operating in the North.[3] Under these circumstances it is probable that Mainwaring again acted as Pennington's Vice-Admiral, but owing to the absence of documentary evidence on this point, it is impossible to state definitely whether this was so.

The mission with which the Navy was entrusted was identical to that of the previous

---

[1] Gardiner, ix. 45.

[2] *S.P. Dom.*, Charles I, ccccxlii. 55 ; ccccxliv. 8 ; cccclxiii. 45.

[3] It was not uncommon at this period to find naval captains filling the rôle of commanders in the army, or landsmen appointed to the command of men-of-war. In February 1640 Mennes was ordered by Northumberland to raise and command a troop of carabineers, which troop he took to Newcastle in April, and continued with the army to the end of the year (*S.P. Dom.*, ccccxlvi. 7; ccccli. 72; cccclxxi. 50).

year, and on the 13th of April orders were given
to make stay of all Scottish shipping that came
into any parts of England, Ireland, and Wales.
At the beginning of May some of the King's
ships were cruising off the coast of Northumber-

Ships	Men.	Captains.
James . .	260	Sir John Pennington, Admiral.
St. George .	260	John Mennes, Vice-Admiral.
Swiftsure .	260	John Povey, Rear-Admiral.
Charles . .	250	Sir Henry Mainwaring.
Rainbow .	240	David Murray.
Convertive .	200	Henry Stradling.
Garland . .	170	Richard Fogge.
Leopard . .	160	Captain Fielding.
Happy Entrance	160	Robert Slingsby.
Antelope .	160	Edward Popham.
Expedition .	100	Richard Seaman.
Mary Rose .	100	Thomas Price and Richard Swanley *successively.*
Providence .	100	Richard Hill.
1st Whelp .	60	John Bargrave.
2nd Whelp .	60	Robert Fox (*from August* 1).
3rd Whelp .	60	Robert Fox (*up till August* 1).
8th Whelp .	60	Anthony Woolward.
10th Whelp .	60	Baldwin Wake.
Greyhound .	50	Abraham Wheeler.
Roebuck . .	45	Thomas Rockwell.
Nicodemus .	45	John Lambert.

land for this purpose, and by the end of the
month Captains Fielding and Stradling between
them had captured six vessels laden with provisions and munitions of war, which were brought
into Berwick.[1]   While part of the fleet were thus
engaged in a war against the maritime trade

---

[1] *S.P. Dom.*, Charles I, ccccliii. 24, 54.

of Scotland, the rest were cruising in the Downs protecting English merchantmen. The dangers that beset our merchant shipping were many, and those of the fleet that were detailed for convoy duty were instructed to give the merchants ' speedy convoy,' and ' not to leave them till they see them out of danger.'[1] It was not long before the Scotch began to realise what a serious menace was confronting them on sea. By the end of June their vessels were reported to be ' laid up and unrigged,' a state of things ' which they much grudge at.'[2] Accordingly, a petition was sent to the King desiring ' the rendition of all ships ' that had been taken from the merchants of Scotland;[3] but Charles was not in a frame of mind to consider it, and on the 18th of July it was decided to strengthen the English fleet in order that it should more effectually continue the campaign. For this purpose the Lords of the Admiralty ordered five merchant ships to be armed and placed under the command of Pennington.[4] By the end of the month eighty vessels with consignments for Scottish ports had been captured, and a contemporary records that the English fleet had so ' blocked up the seas ' that the Scots ' could have no trading.' Under these circumstances it is not surprising that they viewed the situation with alarm. Their petition to the King had remained unanswered, so now they ' publicly professed ' that if their shipping was not restored they would invade England.[5] In this respect they were as good as their word, and in August they crossed the Border, defeating the King's army

[1] *S.P. Dom.*, Charles I, cccclviii. 86.
[2] *Ibid.*, No. 58.   [3] *Ibid.*, cccclvii. 37.
[4] *Ibid.*, cccclx. 36.   [5] *Ibid.*, cccclxi. 81.

near Newcastle on the 28th. On the 8th of September seventeen of the King's ships sailed into the Firth of Forth, and a week later two of them were sent to lie off the mouth of the Tyne, with instructions to hinder all trade while the rebels held Newcastle.[1]

Though up till now the fleet had accomplished its work in an efficient and effective manner, its activity during the autumn was far from successful. Scottish vessels sailing from Sweden with much-needed supplies managed to elude their vigilance, and on the 3rd of October a prominent official wrote that the King's ships were doing 'little good upon the coast of Scotland,' and he ventured an opinion that it would be 'more credit to his Majesty to recall his ships than suffer them to remain to be laughed at.'[2] In spite of the presence of men-of-war off Tynemouth and elsewhere, Northumberland was informed that 'there had been the greatest commerce at Gottenburg with Scotland ever known.'[3]

Without a powerful army and fleet, Charles could never have hoped to subdue the Scots, and the possibility of the failure of the campaign for want of financial assistance was apparent from the first. In July Northumberland had estimated that in order to maintain the land and sea forces till the end of October it would require a sum of £300,000, 'towards which,' he stated, 'we have not in cash nor in view above £20,000 at the most.'[4] Northumberland's cry for money was echoed by the King. 'If they send us none or too little,' he wrote, 'the

---

[1] *S.P. Dom.,* Charles I, cccclxvii. 46, 76.
[2] *Ibid.,* cccclxix. 25.   [3] *Ibid.,* cccclxix. 91.
[4] *Camden Soc.,* 100, xxiii.

rebels will beat us without striking stroke,'[1]
and his prognostication proved only too true.
With the few troops that he commanded, un-
disciplined and mutinous, and an impoverished
exchequer, it was impossible to bring the war
to a successful termination, and when the Scots
seized Durham, the King was brought face to
face with the fact that his campaign against
them had failed. Before the end of October
the fleet was back in the Downs, and a temporary
truce was agreed on until such time as an English
Parliament could be summoned to make a final
settlement.[2] For this purpose the ' Long Parliament ' met at Westminster on the 3rd of
November, but the session was barely a month
old when the legality of ship-money was vigorously
attacked.

The claim put forward by Charles to the
Sovereignty of the Sea received little support
from Parliament, and in January of the following
year the Lords declared ship-money to be illegal.
Nevertheless, preparations were in progress for
the summer's fleet, and by June, Pennington,
with 15 royal ships and 10 merchantmen, was
in the Downs. Mainwaring, either on account
of his advancing years or strong royalist principles,
is not found among the list of captains.[3] The

---

[1] *Camden Soc.*, 100, xxviii.

[2] Rait, *Rels. between England and Scotland*, p. 165.

[3] The fleet for 1641 consisted of the following :—*St.
Andrew*, Admiral Sir J. Pennington ; *Rainbow*, George
Carteret, Vice-Admiral ; *Victory*, John Povey, Rear-Admiral ;
Bonaventure, David Murray ; *Garland*, Richard Fogge ;
Leopard, Richard Blyth ; *Happy Entrance*, Robert Slingsby ;
Lion, Henry Stradling ; *Mary Rose*, Thomas Price (or Richard
Swanley) ; *Expedition*, Richard Seaman ; *Greyhound*,
Abraham Wheeler ; *Providence*, Philip Hill ; *Roebuck*, Thomas
Rockwell ; *Nicodemus*, John Lambert ; *Tenth Whelp*,

Bill that had been brought in to annul the proceedings relating to ship-money received the royal assent in August 1641, and Pennington with other captains who were known to be staunch supporters of the King were viewed with suspicion by the Parliament. In the case of national danger, when the country was at war, ship-money writs had been issued without opposition, but as soon as the King used the tax as a means whereby to support a regular fleet, it became unpopular.

To keep pace with her rivals, the French and the Dutch, there is no doubt that England needed a powerful navy, but the money necessary for its maintenance was always lacking, and the King's efforts to carry out his naval pro-gramme, in spite of the most strenuous opposition, was one of the chief causes that brought about his own downfall. The King's naval ambitions were admirably set forth by the royalists in their arguments against the memorable remonstrance which the Commons made to the people in 1641. ' A sure proof,' they said, ' that the King had formed no system for enslaving his people ' was to be found in the fact ' that the chief object in his government had been to raise a naval, not a military force ; a project useful, honourable, nay indispensably requisite, and in spite of his necessities, brought almost to a happy con-clusion.' [1] Certainly the benefits which Charles conferred on the country by the superior classes

(Baldwin Wake ?) ; and ten merchant ships, *Unicorn, Experi-ence, Leghorn Merchant, Honour, Mayflower, Thomas and Lucy, Paragon, Anne Percy, True Love,* and *Lucy* (*S.P. Dom.,* and *Audit Office Declared Accounts,* 1705, 87).

[1] Derrick, p. 68.

of ships he built, and the fleets he organised, must be acknowledged by all. They proved to the world that the weapon which had been successfully forged by Elizabeth could still be called upon to vindicate England's maritime supremacy in the hour of need, and such gallant seamen as Pennington, Mervin, and Mainwaring, among others, were no unworthy successors of the glorious days of Drake.[1]

In the spring of 1642, when the ships were being prepared for sea as in the previous years, Parliament took the precaution to remove all captains who were suspected of royalist tendencies.[2] A formal message was sent to the House of Lords, 'that the Earl of Northumberland might be moved to constitute the Earl of Warwick his Admiral of the Fleet for that year's service, being a person of such honour and experience as they might safely confide in him.' The King, however, was strongly in favour of Pennington, but Parliament stood firm for Warwick, and on the 25th of March Pennington was sent for to be examined by a Committee of both Houses.[3] On the 2nd of July Warwick came aboard his flagship, the James, then in the Downs, and called on the various captains to accept him as their Admiral. With the exception of Sir John

---

[1] ' Little has been done,' wrote Admiral Colomb, ' towards elucidating the share which Charles' understanding of the naval conditions of the kingdom, and the want of understanding on the part of his opposing subjects, may have had in producing the Civil War, but it seems to be certain that the chief part of the money question was a naval one ' (*Naval Warfare*, 1899, p. 31).

[2] A list of the fleet for 1642 is to be found in Sir W. Penn's *Life*, i. pp. 22–3.

[3] *Commons Journal*, ii. 497.

Mennes, Richard Fogge, John Burley, Robert Slingsby, and Baldwin Wake, the Navy revolted in a body to the side of the Parliament, and these five captains were subsequently forced to surrender their ships on not receiving the support of their crews.[1]

[1] Clarendon, ii. pp. 333-6

CHAPTER XI

1642-46

TRINITY HOUSE—THE CIVIL WAR

THOUGH deprived of his command afloat, Mainwaring soon found other congenial employment. The sound knowledge and judgment he had displayed in all things that concerned the welfare of the Royal Navy and merchant shipping, was in no quarter more highly valued than at the meetings of the Brethren of the Trinity House.[1] In 1642, by consent of the majority of the fraternity, he was for the second time elected to the important post of Master. The election went by seniority, and before admittance to the office of Master it was necessary that a 'corporal oath' should be taken before the wardens and assistants to the effect that from time to time, during his Mastership, he would faithfully and honourably execute the office of Master in all things pertaining to the same. Finally, he was bound to swear allegiance to the sovereign. The oath duly administered, he was enrolled as Master for one whole year.[2]

Unfortunately, details concerning the history

[1] The Trinity House was in 1514, on recommendation of Sir Thomas Spert, granted a charter by Henry VIII.

[2] A copy of the oath is given in the *Royal Charter of the Corporation*, 1685, p. 113.

of the Trinity House during the period in question
are wanting, many of the documents relating
to the Corporation having been destroyed in
the great fire of 1666.   But still, from the meagre
details that are to hand, a few facts may be
gleaned relative to Mainwaring's connection with
this ancient fraternity, which is so closely allied
with the early history of the Navy.

Among the multifarious duties of the Trinity
House at this period, the following may be noted.
Upon them devolved one of the chief duties of the
Naval constructor's department of the present day,
and designs for new ships for the fleet were laid
down by them ; while merchant vessels that
were hired or purchased into the Navy were
accepted or rejected according to their decision.
Besides superintending the ship-building yard
at Deptford, they were responsible for the
victualling of the Navy, and the certifying of
every piece of ordnance and ammunition that
was placed aboard ship.   In time of war, the
equipment of every fleet that left our shores
was under their especial jurisdiction.   Pilots
and masters for the King's ships received
their certificates at the hands of Trinity House ; [1]
while prize disputes and petitions of seamen
were frequently referred to their judgment.   In the
work of this department Mainwaring had already
been engaged many years.   As early as July
1627 his signature is attached to a document
of the Corporation relating to a dispute between
Humphrey Haines, merchant of the City of
London, and Thomas King, mariner, concerning
the division of a prize.   The case had been

[1] Barrett, *Trinity House*, pp. 53–4.   Besides these duties
may be added those of erecting beacons, laying buoys, and
impressing mariners when called upon.

referred to the Trinity House by Sir Henry
Marten, judge of the Admiralty, and on the
26th of July they gave their opinion as follows.
That Thomas King should have a part of the
said prize, and 'such part of the third part as
is proportionable according to the adventure
which he bore in the said ship.' [1] In April 1629
Mainwaring's name figures among others on a
certificate of the Trinity House regarding the
amount of ordnance to be placed aboard the
Trial of London [2] and the Jonas of Dysart,[3] asking
that they should be furnished with 'six minions
of cast-iron ordnance' and 'six sakers and ten
minions' respectively. Earlier in the year Sir
Kenelm Digby had returned from his famous
privateering expedition in the Mediterranean,[4]
and as soon as he landed in England he was confronted with various lawsuits respecting the
prizes he had taken. Finally he appealed to
the Trinity House for their opinion as to 'what
shares are due to such as went out of my voyage;
also to limit what shares do belong to me being
commander.' The House answered on the 27th
of June,[5] that 'there occurreth to us one precedent that we conceive doth satisfy your
question.' They then go on to cite the case of

---

[1] Trinity House, *Court Minutes*, 1626–35. I am indebted
to the courtesy of the officials of Trinity House for permission
to examine these.

[2] *S.P. Dom.*, Charles I, xvi. 148. Signed by Wm. Case,
H. Mainwaring, Walter Coke, John Totton, etc., etc.

[3] *Ibid.*, 147. MS. Dizart.

[4] He left England in December 1627, with two ships,
The Eagle, of 400 tons (Captain Milborne), and the *George
and Elizabeth*, 250 tons, commanded by Sir Edward Stradling.

[5] *Court Minutes*, 1626–35. It is possible that Mainwaring
was Master at the time, as his signature is first.

Sir James Lancaster,[1] who having two ships under his command did take great purchase, and at his return home ' he had allotted him for his part two captain's shares, and had presented unto him for an acknowledgment of his merit, one thousand pounds by the adventurers out of their parts of the goods.'

In the following year, John Browne, founder of his Majesty's iron ordnance and shot, petitioned Lord Vere, Master of the Ordnance, concerning the restraint of small iron ordnance, called drake, to the King's particular service, the use of them being much desired by the King's subjects. This was in due course referred to the Trinity House, of which Mainwaring was Master at the time, with a request that if they recommended the use of drakes they were to set down their opinion in writing. On the 25th of November they informed Lord Vere of the convenience and use of drakes in merchant ships, going fully into the question, and stating ' that they which hinder the sale of drake to the King's subjects are ill advised.' [2]

During the years 1632 and 1633, as has been recorded, Mainwaring was engaged with others of the Trinity House in measuring the King's ships, and certifying as to the number of men and guns that were requisite for each, the original document drawn up by them being reproduced in a previous chapter.[3] In April 1632 Secretary Coke and the rest of the Commissioners of the Navy requested the opinion of the Trinity House as to the number of ships and men to be employed against the pirates of Algiers.

---

[1] Pioneer of the English trade with the East Indies ; died 1618.

[2] *Court Minutes.* Browne's petition is also to be found in *S.P. Dom.*, Charles I, clxxv. 97.   [3] See p. 223.

They replied on the 16th of the month (Main-waring's signature is second): ' We say 8 ships : 4 of 500 tons, 4 of 400 tons.' Each of these ships fitly and fully furnished, they informed the Commissioners, would cost £6,000. The number of seamen they suggested for each ship was 140, and for armament they proposed 10 whole culvereins, 10 demi-culvereins, 8 sakers, and 40 muskets for each ship. They concluded their report by stating, ' our opinion is to build, not to buy.'[1] Mainwaring's name is next met with on a certificate of the Corporation, dated 6th of July 1633, relating to the Joseph of London, in which permission was asked to place aboard her ' 2 sakers, 5 minions, and 2 falcons.'[2] In 1634 the Lords of the Admiralty called in the aid of Trinity House to determine what steps could be taken to remedy the defects in the Unicorn, launched the previous year at Woolwich. Her keel measured 107 feet ; beam, 36·4 feet ; depth, 15·1 feet. She mounted 46 guns, and her gross tonnage was returned at 823 tons. Pennington had reported that on joining her at Tilbury she was unable to carry sail, being so crank.[3] He found her dangerous and unserviceable, unable to work her guns, and stated that she would not live in a gale. Edward Boate was her shipwright, and Pennington, ' in regard to the poor man's disgrace that built

---

[1] *Court Minutes.*

[2] *S.P. Dom.*, Charles I, xvii. 72. Signed by Wm. Raineborowe, H. Mainwaring, Ant. Tutchen, John Totton, and Jas. Hockett.

[3] ' We say a ship is crank-sided when she will bear but small sail and will lie down very much, with little wind, the cause thereof is, that her breadth being laid too low, she hath nothing to bear her up ' (*Seaman's Dict.*, p. 30).

her,' gave her a trial at sea ; the result of which
he stated as above.

Pennington, who was admiral for the guard
of the Narrow Seas, joined the Unicorn as his
flagship on the 30th of April 1634. His journal
for the three following days gives an account of
the unseaworthy condition of the ship.

May 1. We weighed and stood to and again in the
River to try our ship, and found her so tender-sided that
all our company affirmed she was not fit to go to sea,
for she laid the ports of her lower tier under water,
yet Captain Pett and Mr. Austin were of opinion that
if she took in more ballast she might serve to lie in the
Narrow Seas the summer season.

May 2. We took in 100 tons of ballast, which brought
her down some 4 or 6 inches below her breadth.

May 3. Captain Pett and Mr. Austin left us, but Mr.
Boate stayed behind to see what our ship would do. . . .
Our ship stooped so much that we durst not open a port
of our lower tier, for they were for the most part under
water.[1]

The ports of the Unicorn were intended to
be 5 feet above the water-line, but in reality
they were only 3 feet 7 inches. Pett recommended to rip off the plank on each side
ten strakes, and upon the bare timbers to bring
on furs of timber, an operation which was known
as furring or girdling her. According to Mainwaring, this method was ' an infinite loss to
owners, and a disgrace to all ships that are so
handled. In all the world,' he reported,
' there are not so many ships furred as are in
England.' [2] Mainwaring, with the Trinity House,
was of the opinion that to remedy her defects

---

[1] *Hist. MSS. Com.*, 10 iv. p. 283.
[2] *Seaman's Dict.*, p. 43.

she should be cut down a deck lower. The Admiralty, however, would not hear of this, and the discussion ended in Pett's suggestion of girdling her being adopted, which increased her stiffness at the expense of her speed.[1]

In the same year, with 'Walter Coke, Ant. Tutchen, and Jonas James,' Mainwaring is found certifying that a merchant ship, being built at Aldeburgh in Suffolk, called the Squire of Aldeburgh, of 105 tons, should have '8 minions of cast-iron ordnance' laid aboard her.[2]

Of Mainwaring's second tenure of office as Master practically no documents exist that throw light on the doings of the Trinity House at this period. All we know is, that the Corporation was looked on with suspicion by the Parliament. On the 20th of June 1642 an ordinance was passed in the Commons empowering Sir Robert Harley, Sir John Evelyn, Mr. Bence, and the citizens of London, to treat with the Trinity House for the loan of money ' for these great occasions.' [3] What results attended their efforts is uncertain, but Parliament, knowing the risks to which they were exposed if they failed to enlist the sympathies of such a powerful body in their cause, removed, as a matter of precaution, any of the officials who were suspected of royalist tendencies. Mainwaring being among the latter category, the Commons on the 9th of November passed the following resolution [4] :

That Sir Henry Mainwaring be forthwith sent for as a Delinquent, by the Sergeant at Arms attending on this House. That this House holds it not fit, that Sir Henry Mainwaring should any longer continue

[1] *Cal. S.P. Dom.*, Charles I, 17th July 1634.
[2] *S.P. Dom.*, Charles I, xvii. 85. MS. Alborough.
[3] *Commons Journals*, ii. 633, 722.   [4] *Ibid.*, 841.

Master of the Corporation of the Trinity House. That the Corporation of the Trinity House be informed forthwith to make election of a new Master of their Corporation, and that the Lords' concurrence be desired.

Two days later they added to their resolution a clause debarring Mainwaring from being one of the Brethren.[1] Who the person was that succeeded Mainwaring is not recorded, but Parliament felt that for the safety of their cause the real danger could only be met by dissolving the charter of the Trinity House, which they did in 1647, the affairs being placed *pro tempore* in commission.[2] Whether Mainwaring was actually arrested under the order of the House is not known. Possibly like others he took to flight, for on the outbreak of the Civil War he took the field in support of the King, and when the royalist forces withdrew to Oxford at the end of November he is found among their ranks. For a number of months Oxford remained the royal headquarters, and during the King's sojourn there, Mainwaring, on the 31st of January 1643, was honoured by the University with the degree of Doctor of Physic.[3]

A considerable time now elapses before Mainwaring, like many other royalists, is heard of again. One thing, however, is certain, that he remained in England during these troublesome times. As a sailor he had little chance of a command in an army where there were ten applicants for every post. Advancing years unfitted him for service in a subordinate rank, and it is unlikely that he took part in the various marches and vicissitudes of the main army under

[1] *Commons Journals*, ii. 844.   [2] Barrett, pp. 74-6.
[3] Wood, *Athenae Oxon.*, ed. Bliss, IV ii. p. 48.

Charles, which culminated on the 20th of September in the indecisive battle of Newbury. In the following year a copy of Mainwaring's ' Nomenclator Navalis ' was brought to light, and Parliament being in possession of the fleet, it is not surprising that its worth should have been recognised. It was accordingly printed, and the high value placed on the information it contained may be judged from the imprimatur on the title page, which stated that it was conceived to be very ' fit to be at this time imprinted for the good of the Republic.'

The book was entered in the registers of the Stationers' Company 13th of March 1644, and after being duly licensed by John Booker,[1] was sold by ' John Bellamy at the sign of the three golden Lions in Cornhill.' It is entitled

The Sea-mans Dictionary : or, an Exposition and Demonstration of all the Parts and Things belonging to a Ship. Together with an Explanation of all the Terms and Phrases used in the Practique of Navigation. Composed by that Able and Experienced Sea-man Sir Henry Manwayring, Knight : and by him presented to the late Duke of Buckingham, the then Lord High Admiral of England.[2]

Its object was set out in a preface, ' showing the scope and use of this book,' from which the following is extracted :

My purpose is not to instruct those, whose Experience and Observation, have made them as sufficient (or more)

---

[1] Booker was licenser of mathematical works, and his license is imprinted on the title page thus :—' I have perused this Book, and find it so universally necessary for all sorts of men, that I conceive it very fit to be at this time imprinted for the good of the Republic.' September 20, 1644.

[2] The original MS. is dedicated to Buckingham, whom Mainwaring described as ' my most honored Lord and Patron

then myself : yet even they should lose nothing by remembering : (for I have profited by mine own labour, in doing this). But my intent, and the use of this Book, is, to instruct one, whose Quality, Attendance, Indisposition of body (or the like) cannot permit to gain the knowledge of Terms, Names, Words, the Parts, Qualities and manner of doing things with Ships, by long experience : without which there hath not any one arrived (as yet) to the least judgment or knowledge of them : It being so, that very few Gentlemen (though they be called Sea-men) do fully and wholly understand what belongs to their Profession ; having only some scrabbling Terms and Names belonging to some parts of a Ship. But he who will teach another must understand things plainly, and distinctly himself (that instead of resolving another man's doubts, he do not puzzle him with more confusion of Terms of Art), and so (to appear to know somewhat) will still expound *Ignotum per ignotius.* And for professed Sea-men, they either want ability, and dexterity to express themselves, or (as they all do generally) will, to instruct any Gentleman : If any will tell me why the vulgar sort of Sea-men hate landmen so much, either he or I may give the reason, why they are so unwilling to instruct them in their Art : whence it is that so many Gentlemen go long Voyages, and return (in a manner) as ignorant, and as unable to do their Country service, as when they went out. . . . To understand the Art of Navigation is far easier learned than to know the Practique of Mechanical working of Ships, with the Proper Terms belonging to them : In respect that there are helps for the first by many books (which give easy and ordinary rules for the obtaining to it), but for the other, till this, there was not so much as a means thought of, to inform any one in it.[1] . . . But I will speak it with as much confidence as truth, that in six months, he, who would but let me read this

This of course refers to the work when it was originally compiled. Captain John Smith's *Accidence for all young Sea-men* appeared in 1626, but was a mere tract compared to Mainwaring's work.

book over with him, and be content to look sometimes at a Model of a Ship, and see things how they are done, shall without any great study, but conversation, know more, be a better Sea-man, and speak more properly to any business of the Sea, than any other Gentleman, who shall go (two or three years together) to Sea, without this : for by the perusing of this Book, he shall not only know what to question, or doubt of, but likewise be resolved.

To Mainwaring belongs the distinction of helping to spread a practical knowledge of the sea profession, and his remarks quoted above throw an interesting sidelight on one of the outstanding evils of the age—the employment of gentleman commanders who were ignorant of naval affairs, and who, owing to influence at court, or land service in the low countries, were frequently appointed to the command of men-of-war, much to the disgust of the seamen who had been bred to the profession.[1]

On the failure of the treaty of Uxbridge towards the end of February 1645, the King resolved to send the Prince of Wales to the West of England. The care of the young Prince was entrusted to Sir Edward Hyde, and on the 4th of March father and son finally parted. That same day at the head of 300 horse the Prince left Oxford, and the move brought Mainwaring definite employment. Though the Royal Navy was entirely in the hands of the Parliament, several merchant vessels had been hired or purchased for the King's service and fitted out as men-of-war. Among the latter was the St. George or Great George, belonging to Dartmouth, which had been purchased in November 1643 by Thomas Cholwick and Captain John Smith

---

[1] *See* volume ii., *Gentlemen & Tarpaulin Commanders.*

for £1300.[1] As soon as it became known that
the King intended sending the Prince into the
west, Mainwaring was appointed to command
this vessel, with instructions to have her in readiness at Falmouth to convoy the Prince to Scilly
in the event of danger. On the 5th of March the
royal retinue reached the garrison at Devizes,
and on the following day entered Bath. This
town, Clarendon states, offered the Prince such
serenity, that he stayed there two or three days.
At Bridgewater on the 23rd an attempt was made
to reorganise the royalist forces in the west, but
the rapid advance of Fairfax's army caused the
Prince and his followers to withdraw into Cornwall. On the 12th of February 1646 the royal
party came to Truro, and after a short stay there
a visit was paid to Pendennis Castle, Falmouth,
the Prince 'intending only to recreate himself
for two or three days, and to quicken the works.'
On the morning of his intended return a despatch
was received from the Lords Hopton and Capel,
to the effect that 'they had severally received
intelligence of a design to seize the person of
the Prince, and that many persons of quality
of the country were privy to it.'[2] Some of the
royal servants were supposed to have been
implicated in the plot, and after the receipt of

[1] *Clarendon State Papers in the Bodleian*, i. No. 1730.
In this vessel the Queen was conveyed to France on the 14th
of July 1644, and £400 was paid to Sir Nicholas Crispe for
expenses incurred in conveying her Majesty thither. Crispe
received a commission from the King on the 6th of May 1644,
to equip at his own and his partner's charge not less than
fifteen ships of war for the royal service, with power to make
prizes, receiving a tenth as his own share. Among the
Clarendon State Papers is a list of the disbursements of the
St. George, 1640–5 (i. 1768, 2073 ; *Dict. of Nat. Biog.*, article
Crispe).   [2] Clarendon, *Rebellion*, 1826, v. 317.

this startling information the Prince's councillors deemed it prudent to remain at Pendennis. Finally, as a matter of precaution, instructions were given ' to cause the frigate belonging to Hasdunck, and the other ships, to be ready upon an hour's warning.' [1] On Monday morning, the 2nd of March, news reached Pendennis of the advance of the Parliament's forces, and the governor, Colonel John Arundel, was informed of the Prince's resolution ' that night to embark for Scilly, being a part of Cornwall ; from whence, by such aids and relief as he hoped he should procure from France and foreign parts, he should be best able to relieve them.' [2] About 10 o'clock he embarked on the frigate Phoenix, and on the Wednesday afternoon landed safely at St. Mary's. Mainwaring's ship, however, instead of forming one of the Prince's convoy as originally intended, was detained by the governor of Pendennis for the assistance of the garrison, much against the royal command, as is shown in a letter of Lord Hopton's to the Prince, in which he says :

As for the Great George, the ship appointed by your Highness's order to be brought after your Highness by Sir Henry Mainwaring, how she was stayed by the importunity of the Governor and Officers of Pendennis for the service of that castle, and that I used my best endeavour to have your Highness's order observed concerning that ship, will appear by several letters that passed between me and them, which I have ready to show.[3]

[1] Clarendon, *Rebellion*, 1826, v. 319. John van Haesdonck was in the Prince's service, and among the *Clarendon State Papers* in the Bodleian is a list of ten ships at sea under his command in 1645. (No. 1913.)

[2] Clarendon, v. 320.

[3] Ormonde, *Letters*, ed. Carte, i. 125.

Unfortunately Hopton's letters, of which he speaks, are not forthcoming ; they would, no doubt, provide interesting reading were it possible to recover them.   The reluctance of the officers of Pendennis to obey the royal command is perhaps, under the circumstances, pardonable. A man-of-war, mounting 40 guns, in the hands of a first-rate seaman, was a distinct asset to the beleaguered garrison.

The castle of Pendennis is situated on a bold promontory some 200 feet above the sea, and with the castle of St. Mawe's on the east commands the whole entrance to Falmouth Harbour.   It was therefore a fortress of great importance to the royalists, and on account of its strategical position gave the Parliamentary forces considerable trouble.[1]

After the surrender of Hopton's army at Truro, Fairfax despatched two of his regiments under the command of Colonel Hammond for the purpose of blocking up Pendennis by land. On the 17th of March his troops occupied the village of Pennycomequicke, while Batten, the Parliament's Vice-Admiral, laid siege to Pendennis by sea.   Meanwhile the Great George appears to have run aground on the north side of the castle, whether from design or accident is uncertain; but in spite of her position she was able to use her guns to good effect, and when Fairfax's party proceeded to view the works they met with a warm reception, as is shown in the following extract.   The writer was one of the officers under Fairfax, and the incident he relates no doubt refers to the Great George.   In his letter, which

---

[1] With the exception of Raglan Castle, Monmouthshire, Pendennis was the last royalist stronghold to surrender.

is dated 19th March 1645-6, the writer carefully conceals his identity under the initials ' T. M.'

> The General [he writes] went into Arwenack, Sir Peter Killegrew's house, where and in the village of Pennycomequicke we had quartered two regiments for the blocking up of Pendennis Castle on the land side. The day before the General sent thither those two regiments, the enemy in the castle set on fire Sir Peter's house, and burned a great part thereof down to the ground, and would have done the like with Pennycomequicke, had not our men's unexpected coming prevented them in the castle. . . . The man-of-war that hath 40 pieces of ordnance in him which lieth aground on the north side of the fort let us pass very quietly through Pennycomequicke and to Arwenack, which lies within half musket shot of the enemy's outworks, but is blinded by the houses and the trees, so that they cannot see those that are on the other side of the house; but when we came off and were past Pennycomequicke, and advanced into an open field on our way back to Penryn, the ship that lay on the north side of the castle let fly at us, but their shot (by God's mercy) did us no harm, though the bullets flew very near us, and one grazed not far from me, which we found, and was a bullet of some 12 *lb.* weight.[1]

The castle was known to contain ' many very considerable men, and the most desperate persons, and the violentest enemies that the Parliament hath in this kingdom.' [2] Besides 40 guns in the ship, the garrison were reported to have at least 80 pieces of ordnance mounted.

On the 18th of March Fairfax summoned the governor to surrender, and the latter's reply, after ' less than two minutes' resolution,' was to

---

[1] Cited in Oliver's *Pendennis*, pp. 39-42.
[2] ' T. M.'s ' letter.

the effect that sooner than yield to the King's enemy he would bury himself in the castle.[1]

Therefore, preparations for a more stringent blockade were at once undertaken, and, acting under Colonel Hammond's instructions, fortifications were gradually raised upon the narrow isthmus. By the 28th of the month Pendennis was reported 'almost lined about.'[2] So successfully had the besiegers drawn their net round the staunch little garrison, that by the second week in April the Lords Hopton and Capel deemed it advisable to leave Pendennis and join the Prince of Wales at Scilly. Mainwaring must have also left about this time, as he certainly joined the Prince's followers at Scilly before the lines of fortification were completed at Pendennis.[3]

The destitute state of the royal party while at St. Mary's, one of the Scilly Isles, is revealed by Lady Fanshawe, wife of Sir Richard Fanshawe, the Prince's Secretary of War. Speaking of her own privations she says[4]:

When we had got to our quarters near the castle, where the Prince lay, I went immediately to bed, which was so vile, that my footman ever lay in a better, and we had but three in the whole house, which consisted

---

[1] Oliver, p. 43. This gallant old commander, who was seventy years of age, after resisting the enemy for five months, finally capitulated on the 17th of August.

[2] *Ibid.*, pp. 42–3.

[3] At the surrender of Pendennis mention is made of ' one great ship that bore the Queen formerly between France and England.' This ship is known to have been the *St. George.* There was also in the Prince's service the *Little George,* and probably the *St. George* was called the *Great George* to designate her from the sister ship.

[4] Lady Fanshawe's *Memoirs,* pp. 59–60, 1829 ed.

of four rooms, or rather partitions, two low rooms and two little lofts, with a ladder to go up : in one of these they kept dried fish, which was his trade, and in this my husband's two clerks lay ; one there was for my sister, and one for myself, and one amongst the rest of the servants ; but when I waked in the morning, I was so cold I knew not what to do, but the daylight discovered that my bed was near swimming with the sea, which the owner told us afterwards it never did but at spring tide. With this we were destitute of clothes, and meat, and fuel, for half the Court to serve them a month was not to be had in the whole island, and truly we begged our daily bread of God, for we thought every meal our last. The Council sent for provisions to France, which served us, but they were bad, and a little of them.

On the Sunday following the arrival of Hopton and Capel a fleet of about twenty-seven Parliamentary ships encompassed the islands; but owing to a violent storm, which raged for two or three days, they were all dispersed. The 16th of the month, Charles and his retinue embarked on the Proud Black Eagle, commanded by Captain Baldwin Wake, and attended by two other vessels the little party set sail for Jersey.[1]

[1] Clarendon, v. pp. 359–60.

CHAPTER XII

1646–47

WITH THE ROYALISTS IN JERSEY

THERE comes a time in the lives of most men
when they can look forward with pleasure to
well-earned rest and retirement, but Mainwaring's
fortunes on the threshold of his old age had
almost reached their lowest ebb. Though formerly
he had ' lived in great state,' and entertained a
large retinue when on shore,[1] on coming to Jersey
he was as poor as the rest of the royal followers.
Had he taken the side of the Parliament in the
Civil War, he would have probably achieved
fame and profit, whereas now he was an exile
attached to a hopeless cause, without any hope
of gain. The vicissitudes through which the
royalists had passed during the last three years
had proved a serious drain on their resources,
and on landing at Jersey, Mainwaring had only
a single person—his own nephew—to attend on
him.[2] Yet during this period of exile he was
able to render a service which produced a most
lasting effect on the future of the Navy. From
Pepys it is well known that Charles II possessed
an intimate knowledge, ' a transcendent mastery,'

[1] Chevalier's Journal (in Hoskins, i. pp. 357–8).
[2] *Ibid.*

as he styles it, in all nautical affairs.[1] Where the rudiments of that knowledge were gained is a point which has never been explained ; it will now appear that it was from Mainwaring.

This extraordinary insight into maritime affairs displayed by Charles in after life is a point on which all his historians are agreed, and it is recorded of him, that 'almost the only pleasure of mind he seemed addicted to was shipping and sea-affairs.'[2] It is an undoubted fact that the foundation of that knowledge was acquired during his stay in the hospitable island of Jersey. Here in company with the first seaman of the day, whose *magnum opus* had just been issued to the world, it is not too much to assume that the Prince learnt the rudiments of his seamanship from Mainwaring. Even during the voyage from Scilly he had greatly enjoyed the experience of taking the helm of the Proud Black Eagle, and remaining there for a couple of hours on end. Though barely sixteen years of age he showed marked interest and intelligence ; and the course of instruction followed was identical to that laid down by Mainwaring ; that is, besides having the art expounded to him, a pupil should see for himself how things were done, and 'look sometimes at the model of a ship.' For this purpose, soon after his arrival in Jersey, the Prince ordered a model of a pinnace to be built for him at St. Malo. On the 8th of June the vessel reached Jersey, and a contemporary account describes her as a perfect model; of great length, fore, and aft ; elegantly painted and emblazoned with the royal arms, and fitted with twelve pair

[1] Cited in Derrick, p. 84.
[2] *Character of Charles II* (Buckingham's *Works*, ii. 1715, p. 239).

of oars. She was equally suited for sailing as
well as rowing, and for that purpose was fitted
with a couple of masts, and the like number of
sails.[1] Here in the secluded waters of St. Aubin's
Bay, land-locked and encompassed by rocks,
the Prince was free to sail his pinnace and enjoy
his first lessons in seamanship, undisturbed by
the attentions of the Parliament's fleet. A more
touching picture than this is difficult to imagine.
On the one hand we have the Prince entering
into the spirit of his new hobby with all the
enthusiasm of youth, while on the other we have
the old sea-captain rendering a last service to the
cause he loved so well, by successfully fostering
in the son that same interest in England's maritime
greatness which had distinguished his unfortunate
father.

On the Sunday following the Prince's landing,
great rejoicings took place throughout the Island.
Soon after nightfall all the prominent hill-tops
were lit with blazing bonfires, every man contri-
buting a faggot as a token of his loyalty. The
next few days were devoted to holding levées in
the great hall of the castle, when the principal
personages of Jersey were presented to his
Highness. The governor, Captain George Carteret,
was created a baronet, and the captain of the
royal frigate, Proud Black Eagle, became Sir
Baldwin Wake. The Prince had now been a
whole week in Elizabeth Castle without having
attempted to set foot on the mainland. On
Sunday the 26th it was announced that he and
his suite would attend divine service at St.
Helier's,[2] and the gentry of the Island, amounting

---

[1] Hoskins, *Charles II in the Channel Islands,* i. 413.
  Ibid., i. p. 370.

to nearly 100 horse, proceeded to the castle to escort him from the gates. Accompanied by the governor's troop and a guard of honour, the royal cavalcade wended its way to the church, where the service was conducted by one of the clergymen attached to the Prince's train.

On the 27th of April Lord Digby arrived at Jersey in a small frigate, the St. Francis of Dunkirk, of about 140 tons burden. This vessel, which was reputed to be 'one of the fastest sailing vessels in the world,' mounted 12 guns, and besides passengers and sailors, carried over a hundred Irish soldiers. Digby, who happened to be in Ireland when the Prince retreated to Scilly, sailed from Waterford with 3 frigates to his assistance; but on reaching Scilly, finding that the Prince had already departed, sent the other two back to Ireland.[1]

At the beginning of June instructions were issued for the Doggerbank, under the command of Captain Dayman, to be laden with provisions, with the idea of running the blockade at Pendennis. She was fully armed and equipped for her dangerous mission, and in addition to her ordinary armament she mounted four swivels. On the 4th of the month she sailed, but meeting with contrary winds she was forced to fly for shelter in the small haven of Perraulx, on the coast of Brittany. Here the soldiers and crew spent most of their time carousing on shore, with the result that news reached the enemy that she might easily be surprised at her anchorage. The commander of the Parliamentary squadron, who had long been on the look out for the Doggerbank, seized the opportunity offered him, and

---

[1] Cary, *Memorials*, i. p. 60; Hoskins, i. pp. 373-4.

despatched two of his ship to Perraulx. On their arrival, such of the crew that had been left on board, realising that it would be hopeless to engage the enemy, fired some pieces at random, then abandoned the ship, and escaped ashore.[1]

About this time the Prince and his council turned their attention to strengthening and modernising the defences of the castle. Acting on the advice of an engineer, who had been specially summoned from Paris, the rocks round the castle were scarped, to prevent them being easily scaled, and the space beyond the old works was surrounded by a rampart and ditch. While the Prince was thus occupied with his pinnace and fortifications, entreaties reached him from his mother to join her in Paris. The Queen had received information of a supposed conspiracy to deliver her son over to the Parliament, for the sum of 20,000 pistoles, and forthwith the Lords Capel, Culpepper, Jermyn, and Wentworth, among others, were despatched to Jersey, with instructions to prevail upon the Prince to come into France. Jermyn handed to the Prince the letters and papers with which he had been entrusted, and a council was summoned in his Highness's bed-chamber, at which the Queen's letter was read, with extracts from those of the King. The silence which followed the reading of the King's letter was only broken by Hyde rising and desiring ' that in a matter of so great importance, upon which the fate of three kingdoms might depend,' that they ' might not be put suddenly to deliver an opinion.' After much discussion the council was postponed till the next day, which was Sunday, when the royal

---

[1] Hoskins, i. pp. 405–10.

letters were again read. Hyde records that after an hour's debate, ' it was agreed that every man should deliver his opinion as he thought fit.' The Earls of Berkshire and Brentford, and the Lords Capel, Hopton, and the Chancellor, were of the opinion that the Prince should suspend the idea of journeying into France. Culpepper's view was, that the King's command was positive, and he advised the Prince to submit ; while the other three, Jermyn, Digby, and Wentworth, would not express their opinions. The Prince, however, resolved to obey the royal command, and gave out his intention of starting on the Tuesday morning ; [1] but contrary winds and mutinous seamen delayed his embarkation till the following Thursday. During the time he was stayed, Hyde informs us that the Prince showed ' great impatience, and would never suffer any of his attendants to go out of the castle, lest they might be absent in that article of time when the wind would serve, which he resolved to lay hold of, so that nobody went to bed.' About five o'clock in the afternoon of Thursday, 25th of June, the Prince, supported by Jermyn and Digby on either side, embarked on the frigate, and reached the French coast about eleven o'clock at night, where he lay at anchor till daybreak.

Hyde, who had so strongly expressed himself against the Prince's removal, refused to accompany his royal master into France, as did two other members of the Prince's council, the Lords Capel and Hopton, who preferred ' a loyal part of the King's dominions to the wilderness of a foreign kingdom.' Besides these three dissentient

[1] Hoskins, i. pp. 435, 440.

members of the council, many other gentlemen
of the Prince's suite declined to accompany him
into France, taking up their abode in Jersey,
' not knowing where to be better or so well.'
Amongst them may be named : Sir Henry
Mainwaring, Sir David Murray, Sir John Macklin,
Sir Edward Stawell, and Sir Richard Fanshawe.
The Prince's governor, the Earl of Berkshire,
also remained ; but two days after the departure
of his royal charge he set sail for St. Malo, where
he embarked in a Dutch ship bound for Holland.
En route the vessel passed close to Jersey, and
the Earl caused a salute to be fired, as a leave-
taking to his old friends on the Island.[1]

The most central and interesting figure among
this little band of royalists is, without doubt,
that of the chancellor, Sir Edward Hyde, better
known to posterity by his later dignity as Earl of
Clarendon.   Of the others we may note that Sir
David Murray was an old cavalier nearly eighty
years of age ; Sir Edward Stawell was the son of
Sir John Stawell, governor of Exeter ; while Sir
Richard Fanshawe was the Prince's Secretary
of War.   During Hyde's sojourn in the Island,
besides conducting a voluminous correspondence,
he found time to continue his studies and

enjoyed the greatest tranquillity of mind imaginable.
Whilst the Lords Capel and Hopton stayed there, they
lived and kept house together at St. Helier's, where,
having a chaplain of their own, they had prayers every
day in the church at eleven of the clock in the morning ;
till which hour they enjoyed themselves in their chambers
according as they thought fit : the chancellor to the
continuation of the History which he begun at Scilly.[2]

[1] Hoskins, ii. 1-2.
[2] Clarendon, *Life*, i. p. 239.   *The History of the Rebellion*
was first published at Oxford in three volumes, folio, 1702-4.

Whilst Hyde and his fellow royalists were enjoying the seclusion and hospitality offered by the Island of Jersey, those that had been left behind for the defence of Pendennis were on the eve of capitulation. On the 13th of July, over a fortnight after its despatch, a letter reached Jersey, signed by the principal officers of the castle, containing heart-rending details from the famished and beleaguered garrison, who, for want of victuals, were forced to kill their horses to provide food. The letter, which was addressed to the Prince, was immediately forwarded to him in Paris by the one-armed colonel who had brought the intelligence to Jersey. This touching appeal, however, failed to bring the prompt assistance that was needed, and the courageous defenders were forced to surrender on the 17th of August. Some of the loyal officers eventually found their way to Jersey, where they were warmly welcomed by their old friends.

About the end of September, the ' tranquillity of mind ' enjoyed by Hyde and the other cavaliers was disturbed by an alarming report from France, to the effect that the Channel Islands were to be sold to the French. The originator of this scheme was reported to be Lord Jermyn, who, for delivering up the islands of Jersey and Guernsey, was to receive 200,000 pistoles and a dukedom. The plot was to levy 2000 Frenchmen, under a pretence that they were for the English service, to help in reducing the Island of Guernsey, whereby it was hoped that their commander, Jermyn, would be able to seize both islands.[1] The scheme, Hyde informs

---

[1] Hoskins, ii. pp. 55–6. Guernsey at the time was strongly Parliamentarian.

us, was so far advanced that ships had already been chartered for transporting the men. On the 19th of October articles were drawn up by Sir George Carteret, the governor of Jersey, and the others, in which they set forth their determination to resist at all costs any attempts that the French might make ' on the greatest road of trade in the world.' [1] If the French had any such designs, their scheme did not progress any further, and Jermyn denied all knowledge of the transactions, telling Hyde that he hoped his friends did not conceive him guilty of ' so infamous a piece of villany.' In spite of Jermyn's denial, the evidence was the testimony of a number of trustworthy individuals, and it is probable that the idea was entertained by the French, but abandoned when they found that the intelligence had leaked out. On the 26th of the month Lord Capel left the Island, and passed through Paris on his way to Holland.

The next two months passed without any attempt by the Parliamentary ships to reduce Jersey. In the interval Sir George Carteret took the opportunity of replenishing the magazine and stores of the castle.

On the 25th of February, 1647, Lord Hopton received news of the death of his wife in England, and the following day he left the Island on his way to Rouen, much to his own regret and the grief of the handful of honest fellows who, as Hyde wrote to Cottington in Paris, ' love each other heartily, which, they say, is a charity not

---

[1] Hoskins, ii. p. 60. *See* also 'Articles of association entered into between Hopton, Hyde, and Carteret, for the defence of Jersey against the supposed design of Lord Jermyn ' (Clarendon, *State Papers*, ii. 279–82).

yet translated into the language of the climate in which you inhabit.' [1]

Hyde, now bereft of his two friends, left his lodging in St. Helier's, and betook himself to Elizabeth Castle, where a chamber was allotted to him in which to pursue his studies. At the time when Hyde joined the family circle of Sir George Carteret, the new fortifications, begun about nine months previously, were nearing completion. Guns had been mounted on the ramparts of the new outwork, and a barbican placed in advance of the drawbridge. Every Thursday a council of war was held in the precincts of the castle, at which suggestions for defensive operations were eagerly discussed.[2] The 6th of May, a man-of-war mounting 26 guns, and a pinnace of 6 guns, anchored in the roadstead before the castle, and a messenger was despatched under a flag of truce to the governor. As a matter of precaution he was blindfolded, and led to the council chamber, where he handed a letter to Carteret from the Earl of Warwick, summoning him to deliver up the island to the Parliament. A council of war was called, and within an hour the messenger was on his way back with Carteret's answer, which was to the effect that he did not intend to make himself ' a real and avowed villain by betraying a trust.' The summons was really intended as an ultimatum to the attack which was to be made in earnest during the month of May, and on the 1st of that month the Commons ordered the Committee of the Army to furnish Colonel Rainborowe with four mortar pieces and munitions for reducing the Island of Jersey,

---

[1] Hoskins, ii. pp. 99–100.
[2] *Ibid.*, ii. pp. 121–2.

for which purpose a sum of £6000 was voted.[1]
Carteret's secret emissaries in London confirmed
the intelligence, and informed him that 12,000
men were to be employed for that service. On
receipt of these alarming tidings, the energies
of all on the Island were redoubled, in order
to place the defences on a sound footing. The
militia were drilled and armed, the governor's
company was formed into a light brigade, while
another company of 200 picked men was raised
and designated 'The Prince's Own.' Their
vigilance and resources were soon to be put to
the test. One fine morning three large and six
smaller ships of the enemy were observed steering
towards the Island. They were believed to be
the vanguard of the hostile squadron, and one
of their number was the Convertive of 42 guns.
The pre-arranged signal, that the beacons were to
be fired in the advent of danger, was given, and
the call to arms was sounded in every district.
The now well-disciplined troops were soon on
the spot, and a brisk fire was exchanged between
the ships and the soldiers. Carteret was quickly
on the scene, and seeing that the enemy did not
intend to effect a landing, but merely to make
a demonstration, ordered his men to retire.[2]

In the meantime Parliament was so much
occupied with the problem of disbanding the
army that the proposed expedition against

---

[1] *Commons Journals*, v. p. 159; Whitelocke's *Memorials*,
p. 245.

[2] In 1632 Sir George Carteret was Lieutenant in the
Convertive, and in 1637 he was second in command of the
Sallee expedition. Five years later he was raised to the rank
of Vice-Admiral, and the year following he was appointed
Governor of Jersey. He was Treasurer of the Navy from
1661 to 1667, and died in 1680 (*Dict. of Nat. Biog.*).

Jersey was for the time abandoned. The vote for money was withdrawn, and on the 28th of May Rainborowe was suddenly ordered ' to repair to his regiment with all speed, and take course to stay it' till further orders from the Parliament.[1] The order to Rainborowe[2] from the House to repair to his regiment, and detain it in the place where he should find it, is in some respects worthy of notice. On the 12th of May the House had reason to believe that his soldiers were quartered in Hampshire, at Portsmouth and Petersfield respectively, ready to embark at notice for Jersey. Between that date and the 28th of the month they had evidently received intelligence of their mutiny, ' and knew probably they were on the march northward to join their comrades, but were ignorant of the precise line of march they had taken, or the exact point at which they were aiming.'[3]

As soon as the news of the postponement of the expedition reached Jersey, the glad tidings were diffused through the Island, and gave fresh zest to the rejoicings which were to take place in the castle in honour of the Prince's

---

[1] *Commons Journals*, v. 193.

[2] At the outbreak of the Civil War Rainborowe joined the Parliamentary forces, and in 1643 was in command of the *Swallow* of thirty-four guns. He assisted Fairfax in the defence of Hull, and appears to have deserted sea service for that on land. In 1646 he sat as M.P. for Droitwich, and in September 1647 he was appointed Vice-Admiral for the winter guard of the seas. With the seamen he was very unpopular, and his commission lasted only five months. On the 29th of October 1648 he was kidnapped by a party of royalists at Doncaster, and in the struggle was mortally wounded.

[3] Mr. E. Peacock's Notes on the life of Rainborowe, in *Archaeologia*, xlvi. 3.

seventeenth birthday. To celebrate the joyous occasion a sumptuous banquet was spread in the great hall of the castle, to which the principal personages of the Island were invited, among whom were Sir Edward Hyde, Sir David Murray, Sir Henry Mainwaring, Sir John Macklin, and Sir Edward Stawell. Nor did Carteret forget his soldiers, and they in company with the tradesmen were feasted in another part of the castle. By the aid of our worthy chronicler, Chevalier, we are enabled to get a glimpse of this convivial gathering. The feasting over, he informs us, ' the garrison manned the ramparts ; hosts of spectators lined the parapets ; wine flowed in abundance ; the health of the King, Queen, Prince of Wales, and other members of the royal family was drunk with loud acclamations amid repeated charges of ordnance and musketry.' [1]

Soon after the suspension of hostilities, Chevalier informs us, ' many persons of all ranks and conditions,' who had sought refuge in Jersey, took their departure ; some making their way to the King, whilst others returned to their estates in England, from which they had been absent so long. Towards the end of February 1648 Mainwaring was amongst the little band that came to bid farewell to the governor, Sir George Carteret, with whom they had spent the last 22 months.[2] The only royalists of note who remained were Hyde, Sir David Murray, and Sir John Macklin. Hyde, not daring to venture into England, continued to reside at his lodging in Elizabeth Castle.[3]

During the time that Mainwaring passed on

---

[1] Hoskins, ii. 137.   [2] Chevalier's *Journal*, p. 530.
[3] Hoskins, ii. 163.

the Island he became on very intimate terms
with the Jersey chronicler, Jean Chevalier, and
to pass away an idle hour frequently entertained
that worthy with stories of his early sea life,
which must have duly impressed him, for in
a subsequent part of Chevalier's Journal there
appears an account of the 'heroic feats of Sir
Henry.'[1]

[1] *See* volume ii.

CHAPTER XIII

1648–53

SERVICE WITH THE ROYALIST FLEET—LAST YEARS AND DEATH

DURING the period preceding the execution of Charles I, and onwards up to the time of the Restoration, it is difficult to trace the travels of many who adhered to the royalist cause, and among them must be classed Sir Henry Mainwaring.[1] For four months after he bade adieu to the hospitalities of the Island of Jersey no mention of his name is to be found, though it is known that he managed to join the revolted ships in Holland about the end of June in that year. Under these circumstances it will perhaps not be considered out of place to give a brief résumé of the doings of the Navy during this period. Batten, who had connived at the supply of arms for the Essex insurgents, had been dismissed from his command as Vice-Admiral of the Parliament's fleet, and Rainborowe

---

[1] The reason is not difficult to ascertain. ' It is no secret,' writes Mr. Ewald, ' that the Domestic *State Papers*, after the year 1640, are as meagre in bulk as they are in interest. . . . During the Civil War numerous documents were destroyed by the Parliamentary party. . . . The State Paper Office was the King's repository, and the officers who transmitted papers there were his servants ' (Ewald, *Stories from the State Papers*, ii. 182–3).

appointed in his stead.[1] This caused great
dissatisfaction among the seamen, with whom
Batten had become very popular ; and when
part of the fleet was lying in the Downs on the
27th of May 1648 they took advantage of the
occasion while Rainborowe was on shore to
declare for the King. Those that revolted were :
Constant Reformation, Swallow, Convertive,
Antelope, Satisfaction, Roebuck, Hind, Crescent,
and Pelican,[2] and under their guns the castles
of Deal, Walmer, and Sandown were recovered
for the royalist cause. The Duke of York being
then in Holland, the ships made their way to
Helvoetsluys, where they arrived about the end
of the month. From here a message was despatched to the Prince, then at St. Germains,
to come over and place himself at their head,
and on the 25th of June, with Prince Rupert, the
Lords Hopton, Culpepper, and others, he started
to join his brother in Holland. The royal party
sailed in an English frigate from Calais, and
on the Prince's arrival he was received by the
sailors 'with all those acclamations, and noises
of joy, which that people are accustomed to.'[3]
Mainwaring was now appointed by the Prince
to the command of the Antelope, a 30 gun ship,[4]
and after a stay of about a week, in which to
refit, the royalist squadron sailed for the Thames,
with Lord Willoughby as its Vice-Admiral. On
the 22nd of July the Prince anchored in
Yarmouth roads, but having no land force with
him, and finding that nothing was to be gained
by prolonging his stay, sailed for the Downs,

[1] *Cal. S.P. Dom.*, Charles I, 1648-9, pref. xxi.

[2] *Ibid.*, 1648-9, p. 124. In Sir W. Penn's *Life* mention
is made of another, the *Blackamoor Lady* (ii. 261).

[3] Clarendon, v. p. 33.   [4] Chevalier's *Journal*, p. 683.

where he found the Kentish castles still holding
out for the King. During their stay in the
Downs the fleet seized a ship sailing from London
to Rotterdam, laden with cloth. This was owned
by the Company of Merchant Adventurers, and
the value of her cargo was returned at £40,000.
Another royalist prize was an East Indiaman
homeward bound and richly laden, which
Clarendon informs us was very welcome, 'because
the ship itself was a very strong ship, and would
make an excellent man-of-war.[1] The city of
London was greatly alarmed by the seizure of
its merchant shipping, and one of them, the
cloth ship, they petitioned Charles to restore.
The substance of his reply was to the effect that
he had to provide money for the maintenance
of the navy under his command, and desired
the city to supply him with £20,000, for the
expenditure of which sum he undertook to give
account ; and on receipt of which he stated the
ship should be restored to her owners. After
about a month's negotiation, the sum of £12,000
was eventually handed over to the Prince, and
the cloth ship released. It is quite probable
that her cargo was considerably under-estimated,
and, as Clarendon shrewdly remarks, 'there was
somewhat else besides cloth in the body of it,
for which there was not any search suffered to
be made.[2]

The Prince was now joined by Batten, who
had succeeded in bringing over the Constant
Warwick, one of the best of the Parliamentary
ships, with him. On his arrival Batten was
cordially received by the Prince, who knighted
him, and appointed him his Rear-Admiral.

[1] Clarendon, *Rebellion*, vi. 64.   [2] *Ibid.*, 67.

From the Downs the fleet sailed for the mouth of the Thames, where it remained inactive till the end of August. The Prince, now finding himself running short of provisions and with no prospect of support on land, determined to return to Helvoetsluys and refit his ships. The seamen, however, were eager to try conclusions with Warwick, and when the news was conveyed to them of the intended return, they mutinied, and insisted in sailing up the Thames to meet the enemy. They would sooner live on half rations, they stated, than go back to Holland without engaging Warwick's ships.[1] Knowing that all depended on his seamen, the Prince forthwith resolved to strike a blow before returning. On the 30th of August both the fleets were within striking distance, preparing for action, when they were suddenly separated by a violent storm, and the desire of the Prince's sailors was not gratified. The gale continuing on the next day, the royalist fleet was confronted with the prospect of starvation ; and with their water casks empty, and one solitary butt of beer, there was no alternative but to return to Holland.[2]

At the beginning of September the fleet arrived in Goree Road, but Warwick's ships followed so closely, that both raced for possession of the harbour. One account states that the Constant Reformation was nearest the anchorage, but ' Warwick sent a good sailing frigate to get in before, so the Prince's boat and the other rowed

---

[1] Gardiner, *Civil War*, iii. 467–8.

[2] *Ibid.*, p. 468. The Prince is blamed by some for remaining so long at the mouth of the river, when he might have sailed to the Isle of Wight, and tried to effect the release of his father. (*See* Lediard, ii. 532 ; Clarendon, vi. 80.)

à vi for the harbour.' Warwick's frigate had
apparently gained the day, when Captain
Allen,[1] who happened to be on shore, pretending
to be their friend, called for a rope to make it
fast, but as the boat was putting off again he
let slip the rope, and back went Warwick's ship.
After this the Prince's fleet were hauled in,
except the Convertive, which came in on the
next spring tide.[2] Another account, also contemporary, which shows that Mainwaring was
with the fleet, is contained in the petition of
George Rosewell, a seaman of the merchant ship
Love, which had been captured in the Downs
and brought over to Holland. Rosewell states
that he 'lost his wherry and chest and all he
had in the ship, which was plundered by the
merciful Parliament, he being ashore that night
that his captain went away with the ship, and
he cut away the Tenth Whelp's hawsers, or else
your Highness' great ships should not have come
into the Sluice (*i.e.*, Helvoetsluys), which Sir
Henry Mainwaring can witness.' [3]

[1] Captain Thomas Allen was knighted, and made captain
of the Guinea frigate of 300 tons, which formed one of Prince
Rupert's squadron.

[2] Warburton, *Prince Rupert*, iii. 253.

[3] *Pepys MSS.* at Magdalene College, Cambridge. (*Hist.
MSS. Com.*, 1911, p. 239, dated November, 1648.) This
incident has hitherto apparently been unnoticed. In the
State Papers, Domestic, Charles I, ccccxviii. 164, there is a
petition of the owners of the *Love* to the Commissioners of
the Navy. The *Tenth Whelp* was commanded by Captain
W. Brandlyn, and was one of the Parliament's fleet in the
Downs. There is still another version, by one who was in
the *St. George*, entitled :—' A letter from the Navy with the
Earl of Warwick, Lord High Admiral: from Hellevoyt
Sluice, Novem: 24, 1648,' London. Printed for Laurence
Blaikelocke, 1648. 'The next morning,' the writer states,
'being the ninth (*i.e.*, of November). . . instead of firing on

Warwick, however, followed the ships into the harbour, summoning the Prince to lower the royal standard, and to render the ships to him as Lord Admiral of England. The States of Holland informed Warwick that no hostile act would be countenanced in their waters ; and to enforce this neutrality Tromp was soon on the scene, with sixteen men-of-war, having received orders to lie midway between the rival fleets, and in case the roadstead was violated, to join against the aggressor. Many of the royalist seamen during the blockade that ensued, finding their provisions running short, and their pay in arrears, were induced by Warwick's sailors to desert, and the Constant Warwick, which Batten had brought to the Prince, ' either voluntarily left the fleet, or suffered itself to be taken by Warwick's squadron.' [1]

On the 21st of November Warwick, finding his own ships needed revictualling, and being prevented from obtaining supplies on shore, was compelled to raise the blockade and sail for the Downs, where he arrived on the 23rd.

us, they all hastened to gain the Sluice, which we might have prevented had there not been slackness in some . . . We had one Frigate in their Admiral's way, and lay before the Sluice mouth, where our Vice-Admiral might have been also, if ordered, and then the valiant Prince could not have run his head into that hole, as presently afterwards he did, by carrying a Hawser on shore, and the Guinea Frigate also, the rest being all at an anchor as near the pier as they could get. In the night they cut the cables of five more, and hauled them all but one into the Sluice, where one lay athwart the other's sterns . . . The next morning, being the 10th, as soon as it was light . . . the *Love* (a ship of 38 guns) weighed and ran right for the Sluice. One of our ships laid her cross the Hawser, forcing her to an anchor, some of the soldiers on board her cried fire, but immediately she yielded.'

[1] Clarendon, vi. 135.

The Prince was now confronted with the double
difficulty of victualling his ships and finding
money to pay the clamouring seamen. Many
rich prizes had been brought into the Hague,
and their cargoes sold at a considerable loss in
order to appease the demands of his crews.
Willoughby, who was inexperienced in naval
affairs, was now superseded by Prince Rupert,
though the latter was not favoured by the seamen.
The ships were hastily surveyed, and Mainwaring's
ship, the Antelope, being unfit for further service,
her ordnance was sold, and the proceeds devoted
to victualling and fitting out the rest.[1] In the
meantime Rupert had by vigorous methods of
procedure, such as throwing 'two or three
seamen overboard by the strength of his own
arms,' succeeded in restoring some form of order
among the seamen.[2]

The royalist exiles had long entertained the
idea of assailing England through Ireland, and
on the 11th of January 1649 Rupert sailed
from Helvoetsluys with eight warships and three
Dutch East Indiamen. His squadron made such
an imposing appearance, that on its passage
through the Downs no attempt was made to
interrupt its progress; and on the 29th Rupert's
fleet cast anchor at Kinsale.[3] The following day
the final catastrophe of the Civil War was enacted,
and 'Charles Stuart, King of England,' was
no more.

The news of his father's death did not reach
the Prince at the Hague till four days later, and
on the receipt of the intelligence much condolence

---

[1] At the end of June 1649 she was destroyed by a boat's
crew from the *Happy Entrance* (Spalding, *Life of Badiley*,
p. 29).   [2] Clarendon, vi. p. 151.
   [3] Gardiner, *Commonwealth*, i. p. 15.

was meted out to him by the States of Holland. For nearly six months after this sad event Charles, King of Scotland, the only title by which he was recognised by the Parliamentarians, continued to reside at the Hague. Here his suite consisted of the Marquis of Montrose ; the Lords Hopton, Wilmot, Culpepper, and Wentworth ; besides Sir Edward Hyde, Sir Edward Nicholas, Sir Edward Walker, Sir Henry Mainwaring, and other poor but staunch cavaliers.

The time had now come for Charles to bid adieu to the States of Holland, and prior to his departure we find a warrant signed by him, and dated at the Hague, June 6th, to pay Mainwaring, amongst others, the sum of 300 guineas. The original document is still preserved, and runs as follows [1] :

1649. June 6. The Hague.—Charles R. our will and pleasure is that out of such moneys as you shall receive that you immediately pay to the several persons specified in the annexed schedule the several sums set on their names. Given under Our Sign Manual at the Hague this sixth day of June, 1649.

The warrant is to Sir Edward Walker, who in February 1649 had been appointed Clerk of the Council to Charles, and the curious instruction, ' out of such moneys as you shall receive,' had no doubt direct reference to the sale of the prizes which Rupert had captured during his voyage to Kinsale, the profits of which helped to

---

[1] *Hodgkin MSS.* (*Hist. MSS. Com.*, 15 ii. p. 113). Some forty names are mentioned in this interesting document, among whom are the following :—Sir Edward Walker, 500 guineas ; Lord Gerrard, 2000 guineas ; Earl of Cleveland, 1000 ; Sir Marmaduke Langdale, 500 ; ' To the mariners of the *Antilop*, 100 guineas ' ; ' To a poor man at Hetforsluce for his ship, 350 guineas.'

maintain his fleet, and partly support the court
of Charles at the Hague. At the beginning of
the following November, Rupert, with seven
ships, left Kinsale on his famous buccaneering
expedition.[1] In the opinion of men such as
Mainwaring, the King's only chance of regaining
the throne depended on what measure of success
attended his efforts on the sea, and when the
last remnant of the royalist fleet quitted the
coast of Ireland, it is safe to assume that Mainwaring returned to England. The many
vicissitudes through which he had passed had
left their mark, and now prematurely aged and
worn,[2] his one desire was to end his days in the
England he loved so well. He presents a truly
pathetic figure, only too common amongst the
King's adherents, who, when they realised that
their cause was lost, determined to return to
England and make their peace with the Parliament. The news of the death of his elder brother,
Sir Arthur Mainwaring, at the end of the previous
year, had no doubt been conveyed to him in
Holland, and it is probable that one of his first
visits on reaching England was to Sayes Court,
Chertsey. This fine Elizabethan mansion, which
James I is reported to have occasionally occupied,
was demised by Charles I to Sir Arthur Mainwaring in 1634, and after his decease it remained
for some time in the possession of his widow,
Grissell, Lady Mainwaring. Sir Arthur is buried

---

[1] Rupert had succeeded in relieving the Scilly Isles, which
Sir John Grenville held for the King. On the 22nd of May
he was blockaded by Blake at Kinsale, but in the following
October a gale forced Blake to raise the blockade, and Rupert
escaped to sea.

[2] He is variously stated to have been between seventy and
eighty, and also about seventy, whereas he was only sixty-two.

at Chertsey, and on a marble gravestone was this inscription [1] :

Here lies the Body of Sir Arthur Mainwaring of Sayes, in the County of Surrey, Knight, Son & Heir of Sir George Mainwaring of Ightfield, in the County of Salop, Knight, whose second Wife was Grissell, the eldest daughter of Sir David Woodroofe of Poyle in the said County of Surrey, Knight, by whom he had issue two Sons named Charles & Arthur, and one daughter named Margaret, which Arthur lies hereby interred ; and the said Charles & Margaret surviving, departed this Life the 29 day of December, An. Dni. 1648.

Where Mainwaring resided, or what pursuits he indulged in, cannot be ascertained ; but the remainder of his life was evidently spent in comparative poverty. He had served his King with unshaken loyalty and integrity, and, in common with many others, had spent what means he possessed in the royalist cause. These devoted men who supported Charles I, and afterwards followed his son across the seas, were indeed men of spirit. When poverty pressed them hard, they would say like one of Hyde's correspondents, ' yet I have a mad kind of humour that keeps me alive and merry in every place where I come.' [2] For the sake of their King they freely sacrificed all, not counting the cost of their actions, and faced the world with a brave and cheerful countenance. The miserable plight of the royal finances did not allow of much margin for the King's faithful retinue, and they were forced to eke out an existence as best they could, the best being often very precarious.

[1] Aubrey, *Surrey*, 1718, ii. 177.
[2] Clarendon, *State Papers*, ii. 255. Cited in Miss Eva Scott's *King in Exile*, pp. 1–2.

During the sojourn of the court in France, Sir Edward Hyde and others were forced to go into ' pension ' together, subsisting on one meal a day, for which they paid (when they had the money) one pistole a week. The King and his followers lacked the necessaries of life – food, fire, and clothing. Hyde, writing to a friend, stated he had not three sous to enable him to buy a faggot, and was so cold he could not hold his pen. Reduced to these dire straits, the royalists were quite resigned and even cheerful over their many misfortunes. Hyde in a merry mood wrote, ' The conditions will grow a second nature with us. I do not know that any man is yet dead for want of bread, which really I wonder at ! ' [1]

The lines reproduced here, which were written by Alexander Brome, admirably set forth the royalist sentiment of the time.[2]

> We do not suffer here alone,
> Though we are beggared so's the King ;
> 'Tis sin t'have wealth when he has none,
> Tush ! poverty's a royal thing !

Towards the close of the year 1651 Mainwaring was in such reduced circumstances that, besides his clothes, his only other possession was a horse ! This pathetic side of his life is revealed when he sought to make his composition with the Committee for Compounding the estates of royalists at Goldsmiths' Hall. The intensely human records of this Committee, which lay bare every detail regarding the possessions of those that took the King's side in the Civil War,

---

[1] Scott, pp. 434–4.
[2] ' The Royalist,' written 1646 (reprinted in Mackay's *Cavalier Songs*).

are preserved among the archives in the Public Record Office, and Mainwaring's petition, which is dated 4th of November 1651, is as follows :

To the Honourable the Commissioners for Compounding.

The petition of Sir Henry Mainwaring, Knight, Humbly showeth that whereas being a servant of the late King he did adhere to him in the late war against the Parliament and then went into Holland, and hath never acted anything since the late King's death, nor was never sequestered. He being about 70 years of age, and desiring to end his days in peace, humbly prays he may be admitted to [a] composition for his poor estate in the particulars annexed,

And he shall daily pray, &c.,

HENRY MAINWARING.

4 *November*, 1651.
Referred to Mr. Reading to report.
R. M.
Jo: LEECH.

A particular of my estate for which I desire to compound.

I am possessed of a horse and wearing apparel to the value of £8. This is a true particular of my estate for which I desire to compound, and do humbly submit to such fine as shall be imposed upon me. And I do affirm that I am not comprised in any qualifications or exceptions of Parliament nor have committed any act of delinquency since the 1st of February, 1648.[1]

HENRY MAINWARING.

On the 25th of November the fine was fixed at one-sixth,[2] and it was 'ordered that Sir Henry

[1] *I.e.,* 1st February 1648–9.

[2] It is interesting to note that the fines were levied in the following ratios: one-half from a delinquent M.P.; one-sixth from those who had taken part in the former or latter war; one-third from those who had taken part in both.

Mainwaring, Knight, do pay into the Treasury at Goldsmiths' Hall as a fine for his delinquency in the late war against the Parliament the sum of £1 6s. 8d. within six weeks after the date whereof this order.'[1] It is to be hoped that Mainwaring did not have to realise on his horse to raise the necessary £1 6s. 8d., and that some good friend came forth in this hour of adversity with the requisite sum ; at any rate, on the 18th of December the fine was paid, and Mainwaring given a discharge.

He did not long survive his composition, and eighteen months afterwards, in May 1653, his death is recorded at the age of sixty-six. On the 15th of the month he was buried at St. Giles' Church, Camberwell,[2] where his wife had been interred some twenty years before. No record of his last days is available, and no tombstone stands to mark the last resting-place of one of the greatest seamen of the age ; but it is pleasant to think that, dying when he did, a few weeks after the battle of Portland, he was spared to rejoice over the first of the victories against the Dutch, which marked the revival of the Navy, and for which he had done so much to pave the way.

As he lay on his death-bed the country was ringing with the glorious news, and for such a man there could have been no sweeter passing bell. Mainwaring's whole soul was bound up with the welfare of the English Navy, and the knowledge he had accumulated through experience had been freely given for the benefit of his fellow countrymen. A linguist and a

---

[1] *Royalist Composition Papers*, G12, pp. 351, 375 ; G223, p. 116.

[2] *Coll. Topog. et Genealogica*, iii. 165.

scholar of no mean ability, he wielded a pen with as much dexterity as he handled a ship, and was never happier than when committing his views to paper on any subject connected with the Navy and the naval art. Of a studious nature, his indefatigable industry and quickness of perception placed him among the foremost Englishmen of the time. A true patriot at heart, he is one of those forgotten worthies whose enterprise and courage helped to make the British flag known and respected in all seas, and of him it may truly be said, that in his life was exemplified the motto of his family—' Devant si je puis.'

INDEX

I.

2 A

I.

2 B

Printed by SPOTTISWOODE, BALLANTYNE & Co. LTD.
Colchester, London & Eton, England